Published with assistance from the
Lucius N. Littauer Foundation.

Designed by Sonia L. Scanlon.
Set in Minion type.
Printed in the United States of America.

Library of Congress Card Number: 00-100482
ISBN 978-0-300-09413-8

A catalogue record for this book is available
from the British Library.

The paper in this book meets the guidelines
for permanence and durability of the Committee
on Production Guidelines for Book Longevity
of the Council on Library Resources.

10   9   8   7   6   5   4

At Memory's Edge

At
Memory's
Edge

After-Images of the Holocaust in

Contemporary Art and Architecture

James E. Young

NEW HAVEN AND LONDON   YALE UNIVERSITY PRESS

Contents

Acknowledgments

The seeds for *At Memory's Edge* were first planted in a handful of talks and catalogue essays I was invited to do on behalf of a postwar generation of artists who came to know the Holocaust as I did—only, and thankfully, as a "vicarious past." For the extended conversations and studio visits by which I came to know their work, and then for their generous cooperation in providing images by which I could represent their work in this book, I very gratefully thank: Art Spiegelman, David Levinthal, Shimon Attie, Horst Hoheisel, Rachel Whiteread, Renata Stih and Frieder Schnock, Jochen Gerz and Esther Shalev-Gerz, Daniel Libeskind, and Peter Eisenman. I can only hope that my discussion of these artists' and architects' work begins to do justice to their complex and highly nuanced formal articulations of Holocaust memory in this decidedly antiredemptory age.

In addition to the catalogue essays and talks occasioned by the artists and architects themselves, I have presented parts of this book in a number of public lectures and symposia organized by colleagues as preoccupied by these difficult questions as I have been. For inviting me to speak and then providing the lively intellectual settings in which I could refine, elaborate, and always improve on my reflections on "the uncanny arts of memory," I offer warm thanks to: Susan Suleiman at the Center for Cultural and Literary Studies at Harvard University; Marianne Hirsch and Leo Spitzer at Dartmouth College; Tody Judt at the Center for European Studies at New York University; Sander Gilman and the Smart Museum of Art at the University of Chicago; Peter Homans at the University of Chicago; Froma Zeitlin and the Humanities Council at Princeton University; Naomi Sokoloff at the University of Washington, Seattle; Angelika Bammer at Emory University; Christhard Hoffmann at the Center for European Studies at the University of California at Berkeley; Rudy Koshar at the University of Wisconsin at Madison; Murray Baumgarten and Peter Kenez at the University of California at Santa Cruz; Thomas Schumacher and the School of Architecture at the University of Maryland; Marianne Doeszema at the Mt. Holyoke College Art Museum; Bryan Cheyette at the University of London; Barbara Henry at Scuola Superiore at the University of Pisa, Italy; Jörn Rüsen at the Zentrum für interdisziplinäre Forschung at the University of Bielefeld, Germany; Gary Smith at the Einstein Forum in Berlin and Potsdam, Germany; and Jörg Hüber at the Schule und Museum für Gestaltung in Zurich, Switzerland.

Because parts of this book have also appeared in a handful of journals, my writing has also benefited from the editorial eye of editors like W. J. T. Mitchell at *Critical Inquiry* and Martin Morris at the *South Atlantic Quarterly,* as well as editors at the *Frankfurter Allgemeine Zeitung, Berliner Zeitung,* and *Tages Spiegel* in Germany.

Like others in the academic community, I owe great debts both to foundations and to administrators at my home institution for so generously supporting my requests for support and time off from teaching to write. Over the past several years, work on this book has been supported by generous grants from the American Council of Learned Societies, the American Philosophical Society, and the Memorial Foundation for Jewish Culture. I am also extremely grateful to both the Lucius N. Littauer Foundation and its program officer, Pamela Ween Brumberg, for the very generous publication grant that has allowed me to show in images, as well as to describe in words, the uncanny arts of memory here. For helping see this book through its signing and production at Yale University Press, I thank my editor, Jonathan Brent, my manuscript editor, Laura Jones Dooley, and my friend and agent, Deborah Karl. And of course, none of this writing would have been possible without the kind understanding and cooperation of my friend and English department chair, Stephen Clingman, and the dean of the College of Humanities and Fine Arts, Lee Edwards, both at the University of Massachusetts at Amherst.

It becomes almost impossible to acknowledge just how crucial a role my friends and family have played in helping me work through the issues at the heart of this project—on aesthetic, ethical, historical, and personal levels. For both their writings, which have inspired and instructed me, and the conversations we have had over the years, I thank: Susan Shapiro, Froma Zeitlin, Geoffrey Hartman, Natalie Zemon Davis, Saul Friedlander, Christopher Benfey, Lawrence Douglas, Andreas Huyssen, Anson Rabinbach, Jeffrey Herf, and Michael Wise.

Coming as I have from the literary and historical realms to the subtler, if more ephemeral worlds of contemporary art and design, I owe an inestimable debt to my wife, Lori Friedman, and her own uncannily prescient eye for art. In teaching me to see and to think about contemporary art, she has also taught me to see and to think about memory in ways that would have been otherwise lost to me. Finally, it is to our two young sons, Asher and Ethan, that I dedicate this book, for it is from them that I learn all over again how memory and life necessarily generate, and regenerate, each other.

Introduction

"Some people want to forget where they've been; other people want to remember where they've never been."

—*Eli Cohen and Gila Almagor, from their film* Under the Domim Tree

The Holocaust as Vicarious Past

HOW IS A POST-HOLOCAUST GENERATION of artists supposed to "remember" events they never experienced directly? Born after Holocaust history into the time of its memory only, a new, media-savvy generation of artists rarely presumes to represent these events outside the ways they have vicariously known and experienced them. This postwar generation, after all, cannot remember the Holocaust as it occurred. All they remember, all they know of the Holocaust, is what the victims have passed down to them in their diaries, what the survivors have remembered to them in their memoirs. They remember not actual events but the countless histories, novels, and poems of the Holocaust they have read, the photographs, movies, and video testimonies they have seen over the years. They remember long days and nights in the company of survivors, listening to their harrowing tales until their lives, loves, and losses seem grafted onto their own life stories.

Coming of age after—but indelibly shaped by—the Holocaust, this generation of artists, writers, architects, and even composers does not attempt to represent events it never knew immediately but instead portrays its own, necessarily hypermediated experiences of memory. It is a generation no longer willing, or able, to recall the Holocaust separately from the ways it has been passed down. "What happens to the memory of history when it ceases to be testimony?" asks Alice Yeager Kaplan.[1] It becomes memory of the witness's memory, a vicarious past. What distinguishes many of these artists from their

1

parents' generation of survivors is their single-minded knack for representing just this sense of vicariousness, for measuring the distance between history-as-it-happened and what Marianne Hirsch has so aptly called their "post-memory" of it.[2]

By portraying the Holocaust as a "vicarious past," these artists insist on maintaining a distinct boundary between their work and the testimony of their parents' generation. Such work recognizes their parents' need to testify to their experiences, even to put the Holocaust "behind them." Yet by calling attention to their vicarious relationship to events, the next generation ensures that their "post-memory" of events remains an unfinished, ephemeral process, not a means toward definitive answers to impossible questions.

What further distinguishes these artists from their parents' generation, moreover, is their categorical rejection of art's traditional redemptory function in the face of catastrophe. For these artists, the notion either that such suffering might be redeemed by its aesthetic reflection or that the terrible void left behind by the murder of Europe's Jews might be compensated by a nation's memorial forms is simply intolerable on both ethical and historical grounds. At the ethical level, this generation believes that squeezing beauty or pleasure from such events afterward is not so much a benign reflection of the crime as it is an extension of it. At the historical level, these artists find that the aesthetic, religious, and political linking of destruction and redemption may actually have justified such terror in the killers' minds.

Not only does this generation of artists intuitively grasp its inability to know the history of the Holocaust outside of the ways it has been passed down, but it sees history itself as a composite record of both events *and* these events' transmission to the next generation. This doesn't mean that their vicarious memory of the past thereby usurps the authority of history itself, or that of the historians and their research; after all, as they are the first to acknowledge, they inevitably rely on hard historical research for their knowledge of what happened, how, and why. But in addition to the facts of Holocaust history, these artists recognize the further facts surrounding this history's transmission to them, that its history is being passed down to them in particular times and places. These are not mutually exclusive claims or competing sets of facts but part of history's reality. Neither history nor memory is regarded by these artists as a zero-sum game in which one kind of history or memory takes away from another; nor is it a contest between kinds of knowledge, between what we know and how we know it; nor is it a contest between scholars and students of the Holocaust and the survivors themselves. For these artists know that the facts of history never "stand" on their own—but are always supported by the reasons for recalling such facts in the first place.

For American artists like Art Spiegelman, David Levinthal, and Shimon Attie, whose work I explore in this book's first three chapters, their subject is not the Holocaust so much as how they came to know it and how it has shaped their inner lives. Theirs is an unabashed terrain of memory, not of history, but no less worthy of exploration. When they go to represent this "vicarious past," they do so in the artistic forms and media they have long practiced. When "comix"-artist Art Spiegelman remembers the Holocaust, therefore, he recalls both his father's harrowing story of survival and the circumstances under which Spiegelman heard it. In his "commixture" of images and narrative, he is able to tell both stories simultaneously, turning them into a single, double-stranded narrative.

When photographer David Levinthal was asked by his art teacher at Yale why he took photographs of toys in historical tableaux instead of historical reality itself, he answered simply that the vintage Nazi figurines he collected and photographed *were* his historical reality, the only remnants of the past he had experienced. By photographing his imagined re-creations of Nazi pageantry, the fascist war-machine, and the murder of the Jews, Levinthal would limit his representations to an exploration of that which he knows from history books, photographs, and mass-media images. Similarly, in his European environmental installations, artist Shimon Attie has projected archival photographic images of the past—his memory—back onto the otherwise amnesiac sites of history in order to reanimate these sites with his "memory" of what happened there. Haunted by what he regarded as the specter of missing Jews in Berlin's Scheunenviertel, Attie projected photographs of Jews from this quarter taken in the 1920s and 1930s back onto their original sites, among other projects of his I explore in Chapter 3. Here he has literally projected the "after-images" in his mind back onto otherwise indifferent landscapes.

No doubt, some will see such work as a supremely evasive, even self-indulgent art by a generation more absorbed in its own vicarious experiences of memory than by the survivors' experiences of real events.[3] Others will say that if artists of the second or third generation want to make art out of the Holocaust, then let it be about the Holocaust itself and not about themselves. The problem for many of these artists, of course, is that they are unable to remember the Holocaust outside of the ways it has been passed down to them, outside of the ways it is meaningful to them fifty years after the fact. As the survivors have testified to *their* experiences of the Holocaust, their children and their children's children will now testify to their experiences of the Holocaust. And what are *their* experiences of the Holocaust? Photographs, film, histories, novels, poems, plays, survivors' testimonies. It is necessarily mediated experience, the afterlife of memory, represented in history's after-images: the impressions retained in the mind's eye of a vivid sensation long after the original, external cause has been removed.

Why represent all that? Because for those in Spiegelman's, Levinthal's, and Attie's generation, to leave out the truth of how they came to know the Holocaust would would be to ignore half of what happened: we would know what happened to Spiegelman's father but miss what happened to the artist-son. Yet isn't the important story what happened to the father at Auschwitz? Yes, but without exploring why it's important, we leave out part of the story itself. Is it self-indulgent or self-aggrandizing to make the listener's story part of the teller's story? This generation doubts that it can be done otherwise. These artists can no more neglect the circumstances surrounding a story's telling than they can ignore the circumstances surrounding the actual events' unfolding. Neither the events nor the memory of them take place in a void. In the end, these artists ask us to consider which is the more truthful account: that narrative or art which ignores its own coming into being, or that which paints this fact, too, into its canvas of history?

For artists at home in their respective media, whether it is the comix of Spiegelman or the vanguard photography of Levinthal, questions about the appropriateness of their forms seem irrelevant. These artists remain as true to their forms and chosen media as they do to their "memory" of events. But for those less at home in the languages of contemporary art, the possibility that form—especially the strange and new—might overwhelm the content of such memory-work leads some to suspect the artists' motives. Historian Omer Bartov, for example, has expressed his sense of "unease" with what he describes as the "cool aesthetic pleasure" that derives from the more "highly stylized" of postmodern Holocaust representations.[4] Part of what troubles Bartov is that such work seems more preoccupied with being stimulating and interesting in and of itself than it is with exploring events and the artist's relationship to them afterward. Also implied here is an understandable leeriness on Bartov's part of the possibility that such art draws on the power of the Holocaust merely to energize itself and its forms.

Even more disturbing for Bartov, however, is the question historian Saul Friedlander has raised in his own profound meditations on "fascinating fascism," in which Friedlander wonders whether an aesthetic obsession with fascism may be less a reflection on fascism than it is an extension of it. Here Friedlander asks whether a brazen new generation of artists bent on examining its own obsession with Nazism adds to our understanding of the Third Reich or only recapitulates a fatal attraction to it. "Nazism has disappeared," Friedlander writes, but the obsession it represents for the contemporary imagination —as well as the birth of a new discourse that ceaselessly elaborates and reinterprets it—necessarily confronts us with this ultimate question: Is such attention fixed on the past only a gratuitous reverie, the attraction of spectacle, exorcism, or the result of a need to understand; or is it, again and still, an expression of profound fears and, on the part of some, mute yearnings as well?[5]

As the artists whose work I explore here suggest, the question remains open. Not because every aesthetic interrogation of the Holocaust also contains some yearning for "fascinating fascism." But because they believe that neither artist nor historian can positively answer yes or no to this question.

In fact, here we must ask simply: Can the historian ever really know the history of an era without knowing its art and literature? That is, can any historian truly represent events of a bygone era without understanding how the artists and writers of that time grasped and then responded to the events unfolding around them? I would answer simply, No, it is not possible. By extension, I would like to ask how well historians can represent the past without knowing how the next generation has responded to it in its art and literature. That is, without knowing how such history is being mediated for the next generation and why it is deemed so important to remember in the first place. For these phenomena, too, are part of the history that is being told after the fact.[6]

The Arts of Memory in an Antiredemptory Age

On one hand, it's true that the Holocaust, unlike World War I, has resulted in no new literary forms, no startling artistic breakthroughs; for all intents and purposes, it has been assimilated to many of the modernist innovations already generated by the perceived rupture in culture occasioned by the Great War. On the other, what has certainly changed is the redemptory promise that traditionally underlay innovation and "newness" in modern art and culture: where antirealist and fragmentation motifs were seen as redemptory of art's purpose after the Great War precisely because they refused to affirm the conditions and values that made such terror possible, art and literature after the Holocaust are pointedly antiredemptory of both themselves and the catastrophe they represent.

Indeed, of all the dilemmas facing post-Holocaust writers and artists, perhaps none is more difficult, or more paralyzing, than the potential for redemption in any representation of the Holocaust. Some, like philosopher Theodor Adorno, have warned against the ways poetry and art after Auschwitz risk redeeming events with aesthetic beauty or mimetic pleasure.[7] Others, like Saul Friedlander, have asked whether the very act of history-writing potentially redeems the Holocaust with the kinds of meaning and significance reflexively generated in all narrative.[8] Though as a historian Friedlander also questions the adequacy of ironic and experimental responses to the Holocaust, insofar as their transgressiveness seems to undercut any and all meaning, verging on the nihilistic, he also suggests that a postmodern aesthetics might "accentuate the dilemmas" of history-telling.[9] Even by Friedlander's terms, this is not a bad thing: an aesthetics that remarks its own limitations, its inability to provide eternal answers and stable meaning. Works in this vein acknowledge both the moral obligation to remember and the ethical hazards of doing so in art and literature. In short, he issues a narrow call for an aesthetics that devotes itself primarily *to* the dilemmas of representation, an antiredemptory history of the Holocaust that resists closure, sustains uncertainty, and allows us to live without full understanding.

For many artists, the breach between past events and their art now demands some kind of representation, but how to do it without automatically recuperating it? Indeed, the postmodern enterprise is both fueled and paralyzed by the double-edged conundrum articulated first by Adorno: not only does "cultural criticism share the blindness of its object," he writes, but even the critic's essential discontent with civilization can be regarded as an extension of that civilization.[10] Just as the avant-garde might be said to feed on the illusion of its perpetual dying, postmodern memory-work seems to feed perpetually on the impossibility of its own task.[11]

In contrast to the utopian, revolutionary forms with which modernists hoped to redeem art and literature after World War I, the post-Holocaust memory-artist, in particular, would say, "Not only is art not the answer, but after the Holocaust, there can be no more Final Solutions." Some of this skepticism is a direct response to the enormity of the Holocaust—which seemed to exhaust not only the forms of modernist experimentation and innovation but the traditional meanings still reified in such innovations. Mostly, however, this skepticism stems from these artists' contempt for the religious, political, or aesthetic linking of redemption and destruction that seemed to justify such terror in the first place. In Germany, in particular, once the land of what Friedlander has called "redemptory anti-Semitism," the possibility that public art might now compensate mass murder with beauty (or with ugliness), or that memorials might somehow redeem this past with the instrumentalization of its memory, continues to haunt a postwar generation of memory-artists.[12]

Memorial artists in Germany, moreover, are both plagued and inspired by a series of impossible questions: How does a state incorporate shame into its national memorial landscape? How does a state recite, much less commemorate, the litany of its misdeeds, making them part of its reason for being? Under what memorial aegis, whose rules, does a nation remember its barbarity? Where is the tradition for memorial mea culpa, when combined remembrance and self-indictment seem so hopelessly at odds? Unlike state-sponsored memorials built by victimized nations and peoples to themselves in Poland, Holland, or Israel, those in Germany are necessarily those of former persecutors remembering their victims. In the face of this necessary breach in the conventional "memorial code," it is little wonder that German national memory of the Holocaust remains so torn and convoluted. Germany's "Jewish question" is now a two-pronged memorial question: How do former persecutors mourn their victims? How does a nation reunite itself on the bedrock memory of its crimes?

One of the most compelling results of Germany's memorial conundrum has been the advent of its "countermonuments": brazen, painfully self-conscious memorial spaces conceived to challenge the very premises of their being. At home in an era of earthworks, of conceptual and self-destructive art, postwar artists now explore both the necessity of memory and their incapacity to recall events they never experienced directly. After examining in the first half of this book how three American artists—Spiegelman, Levinthal, and Attie—have represented their "vicarious past," therefore, I turn to the ways that the public "counter-arts" of memory in Germany have begun to resist the certainty of monumental forms, the ways European artists have begun to challenge the traditional redemptory premises of art itself.

I thus explore both the early critique of Germany's "memorial problem" by Berlin-born Jochen Gerz, as embodied in his *EXIT / Dachau* project of 1971 as well as his disappearing and invisible memorials in Harburg and Saarbrücken, among other installations. In his and Esther Shalev-Gerz's *Monument Against Fascism* in Harburg-Hamburg, for example, a forty-foot-high lead-covered column was sunk into the ground as people inscribed their names (and much else) onto its surface; on its complete disappearance in 1993, the artists hoped that it would return the burden of memory to those who came looking for it. With audacious simplicity, their "countermonument" thus flouted a number of memorial conventions: its aim was not to console but to provoke; not to remain fixed but to change; not to be everlasting but to disappear; not to be ignored by its passersby but to demand interaction; not to remain pristine but to invite its own violation; not to accept graciously the burden of memory but to throw it back at the town's feet.[13] How better to remember a now-absent people than by a vanishing monument?

In this vein, I explore the negative-form monuments and installations of Horst Hoheisel in Kassel and Weimar, as well as his proposal to blow up the Brandenburger Tor in Berlin in lieu of Germany's national Holocaust memorial. In two further installations by Micha Ullman and Rachel Whiteread, one realized and the other as yet only proposed, I look at how these artists have also turned to both bookish themes and negative spaces to represent the void left behind by the "people of the book." Like Attie, other artists in Germany have also attempted to reanimate otherwise amnesiac sites with the dark light of their pasts, reminding us that the history of such sites also includes their own forgetfulness, their own lapses of memory. Berlin artists Renata Stih and Frieder Schnock have thus mounted eighty signposts on the corners, streets, and sidewalks near Berlin's Bayerische Platz. Each includes a simple image of an everyday object on one side and, on the other, a short text excerpted from Germany's anti-Jewish laws of the 1930s and 1940s. Where past citizens once navigated their lives according to these laws, present citizens now navigate their lives according to the memory of such laws.

If part of these artists' work has been the reinscription of Jewish memory and the memory of the Jews' murder into Berlin's otherwise indifferent landscape, another part has been to reveal the void in postwar German culture that demands this reinscription. To this end, architect Daniel Libeskind has premised his design for Berlin's new Jewish Museum on the very idea of the void. In my chapter on Libeskind's design for Berlin's Jewish Museum, I begin with the prewar story of the museum itself, its own fraught past and ill-fated opening only weeks before Hitler was installed as chancellor in January 1933. But here I also ask the impossible questions facing the architect at the outset of his project: How does a city like Berlin "house" the memory of a people that is no longer at "home" in Germany? How does a nation like Germany invite a people like the Jews back into its official past after having driven them so murderously from it? I suggest here that a "Jewish museum" in the capital of a nation that not so long ago drove its Jews from a land they had considered "home" cannot be *heimlich* but must be regarded as *unheimlich*—or uncanny. My aim in this penultimate chapter is not merely to explain Libeskind's difficult design but to show how as a process, it uncannily articulates the dilemma Germany faces whenever it attempts to formalize the self-inflicted void at its center—the void of its lost and murdered Jews.

Finally, in a self-examining coda, I tell the story of Germany's proposed national Holocaust memorial and my own role in it, my evolution from a highly skeptical critic on the outside of the process to one of its arbiters on the inside. Although I had initially opposed a single, central Holocaust memorial in Germany for the ways it might be used compensate such irredeemable loss, or even put the past behind a newly reunified Germany, over time I began to grow skeptical of my own skepticism. Eventually, I was invited to become the only foreigner and Jew on a five-member *Findungskommission* charged with choosing an appropriate design for Germany's national memorial to Europe's murdered Jews. In this coda, I tell the story of Berlin's "memorial for the murdered Jews of Europe" on one hand even as I explore the collapsing line between my role as critic and arbiter on the other—all toward bringing the issues at the heart of Germany's memorial conundrum into clear, if painful focus.

Like my previous studies of Holocaust narrative and memorials, this book is by no means intended as a survey of the contemporary arts of Holocaust memory.[14] Instead, I have tried to present a handful of artists whose works I believe best embody some of the difficult questions faced by all post-Holocaust artists, works that throw complex issues into sharp relief. These essays are thus premised on three interrelated preoccupations shared by these artists and me. First, memory-work about the Holocaust cannot, must not, be redemptive in any fashion. Second, part of what a post-Holocaust generation must ethically represent is the experience of the memory-act itself. Last, the void left behind by the destruction of European Jewry demands the reflection previously accorded the horrific details of the destruction itself. For these artists, it is the memory-work itself, the difficult attempt to know, to imagine vicariously, and to make meaning out of experiences they never knew directly that constitutes the object of memory.

It's also true that dozens of artists other than the ones I discuss could have been included here, many of them well known. In fact, in spite of their profound effect on a postwar generation of artists preoccupied by the Holocaust, the works of Anselm Kiefer, Josef Beuys, and Christian Boltanski are not addressed here—partly because they have been discussed so thoroughly and insightfully before me. Still others, like filmmakers Chantal Ackerman and Abraham Ravett and the performance artist Deb Filler, have profoundly shaped my thinking in this book, as have installation artists Susan Jahoda, Vera Frenkel, Ellen Rothenberg, and Melissa Gould. The musical composition *Different Trains,* by Steve Reich, has similarly inspired me, especially for the ways it echoes his postwar generation's preoccupation with not having been "there" but still being shaped by the Holocaust. All of these artists deserve wide audiences and demand discussions as sophisticated and illuminating as their works are profound.[15]

In the end, this book is also premised on difficult, at times uncomfortable questions directed toward the post-Holocaust generation of artists and architects and their works: How much is this work about the Holocaust, and how much is it about the artist's vicarious memory of the Holocaust? How can contemporary art formalize such questions without making form itself the subject of their works? Finally, is it possible to enshrine an antimonumental impulse in monumental forms? In my discussions of these artists, I don't pretend to answer these questions but rather hope to lay them bare for all to see.

And as also becomes painfully clear, I must direct similarly difficult questions to myself, the critic and explicator of these works: At what point do I cross over from disinterested critic of these works to their explicator? And then, at what point do I go from being explicator of these at times difficult works to serving as their advocate? In my case, such questions cannot be merely academic. For two of these essays were, in fact, written initially as catalogue essays for exhibitions by David Levinthal and Shimon Attie. And as my reflections on my role in Germany's attempt to build a national Holocaust memorial will show, I went from being what I regarded as a principled opponent of the project to spokesman for the Findungskommission appointed to select an appropriate design for the memorial. This crossing-over of roles is not so unusual in an art world where scholars, curators, museum and gallery directors, and artists have long blurred the lines of their work, where interpreters and evaluators of art have also established canons and market value. But it is new terrain for a cultural historian of the Holocaust. If my aim here has been in part to lay bare these connections, the other, more important part of my aim here has been to explore the ways a new generation of memory-artists have made a critique of institutional memory fundamental to their work.

From Friedlander's integrated historiography to Spiegelman's commixture of image and narrative; from Levinthal's "play of memory" to Attie's wall-projections; from the countermemorial installations of Gerz, Hoheisel, Whiteread, Ullman, and Stih and Schnock to the uncanny architecture of Libeskind and Peter Eisenman, these works succeed precisely because they refuse to assign singular, overarching meaning to either the events of the Holocaust or our memory of them. This is the core of their antiredemptory aesthetic. Such artists and historians continue to suggest meaning in history but simultaneously shade meaning with its own coming into being. In side-shadowing both the history and memory of the Holocaust in this way, not only do they resist the temptation for redemptory closure in their work, but they can make visible why such history is worth recalling in the first place.[16]

Some critics, like Michel Foucault, have suggested that because every record of history, even the archival, is also a representation of history and thus subject to all of a culture's mediating forces, the study of history can only be the study of commemorative forms. To date, in fact, I have also made commemorative forms—such as monuments, museums, and days of remembrance—part of the object my historical inquiry. Unlike Foucault, however, I would not displace more traditional notions of history with hypermediated versions but only add the study of commemorative forms to the study of history, making historical inquiry the combined study of both *what happened* and *how it is passed down* to us.

In this way, historical inquiry might remain a search for certainties about substantive realities even as it is broadened to encompass the realities of history's eventual transmission. Extended backward into the notion of history "as it happened," such a conception includes as part of its search for verifiable fact the search for verifiable, yet highly contingent representations of these facts as they unfolded. Instead of enforcing an absolute breach between what happened and how it is remembered, we might also ask what happens when the players of history remember their past to subsequent generations—and then suggest that this is not memory only but also another kind of history-telling.

Indeed, I would suggest here that these memory-artists may even lead the next generation of historians to a more refined, if complex kind of history-telling, one that takes into account both events and how they get passed down to us. In turn, I would like to see their works force scholars to reflect on their own academic commodification of Holocaust history, how the next generation simultaneously feeds on the past and disposes of it in their work. Although academic critics have been quick to speculate on the motives of filmmakers, novelists, and artists, we have remained curiously blind to our own instrumentalization of memory, to the ways an entire academic industry has grown up around the Holocaust. It is time to step back and take an accounting: Where does all this history and its telling lead, to what kinds of knowledge, to what ends? For this is, I believe, the primary challenge to Holocaust art and historiography in an antiredemptory age: it is history-telling and memory that not only mark their own coming into being but also point to the places—both real and imagined—they inevitably take us.

CHAPTER ONE

Art Spiegelman's *Maus* and the After-Images of History

"How does history become 'personal'—only when it is survived, or only when private lives become public knowledge? What constitutes an 'experience' of history—'being there,' being told about it (telling it), being taught it (teaching it), reading about it, writing it? Or does history become 'personal' when an individual cares about it?"
—*Susan Crane, "(Not) Writing History"*

IN SPITE OF THE BRILLIANT EXAMPLE of his work *Nazi Germany and the Jews*, Saul Friedlander is still not convinced that an antiredemptory historiography of the Holocaust is possible.[1] For even that narrative that integrates something akin to the deep, unassimilated memory of survivors as a disruption of "rational historiography" also seems to mend these same disruptions with the inexorable logic of narrative itself. The question arises: To what extent will the introduction of the survivors' memory into an otherwise rational historiography add a destabilizing strain to this narrative, and to what extent will such deep, unassimilable memory be neutralized by the meaning generated in any and all narrative? Or will such a working through always remain the provenance of artists and novelists, whose imaginative flights bridge this contradiction even as they leave it intact? Friedlander is not sure. "Even if new forms of historical narrative were to develop," he says, "or new modes of representation, and even if literature and art were to probe the past from unexpected vantage points, the opaqueness of some 'deep memory' would probably not be dispelled. 'Working through' may ultimately signify, in Maurice Blanchot's words, 'to keep watch over absent meaning.'"[2]

Here Friedlander also draws a clear distinction between what he terms "common memory" and "deep memory" of the Holocaust: common memory as that which

WE WALKED IN THE DIRECTION OF SOSNOWIEC - BUT **WHERE TO GO?!**

"tends to restore or establish coherence, closure and possibly a redemptive stance," and deep memory as that which remains essentially inarticulable and unrepresentable, that which continues to exist as unresolved trauma just beyond the reach of meaning.[3] Not only are these two orders of memory irreducible to each other, Friedlander says, but "any attempt at building a coherent self founders on the intractable return of the repressed and recurring deep memory."[4] That is, to some extent, every common memory of the Holocaust is haunted by that which it necessarily leaves unstated, its coherence a necessary but ultimately misleading evasion.

As his sole example of deep memory, Friedlander refers to the last frame of Art Spiegelman's so-called comic book of the Holocaust, *Maus: A Survivor's Tale*, in which the dying father, Vladek, addresses his son Artie with the name of Richieu, Artie's brother who died in the Holocaust before Artie was even born.[5] The still apparently unassimilated trauma of his first son's death remains inarticulable—and thereby deep—and so is represented here only indirectly as a kind of manifest behavior. But this example is significant for Friedlander in other ways, too, coming as it does at the end of the survivor's life. For Friedlander wonders, profoundly I think, what will become of this deep memory after the survivors are gone. "The question remains," he says, "whether at the collective level . . . an event such as the *Shoah* may, after all the survivors have disappeared, leave traces of a deep memory beyond individual recall, which will defy any attempts to give it meaning."[6] The implication is that, beyond the second generation's artistic and literary representations of it, such deep memory may be lost to history altogether.

In partial answer to this troubling void in Holocaust history, Friedlander proposes not so much a specific form but a way of thinking about historical narrative that makes room for a historiography integrating deep and common memory. For the integrated historian, this means a historiography whose narrative skein is disrupted by the sound of the historian's own, self-conscious voice. As Friedlander writes, such "commentary should disrupt the facile linear progression of the narration, introduce alternative interpretations, question any partial conclusion, withstand the need for closure."[7] These interruptions would also remind readers that this history is being told and remembered by someone in a particular time and place, that it is the product of human hands and minds. Such a narrative would simultaneously gesture both to the existence of deep, inarticulable memory and to its own incapacity to deliver that memory.

Perhaps even more important for Friedlander, though he gives it equal weight in his argument, is the possibility that such commentary "may allow for an integration of the so-called 'mythic memory' of the victims within the overall representation of this past without its becoming an 'obstacle' to 'rational historiography.'"[8] Here, it seems, Friedlander would not only answer German historian Martin Broszat's demand that the mythic memory of victims be granted a place in "rational historiography," but he would justify doing so as a necessary part of an integrated history rather than on the basis of "respect for the victims" (as Broszat has suggested).[9] Such history necessarily integrates both the contingent truths of the historian's narrative and the fact of the victims' memory, both deep and common. In this kind of multivocal history, no single, overarching meaning emerges unchallenged; instead, narrative and counternarrative generate a frisson of meaning *in* their exchange, in the working through process they now mutually reinforce.

The Comix-ture of Image and Narrative

Here I would like to return to Art Spiegelman's *Maus*, not because it answers Friedlander's call for an integrated history of the Holocaust but because it illustrates so graphically the dilemmas that inspire Friedlander's call. At the same time, I find that by embodying what Marianne Hirsch has aptly termed an aesthetics of postmemory, it also suggests itself as a model for what I would like to call "received history"—a narrative hybrid that interweaves both events of the Holocaust and the ways they are passed down to us.[10] Like Hirsch, I would not suggest that postmemory takes us beyond memory, or displaces it in any way, but would say that it is "distinguished from memory by generational distance and from history by deep personal connection. Post-memory should reflect back on memory, revealing it as equally constructed, equally mediated by the processes of narration and imagination . . . . Post-memory is anything but absent or evacuated: It is as full and as empty as memory itself."[11]

As becomes clear, then, especially to the author himself, Art Spiegelman's *Maus: A Survivor's Tale* is not about the Holocaust so much as about the survivor's tale itself and the artist-son's recovery of it. In Spiegelman's own words, "*Maus* is not what happened in the past, but rather what the son understands of the father's story. . . . It is an autobiographical history of my relationship with my father, a survivor of the Nazi death camps, cast with cartoon animals."[12] As his father recalled what happened to him at the hands of the Nazis, his son Art recalls what happened to *him* at the hands of his father and his father's stories. As his father told his experiences to Art

Art Spiegelman, Maus, 1:12.

in all their painful immediacy, Art tells his experiences of the storytelling sessions themselves—in all of their somewhat less painful mediacy.

"In 1970 I drew a short comic strip called 'Maus' for a San Francisco artists' comic book," Spiegelman has written. "It was based on my parents' experiences as Jewish survivors of the ghettoes and death camps of Nazi Europe. In that early work I represented the Jews as mice and the Germans as cats. (Kafka's tale, 'Josephine the Singer, or the Mouse Folk' offered a precedent, as did the Saturday morning cartoons and comics of my childhood.)."[13] That Spiegelman has chosen to represent the survivor's tale as passed down to him in what he calls the "comix" is neither surprising nor controversial. After all, as a comix-artist and founder of *Raw* magazine Spiegelman has only turned to what has always been his working artistic medium. That the comix would serve such a story so well, however, is what I would like to explore here. On the one hand, Spiegelman seems to have realized that in order to remain true to both his father's story and his own experience of it, he would have to remain true to his medium. But in addition, he has also cultivated the unique capacity in the "comixture" of image and narrative for telling the double-stranded tale of his father's story and his own recording of it.

Art Spiegelman,
Breakdowns.

While Spiegelman acknowledges that the very word *comics* "brings to mind the notion that they have to be funny," humor itself is not an intrinsic component of the medium. "Rather than comics," he continues, "I prefer the word commix, to mix together, because to talk about comics is to talk about mixing together words and pictures to tell a story."[14] Moreover, Spiegelman explains, "The strength of commix lies in [its] synthetic ability to approximate a 'mental language' that is closer to actual human thought than either words or pictures alone."[15] Here he cites the words of what he calls the patron saint of comix, the nineteenth-century Swiss educational theorist and author Rodolphe Töpfer: "The drawings without their text would have only a vague meaning; the text without the drawings would have no meaning at all. The combination makes up a kind of novel—all the more unique in that it is no more like a novel than it is like anything else."[16] For unlike a more linear historical narrative, the "comix-ture" of words and images generates a triangulation of meaning —a kind of three-dimensional narrative—in the movement among words, images, and the reader's eye. Such a form also recognizes that part of any narrative will be this internal register of knowledge—somewhere between words and images—conjured in the mind's movement between itself and the page. Such a mental language may not be reproducible, but it is part of any narrative just the same.

Thus, in describing Winsor McKay, another pioneering cartoonist, Spiegelman further spells out what he calls the "storytelling possibilities of the comic strip's unique formal elements: the *narrative* as well as design significance of a panel's size and shape, and how these individual panels combined to form a coherent visual whole."[17] That is, the box panels convey information in both vertical and horizontal movements of the eye, as well as in the analogue of images implied by the entire page that appears in the background of any single panel. The narrative sequence of Spiegelman's boxes, with some ambiguity as to the order in which they are to be read, combines with and then challenges the narrative of his father's story—itself constantly interrupted by Art's questions and neurotic preoccupations, his father's pill-taking, the rancorous father-son relationship, his father's new and sour marriage. As a result, Spiegelman's narrative is constantly interrupted by—and integrative of— life itself, with all its dislocutions, associations, and paralyzing self-reflections. It is a narrative echoing with the ambient noise and issues that surround its telling. The roundabout method of memory-telling is captured here in ways unavailable to a more linear narrative. It is a narrative that tells both the story of events and its own unfolding as narrative.

Other aspects of Spiegelman's specific form and technique further incorporate the process of drawing *Maus* into its finished version. By drawing his panels in a one-to-one ratio, for example, instead of drawing large panels and then shrinking them down to page size, Spiegelman reproduces his hand's movement in scale—its shakiness, the thickness of his drawing pencil line, the limits of miniaturization, all to put a cap on detail and fine line and so keep the pictures underdetermined. This would be the equivalent of the historian's voice, not as it interrupts the narrative, however, but as it constitutes it.

At the same time, *Maus* resonates with traces of Spiegelman's earlier, experimental foray into antinarrative. According to Spiegelman, at the time of his first *Maus* narrative in 1972, he was actually more preoccupied with deconstructing the comix as narrative than he was in telling a story. As Jane Kalir has observed, Spiegelman's early work here grew more and more abstruse as he forced his drawings to ask such questions as "How does one panel on a page relate to the others? How do a strip's artificial cropping and use of pictorial illusion manipulate reality? How much can be elided from a story if it is to retain any coherence? How do words and pictures combine in the human brain?"[18]

Later, with the publication in 1977 of *Breakdowns,* an anthology of strips from this period of self-interrogation, the artist's overriding question became: How to tell the story of narrative's breakdown in broken-down narrative?[19] His answer was to quote mercilessly and mockingly from mainstream comics like *Rex Morgan, M.D.,* and *Dick Tracy,* even while paying reverently parodic homage to comics pioneers like Winsor McKay and his *Dream of the Rarebit Fiend* ("Real Dream" in Spiegelman's nightmarish version). In *Breakdowns,* Spiegelman combined images and narrative in boxes but with few clues as to whether they should be read side to side, top to bottom, image to narrative, or narrative to image; the only linear narrative here was generated by reading, a somewhat arbitrary reassembling of boxes into sequential order. In his introductory panels to *Breakdowns,* Spiegelman even rejects the notion of narrative as story, preferring to redefine story as the "'complete horizontal division of a building .... [From Medieval Latin HISTORIA . . . a row of windows with pictures on them.]'"[20] But although he explodes comix narrative into a kind of crazy quilt to be read in all directions, Spiegelman deliberately maintains a linear narrative for the Holocaust segment of *Breakdowns.* When I asked why, he replied simply that he wasn't interested in breaking the story of the Holocaust itself into incoherence, only in examining the limits of this particular narrative for telling such a story.

In fact, what Spiegelman admires in the form itself, he says, he once admired in Harvey Kurtzman's *Mad* magazine: "It was *about* something—reality, for want of a better word—and was also highly self-reflexive, satirically questioning not only the world, but also the underlying premises of the comics medium through which it asked the questions."[21] For Spiegelman, there is no contradiction between a form that is about reality on one hand and that which questions its own underlying premises on the other. It is clear that part of the world's reality here is the artist's own aching inadequacy in the face of this reality.

As for possible objections to folding the deadly high-seriousness of the Holocaust into what some regard as the trivial low-seriousness of comics, Spiegelman merely shows how the medium itself has always raised—and dismissed—issues of decorum as part of its raison d'être. Here he recalls that even the distinction itself between the high art of the masters and the low art of cartoonists is challenged by the way "modern masters" like Lyonel Feininger, George Grosz, Käthe Kollwitz, and Juan Gris divided their time between painting and cartoons. Indeed, as Kirk Varnedoe and Adam Gopnik have suggested, the comics in the twentieth century have served as a "metalanguage of modernism, a fixed point of reference outside modern painting to which artists could refer in order to make puns and ironic jokes."[22] As an unusually retentive mirror and caricature of styles in modern art, the comics have at once cat-

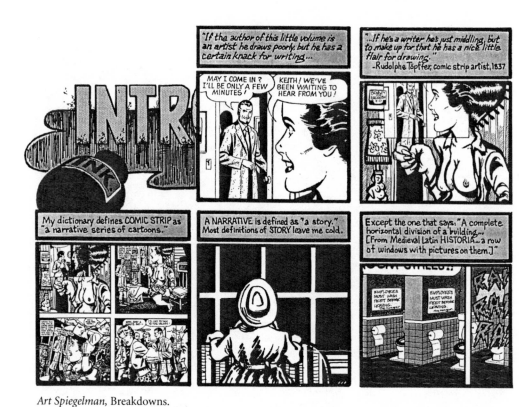

Art Spiegelman, Breakdowns.

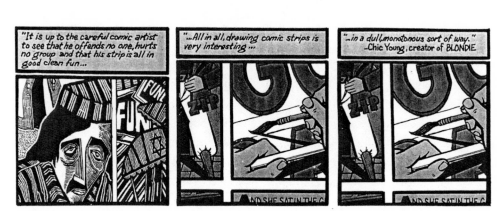

Art Spiegelman, Breakdowns.

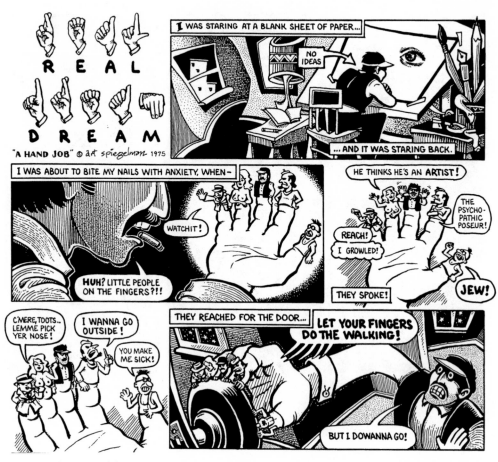

Art Spiegelman, Breakdowns.

alogued and mocked modern art with its own high seriousness—making them the postmodern art par excellence.

Written between 1972 and 1985, the first volume of *Maus* integrated both narrative and antinarrative elements of the comics, embedding the father's altogether coherent story in a medium that constantly threatened to fly apart at the seams. The result is a continuous narrative rife with the discontinuities of its reception and production, the absolutely authentic voice of Spiegelman's father counterposed to the fabular images of cartoon animals. In its self-negating logic, Spiegelman's comix also suggests itself as a pointedly antiredemptory medium that simultaneously makes and unmakes meaning as it unfolds. Words tell one story, images another. Past events are not redeemed in their telling but are here exposed as a continuing cause of the artist's inability to find meaning anywhere. Meaning is not negated altogether, but whatever meaning is created in the father's telling is immediately challenged in the son's reception and visualization of it.

In fact, the "story" is not a single story at all but two stories told simultaneously: the father's story and Spiegelman's imaginative record of it. It is double-stranded and includes the competing stories of what his father says and what Artie hears,   what happened during the Holocaust and what happens now in Artie's mind. As a process, it makes visible the space between what gets told and what gets heard, what gets heard and what gets seen. The father says one thing as we see him doing something else. Artie promises not to betray certain details, only to show us the promise and the betrayal together. Indeed, it may be Artie's unreliability as a son that makes his narrative so reliable.

Throughout *Maus*, Spiegelman thus confronts his father with the record of his telling, incorporating his father's response to Art's record of it into later stages of *Maus*. *Maus* thereby feeds on itself, recalling its own production, even the choices the artist makes along the way (would he draw his French wife who converted to Judaism as a frog or as an honorary

Art Spiegelman, Maus, *1:23.*

mouse?). The story now includes not just "what happened" but how what happened is made sense of by father and son in the telling. At the same time, it highlights both the inseparability of his father's story from its effect on Artie and the story's own necessarily contingent coming into being. All of which might be lost to either images or narrative alone, or even to a reception that did not remark its own unfolding.

By weaving back into his narrative the constant reflection on his role in extracting this story from his father, Spiegelman graphically highlights not only the ways that testimony is an event in its own right but also the central role he plays in this event. Moreover, as Dori Laub has noted, "The listener is a party to the creation of knowledge *de novo*."[23] That is, what is generated in the interaction between father and son in this case is not a revelation of an existing story waiting to be told but a new story unique to their experience together. This medium allows the artist to show not only the creation of his father's story but the necessary grounds for its creation, the ways his father's story hinges on his relationship to the listener. Artie is not just a shaper of testimony during its telling, or after in his drawings, but an integral part of its very genesis, part of its raison d'être. By making this telling and receiving the subject of *Maus,* Spiegelman acknowledges multiple levels of creativity and knowledge-making in the telling and his subsequent drawing. In this way, Spiegelman becomes both midwife to and eventual representer of his father's story.

Maus *as Side-Shadowed History*

Throughout its narrative, *Maus* presumes a particular paradigm for history itself, a conception of past historical events that includes the present conditions under which they are being remembered. The historical facts of the Holocaust, in this case, include the fact of their eventual transmission. This is why the "autobiographical history of the survivor's tale" necessarily begins, then, not in the father's experiences but in Artie's. Neither the three-page 1972 version of "Maus" in *Breakdowns* nor the later, two-volume edition of *Maus* opens in the father's boyhood Poland; rather, both open with the son's boyhood in Rego Park, Queens. The 1972 version begins with Poppa mouse sitting on the edge of his adoring little boy's bed, telling him "bedtime stories about life in the old country during the war": "and so, Mickey, *die Katzen* made all the mice to move into one part from the town! It was wery crowded in the ghetto!" "Golly!" says little mouse in his pajamas. Hence,

Art Spiegelman, Maus, *1:6*.

the "real dreams" that follow in *Breakdowns*.

Maus: A Survivor's Tale opens in 1958, with the young Artie's relationship to his father. Every detail of Artie's childhood is fraught with his father's memory, is shaped by his father's experiences. In the opening panel, something as innocent as being ditched by friends in childhood sparks the father's indignant comparison: "Friends? Your friends? If you lock them together in a room with no food for a week, THEN you could see what it is, friends" (1:6). The father's seemingly inexplicable response to his young son's tears evolves out of a deep memory

that becomes sensible only over the course of the narrative that follows.

After this preamble, Artie appears again, now grown, to visit his father for the first time in nearly two years. He is on a mission, a self-quest that is also historical. "I still want to draw that book about you," Artie says to his father, who answers, "No one wants any way to hear such stories," to which Artie answers, "*I* want to hear it." And then he asks his father to begin, in effect, with his own implied origin: "Start with Mom . . . ," he asks. "Tell me how you met" (1:12). He does not ask him to start with the war, deportation, or internment but with his mother and their union—that is, with his *own* origins. But even here, Artie's needs are frustrated by his father's actual memory: he begins not with Artie's mother, Anja, but with an earlier girlfriend, Lucia, where *his* memory of Anja begins.

Though Vladek tells his son that Lucia and his other girlfriends had nothing to do with the Holocaust, Spiegelman includes them nevertheless. In so doing, Spiegelman extends the realm of Holocaust history not only forward to include its effects on the next generation but also backward to include the rich, prewar tangle of lives lost. For Spiegelman, the Holocaust is much more than the sum of Jews murdered or maimed; it is also the loss of all that came before. By including the quotidian and messy details of his father's love affairs before the war (against the father's wishes), the artist restores a measure of the victims' humanity. More important, he preserves the contingency of daily lives as lived and perceived then—and not only as they are retrospectively freighted with the pathos and portent we assign them now. At the same time, he shows how the victims themselves, for perfectly understandable reasons, are occasionally complicit in the kind of back-shadowed history Spiegelman now rejects.[24]

It is as if Spiegelman realizes that at least part of his aim here as skeptical son, as teller of side-shadowed history, is to show how his father has made sense of his Holocaust experiences through many tellings, even as he would sabotage the ready-made story with his questions, his search for competing and contradicting details. The father might prefer a polished narrative, with beginning, middle, and end; but Artie wants to know the forks in the road, the paths not taken, how and why decisions were made under those circumstances, mistakenly or otherwise. In the nearly fifteen hundred interlocking frames that follow, therefore, the survivor's tale includes life before the war: leaving Lucia; marrying Anja for a mixture of love and money; going to work for his father-in-law; having a baby boy, Richieu; taking Anja to a spa for treatment of severe depression; being called up by the Polish army in the weeks before war.

As a Polish soldier, Vladek sees combat on the front when Germany invades Poland and even kills a German soldier. But the Polish army is overrun, and Vladek is captured. He survives a prisoner-of-war camp and, through a combination of guile and luck, makes his way home to Sosnowiecz. The details of the Polish Jews' ghettoization follow: hiding from selections, the gradual loss of hope and the break-up of the family, various acts of courage and betrayal by Jews and Poles, the painful sending of Richieu into hiding with a relative. The first volume ends with Vladek and Anja being caught and deported to Auschwitz-Birkenau.[25]

Art Spiegelman, Maus, 2:136.

Volume 2 opens in Auschwitz, where Vladek and Anja are separated. Intercut repeatedly with scenes depicting the day-to-day circumstances of his telling, Vladek recounts the arbitrariness of day-to-day life and death in Auschwitz, finding work and learning new skills for survival, making and losing contact with Anja, liberation, the postwar chaos of refugees in Europe, and his search for Anja. The book literally ends with Vladek's description of his joyous reunion with Anja ("More I don't need to tell you. We were both very happy, and lived happy, happy ever after"). Two final panels follow: "So . . . let's stop, please, your tape recorder . . . I'm tired from talking, Richieu, and it's enough stories for now" (2:136). At the bottom of the last page, Art has drawn a picture of a single tombstone for Vladek and Anja, with their names and dates of life. Beneath the tombstone, Art has signed his own name and the dates 1978–1991, not his life span but the span of his writing.

"Which is the true historical project," Alice Yeager Kaplan has asked, "the pin-

Art Spiegelman, Maus, 1:118.

pointing of an empirical cause or the trickier, less disciplined attempt to make links between past and present?"[26] In *Maus*, not only are past and present linked, but they constantly intrude and occasionally even collapse into each other. In relating, for example, the fate of his cousin, Haskel, an infamous *Kombinator* (schemer), the very memory seems to stop Vladek's heart as he grabs his chest. The narrative is one thing, the heart-stopping anxiety it produces in the teller is another. Both are portrayed here—the story and the effect on the teller himself—a kind of deep memory usually lost to narrative alone (1:118).

Earlier, as the father recounts the days in August 1939 when he was drafted, just as he gets to the outbreak of war: "And on September 1, 1939, the war came. I was on the front, one of the first to . . . Ach!" His elbow knocks two bottles of pills onto the floor. "So. Twice I spilled my drugstore!" He blames his lost eye and cataracts for not seeing so well and launches into the story of eye operations and neglectful doctors. On that day and in that chapter of the book, he doesn't finish his story of the Nazi invasion and says it's enough for today. "I'm tired and must count my pills" (1:39–40). Which is fine with Artie, whose writing hand is sore from taking notes.

Both teller and listener need to recover from the storytelling session itself, though whether it is the activity of telling and listening or the content of the narrative that has worn them out is not clear. Throughout *Maus*, the content of the father's tale of survival is balanced against the literal process of its recovery, the circumstances under which it is received and retold.

By making the recovery of the story itself a visible part of *Maus*, Spiegelman can also hint darkly at the story not being recovered here, how telling one story always leaves another untold, how common memory masks deep memory. In Spiegelman's case, this deep, unrecoverable story is his mother's memory of her experiences during the Holocaust. Vladek does not, cannot volunteer this story. It takes Artie to ask what Anja was doing all this time. "Houseworks... and knitting... reading . . . and she was writing always her diary" (1:84). The diaries did not survive the war, Vladek says, but she did write her memoirs afterward. "Ohmigod! Where are they? I need those for this book!" Artie exclaims (1:84). Instead of answering, Vladek coughs and asks Artie to stop with the smoking. It's making him short of breath. What seems to be a mere interruption turns out to be a prescient de-

Art Spiegelman, Maus, 1:84.

Art Spiegelman, Maus, 1:159.

laying tactic. Vladek had, after all, burned Anja's memoirs in a fit of grief after her suicide. Was it the memory of smoke from the burned memoirs or Artie's cigarettes that now made him short of breath?

At the end of the first volume, Spiegelman depicts the moment when his father admits not only destroying his mother's memoirs but leaving them unread. "Murderer," the son mutters (1:159). Here he seems to realize that his father's entire story is haunted by Anja's lost story. But worse, it dawns on the son that his entire project may itself be premised on the destruction of his mother's memoirs, their displacement and violation. "I can tell you," says the father (1:158). Spiegelman does not attempt to retell Anja's story at all, but leaves it known only by its absence; he is an accomplice to the usurpation of his dead mother's voice. It is a blank page, to be presented as blank. Nancy Miller has even suggested, profoundly, that "It's as if at the heart of *Maus*'s dare is the wish to save the mother by retrieving her narrative; as if the comic book version of Auschwitz were the son's normalization of another impossible reality: restoring the missing word, the Polish notebooks."[27] As a void at the heart of *Maus,* the mother's lost story may be *Maus*'s negative center of gravity, the invisible planet around which both the father's telling and Spiegelman's recovery of it revolve.

Here Spiegelman seems also to be asking how we write the stories of the dead without filling in their absence. In a limited way, the commixture of image and narrative allows the artist to do just this, to make visible crucial parts of memory-work usually lost to narrative alone, such as the silences and spaces between words. How to show a necessary silence? Art's therapist, Pavel, suggests at one point that because "life always takes the side of life" (2:45), the victims who died can never tell their stories. Maybe it's better not to have any more stories at all, Pavel says. "Uh, huh," Art nods in agreement and adds, "Samuel Beckett once said, 'Every word is like an unnecessary stain on silence and nothingness.'" "Yes," Pavel answers. And then there follows a panel without words, just an image of Art and his therapist sitting in silence, a moment in the therapeutic context as fraught with significance as narrative itself. For this is not silence as an absence of words but silence as something that passes actively between two people—the only frame in the two volumes without words or some

Art Spiegelman, Maus, 2:45.

other sign denoting words. And yet, Art points out in the next frame, "he said it." "Maybe you can include it in your book," the therapist replies.

How to show the unshowable may also underpin Spiegelman's use of animals for humans here. When Spiegelman is asked, "Why mice?" he answers, "I need to show the events and memory of the Holocaust without showing them. I want to show the masking of these events *in* their representation."[28] In this way, he can tell the story and not tell it at the same time. As ancient Passover Haggadoth used to put birds' heads on human forms in order not to show humans and to show them at the same time, Spiegelman has put mouse heads on the Jews. By using mice masks, the artist also asks us not to believe what we see. They are masks drawing attention to themselves as such, never inviting us to mistake the memory of events for the events themselves.

In his review of *Maus*, Adam Gopnik echoes Spiegelman's words, but with a slightly different twist. It's not just that Spiegelman wants to show this story by masking it, says Gopnik, but that the story itself "is too horrible to be presented unmasked." Moreover, Gopnik finds that Spiegelman may even be extending an ancient Jewish iconographic tradition, if for very untraditional reasons:

> The particular animal "masks" Spiegelman has chosen uncannily recall and evoke one of the few masterpieces of Jewish religious art—the Bird's Head Haggadah of 13th-century Ashkenazi art. In this and related manuscripts, the Passover story is depicted using figures with the bodies of humans and heads of animals—small, common animals, usually birds.
>
> Now, in one sense the problems that confronted the medieval Jewish illuminator and the modern Jewish artist of the Holocaust are entirely different. The medieval artist had a subject too holy to be depicted; the modern artist has a subject too horrible to be depicted. For the traditional illuminator, it is the ultimate sacred mystery that must somehow be shown without being shown; for the contemporary artist, it is the ultimate obscenity, the ultimate profanity, that must somehow be shown without being shown.[29]

Though Gopnik goes on to suggest that this obscenity has also become our sacred subject, we might do better to keep in mind not this apparent conflation of sacred and profane but the medium's essential indirection, its simultaneous attempt at representing and its self-declared inadequacy.

Moreover, as Spiegelman attempts to ironize narrative, he also uses images against themselves. By adopting the mouse as allegorical image for Jews, Spiegelman is able to caricature—and thereby subvert—the Nazi image of Jews as vermin. Subjugated groups have long appropriated the racial epithets and stereotypes used against them in order to ironize and thereby neutralize their charge, taking them out of the oppressors' vocabulary. In this case, the images of mice led in turn to other animal fig-

ures insofar as they are related to mice: the wily and somewhat indifferent cat is the obvious natural enemy of the mouse and, as German, the principal killer of mice here. The hapless Poles are saddled with a more ambiguous figure: though not a natural enemy of the Jews during the Holocaust, as pigs they come to symbolize what is *treif*, or non-Kosher. They may not be as anti-Jewish as the cats, but they are decidedly un-Jewish. The only other animal to resonate a Nazi cast would be the friendly, if none-too-bright dogs as stand-in for Americans, regarded as a mongrel people by Hitler but pictured here as the natural and more powerful enemy of the cats. The rest of the animals are more literally benign: reindeer for the Swedes, moths for Gypsies. But none of these, aside from the mouse, is intrinsic, witness Spiegelman's deliberations over whether to make his French-born wife, Françoise, a frog or a mouse (technically speaking, she has to be a mouse).

Though he has tried to weave the process of drawing *Maus* back into its narrative, Spiegelman is also aware that as a finished text, *Maus* may not truly capture the process. Which is why two exhibitions in New York City, one at the Galerie St. Etienne and the other in the projects room at the Museum of Modern Art, were so central to Spiegelman's project at the time. In these exhibitions, each entitled "The Road to *Maus*," the artist mounted the originals of his finished panels sequentially in a horizontal line along the walls of the gallery. Each panel in turn had all of its earlier drafts running vertically down into it, showing the evolution of each image from start to finish. Cassette players and earpieces were strategically interspersed along the walls of the gallery so that viewers could listen to Art's original interviews with his father. In this way, Spiegelman hoped to bring his true object of representation into view: the process by which he arrived at a narrative, by which he made meaning in and worked through a history that has been both public and personal. Though the ostensible purpose of the exhibition was, according to Robert Storrs, "to illuminate the final entity—a mass-produced work—by showing its complex genesis in the artist's mind and on the draftsman's page,"[30] the artist himself preferred to see the exhibition *as* the total text, he told me. "If I had my way," he said, "this would be the text of *Maus*, replete with how I got to the so-called final panels."[31]

With the advent of CD-ROM, the artist has had his wish at least partly fulfilled, for here is an interactive text in which the panels of *Maus* are accompanied by complete genealogies of their origins. Where did a particular story or set of images come from, and how did they first enter the artist's consciousness? It's all here. We press the interactive screen on one of the colored boxes, and up comes a complete (pre-)history of that panel: Vladek's tape-recorded voice, with Art's interruptions, tells one version. The artist's early sketches done as his father spoke tell another. Photographs and drawings from Art's library that inspired certain images appear one after the other, even video footage of Art's trip to Poland and Auschwitz. By making visible the memory of this memory-text's production, the CD-ROM version of *Maus* reveals the interior, ever-evolving life of memory—and makes this life, too, part of its text.

The Ambivalence of Memory

Like other artists in his antiredemptory generation, Spiegelman cannot escape an essential ambivalence he feels toward his entire memory enterprise. For he recognizes that both his father's story and his own record of it have arisen out of a confluence of conflicting personal, professional, and not always heroic needs. Vladek tells his story, it seems, more for the sake of his son's company than for the sake of history; it is a way to keep his son nearby, a kind of tether. Indeed, as a survivor par excellence, Vladek is not above bartering the story itself to get what he wants: first, as leverage to keep his son nearby, and then later as part of an exchange for food at the local market, where he receives six dollars of groceries for one dollar, a partially eaten box of Special K cereal, an acknowledgment of his declining health, and, of course, a little about "how it was in the camps" (2:90). In a pinch, as it turns out, the savvy survivor can trade even his story of survival for food.

Although this kind of self-interested storytelling might drive the son a little crazy, Art must face the way he, too, has come to the story as much to learn about his origins, his dead mother, his own meshugas, as he does to learn Holocaust history. In fact, the Holocaust-telling relationship literally redeems the father-son relationship for Artie. "I'll get my tape recorder, so today isn't a total loss, okay?" he says after a particularly trying visit with Vladek (2:23). Moreover, he recognizes not only that he, too, has capitalized on his father's story but that in so doing, he has even delayed the rest of the story's publication. What with all the business and promotional deals surrounding *Maus* 1, Art could hardly find time to continue what had been a single project, now broken into two parts for the sake of publication. The Holocaust has been good to a starving artist who admits choosing his life's work partly to spite his father with its impracticality. And now it has made him quite comfortable as well, which becomes part of the story in *Maus* 2—a recognition of his debt to his father's story, the way Art has traded it for his own survival. In this way, history is received as a gift and as a commodity to be traded, the sole basis for any relationship at all between father and son.

All of which generates a certain self-loathing in the artist, even as it saps the author of his desire to continue telling the story. The first five frames of the second chapter in volume 2 open with Art's morbid reflections on the production and success of volume 1. With flies buzzing around his head, he contemplates the stages of his parents' life weighed against the stages of his own, while trying to make sense of the yawning gap between their life experiences and his:

Vladek died of congestive heart failure on August 18, 1982. . . .
Françoise and I stayed with him in the Catskills back in August
1979. Vladek started working as tinman in Auschwitz in the spring
of 1944. . . . I started working on this page at the very end of February 1987. In May 1987 Françoise and I are expecting a baby. . . .
Between May 16, 1944 and May 24, 1944 over 100,000 Hungarian
Jews were gassed in Auschwitz. . . . In September 1986, after 8 years
of work, the first part of MAUS was published. It was a critical and
commercial success. At least fifteen foreign editions are coming out.
I've gotten 4 serious offers to turn my book into a T.V. special or
movie. (I don't wanna.) In May 1968 my mother killed herself. (She
left no note.) Lately I've been feeling depressed. [2:41]

Out of his window, where one of New York City's signature water towers might be
standing, we see what Art sees: a concentration camp guard tower (its base and out-
line not unlike that of the water towers). Now, flies buzz around the crumpled mouse
corpses that litter Art's floor as he slumps dejectedly onto his drafting board.

Part of what gets Art down, of course, is that he is not an innocent bystander
in all this, a grateful vessel into which his father has poured his story. When he remembers his father's story now, he remembers how at times he had to wring it out of
him. When his father needed a son, a friend, a sounding board for his tsouris, Art demanded Holocaust. Before rejoining his father's story in Auschwitz, Art draws himself listening to the tape-recorded session he's about to tell. "I was still so sick and
tired," Vladek is saying about his return from a bout in the hospital. "And to have
peace only, I agreed to make [my will] legal. She brought right to my bed a NOTARY."
To which Art replies, "Let's get back to Auschwitz . . ." "Fifteen dollars he charged to
come! If she waited only a week until I was stronger, I'd go to the bank and take a notary for only a quarter!" "ENOUGH!" screams the son. "TELL ME ABOUT AUSCHWITZ!"
Artie shrinks in his seat and sighs as he listens again to this exchange. Defeated, his
father returns to the story (2:47).

Indeed, Spiegelman is both fascinated and repelled by the way he can actually
assimilate these stories so seamlessly into the rest of his life. At one point, his wife,
Françoise, peeks into Art's studio and asks cheerfully, "Want some coffee?" Art is replay-
ing the tape recording in which his father describes the moments before his brother
was killed. "And then she said, 'No! I will not go in the gas chambers. And my children
will not . . . [clik].'" Art turns off the cassette and answers eagerly, "You bet!" (2:120).

What do these stories do to the rest of the lives in which they are embedded? Shouldn't they foul everything they touch with their stench? Can we keep such stories separate or do they seep into the rest of our lives, and how corrosive are they? Maybe, just maybe, we can live with these stories, after all.

"Why should we assume there are positive lessons to be learned from [the Holocaust]?" essayist Jonathan Rosen has asked in an article that cuts excruciatingly close to the bone of Spiegelman's own ambivalence. "What if some history does not have anything to teach us? What if studying radical evil does not make us better? What if, walking through the haunted halls of the Holocaust Museum, looking at evidence of the destruction of European Jewry, visitors do not emerge with a greater belief that all men are created equal but with a belief that man is by nature evil?"[32]

As we see in the case of Vladek's own racist attitudes toward African-Americans, the Holocaust may have made him even worse. And if the Holocaust does not enlighten its victims, how will its story enlighten the next generation? It is an irony with a very clear judgment built into it: the Holocaust was an irredeemably terrible experi-

Art Spiegelman, Maus, 2:41.

Art Spiegelman, Maus, *2:47.*

ence then, had a terrible effect on many survivors' lives, and endows its victims with no great moral authority now. Categories like good and evil remain, but they are now stripped of their idealized certainties. Neither art nor narrative redeems the Holocaust with meaning—didactic, moral, or otherwise. In fact, to the extent that remembering events seems to find any meaning in them, such memory also betrays events by blinding us with our own need for redemptory closure.

Postmemory and the Evasions of History

At no place in or out of *Maus* does Spiegelman cast doubt on the facts of the Holocaust. Moreover, he is positively traditional in his use of documentary artifacts and photographs as guides to describing real events. When his book made the *New York Times* bestseller list in 1991, Spiegelman was surprised to find it on "the fiction side of the ledger." In a letter to the *Times,* he wrote,

> If your list were divided into literature and nonliterature, I could gracefully accept the compliment as intended, but to the extent that "fiction" indicates that a work isn't factual, I feel a bit queasy. As an author I believe I might have lopped several years off the 13 I devoted to my two-volume project if I could only have taken a novelist's license while searching for a novelistic structure.
>
> The borderland between fiction and non-fiction has been fertile territory for some of the most potent contemporary writing, and it's not as though my passages on how to build a bunker and repair concentration camp boots got the book onto your advice, how-to and miscellaneous list. It's just that I shudder to think how

David Duke—if he could read—would respond to seeing a carefully researched work based closely on my father's memories of life in Hitler's Europe and in the death camps classified as fiction.

I know that by delineating people with animal heads I've raised problems of taxonomy for you. Could you consider adding a special "nonfiction/mice" category to your list?[33]

In the end, the editors at the *Times* did not add this special "nonfiction/mice" category, but they did move *Maus* over to its nonfiction list. But in this context, it is not surprising that the author sees no contradiction between his fabular medium and his devotion to fact in *Maus*. For his positivist stance is not a negation of the vagaries of memory but that which makes the recognition of memory necessary. Together the facts of history and their memory exist side by side, mutually dependent for sustenance and meaning.

Thus will a received history like *Maus* also remain true to the mistaken perceptions and memory of the survivor. What might appear as historical errors of fact in *Maus,* such as the picture of Poles—one in a Nazi uniform (1:140) and others saying, "Heil Hitler" (1:149), when it would have been almost impossible to find any Pole saluting Hitler to another Pole during the war or to find a Polish Nazi—are accurate representations of his father's possibly faulty memory. The truth of such memory is not that Poles actually gave the Nazi salute to each other but that Vladek remembered Poles to be Nazi-like in their hatred of Jews. Whether accurate or not, such a perception may itself have played a role in Vladek's actions during the war—and so deserves a place in the historical record.

Issues of historical accuracy and factuality in a medium like *Maus* are bound to haunt its author, raised as they are by the medium but impossible to resolve in it. Nancy Miller has put the question most succinctly: "The relationship between accuracy and caricature for the cartoonist who works in a medium in which accuracy is an *effect of exaggeration* is a vexed one."[34] But in an era when absolute truth claims are under assault, Spiegelman's *Maus* makes a case for an essentially reciprocal relationship between the truth of what happened and the truth of how it is remembered. The facts of the Holocaust here include the facts surrounding its eventual transmission to him. Together, what happened and how it is remembered constitute a received history of events.

Here I would like to suggest, after Patrick Hutton, that "what is at issue here is not how history can recover memory, but, rather, what memory will bequeath to

Art Spiegelman, Maus, *1:60.*

history."[35] That is, what shall we do with the living memory of survivors? How will it enter (or not enter) the historical record? Or to paraphrase Hutton again, "How will the past be remembered as it passes from living memory to history?" Will it always be regarded as so overly laden with pathos as to make it unreliable as documentary evidence? Or is there a place for the understanding of the witness, as subjective and skewed as it may be, for our larger historical understanding of events?

In spite of (or perhaps because of) their sophistication, even when historians and philosophers of history like Hayden White, Amos Funkenstein, and Saul Friedlander look for models of such history, the best they can come up with are often kinds of fiction, imaginative memoirs, and hybrid forms like the comix. In a parallel vein, Michael André Bernstein has also found that the best examples of what he calls "sideshadowed" and "anti-apocalyptic history" are similarly the fiction of Robert Musil or poetry of Yehuda Amichai. What might this antiredemptory middle voice look like? Very much, according to Bernstein, like the end of Yehuda Amichai's poem "Tourists":

> Once I was sitting on the steps near the gate at David's Citadel and
> I put down my two heavy baskets beside me. A group of tourists
> stood there around their guide, and I became their point of refer-
> ence. "You see that man over there with the baskets? A little to the

right of his head there's an arch from the Roman period. A little to the right of his head." "But he's moving, he's moving!" I said to myself: Redemption will come only when they are told, "Do you see that arch over there from the Roman period? It doesn't matter, but near it, a little to the left and then down a bit, there's a man who has just bought fruit and vegetables for his family."[36]

Prosaic? Yes. Banal? No. Like Friedlander's or Spiegelman's, this is the uncanny middle voice of one who is in history and who tells it simultaneously, one who lives *in* history as well as *through* its telling.

CHAPTER TWO

David Levinthal's *Mein Kampf*

History, Toys, and the Play of Memory

"Photography is an elegiac art, a twilight art . . . "
—*Susan Sontag,* On Photography

"We make, we seek, and finally we enjoy, the contrivance of all experience. We fill our
lives not with experience, but with images of experience."
—*Daniel Boorstin,* The Image

IT MAY BE THE COMPANY I KEEP, but some of my best friends grew up playing with the Holocaust. Not lightheartedly, of course, but in the obsessive earnestness of children trying to work through a family's trauma. For many of my friends growing up in post–World War II America, the Holocaust was a haunting fixture in their households, a constant ache inherited by children ever-watchful of their parents' fears and preoccupations. One friend, in particular, now a philosopher of post-Holocaust theology, recalls that as a six-year-old, she played an ongoing game of "Holocaust hide-and-seek." From morning until night, she bundled her Barbie, Ken, and Shirley Temple dolls, along with her little brother, from closet to closet half a step ahead of the Nazis in her mind. The enemy and chase were easily imagined, she tells me, but what would happen if they caught her and the babies was then literally unimaginable to her, though no less terrifying in its horrible mystery.

As we both realize now, it was here that my friend first learned to imagine history, not as it really happened, but as it mattered in her life. Of course, the Holocaust is a terrible subject for any child's fantasy life, but for a generation of Jewish children growing up in the 1950s—far removed from the killing fields of World War II Europe

—schoolyards and bedrooms strewn with toys were their sites of history, the places where they worked through the whispered terror that still gripped their parents' generation. For it is here, in their play and in the company of toys and make-believe companions, where children first articulate their sense of a vicarious past. It is here where they reenact relationships, recently witnessed discussions, and parental arguments and thus begin to adopt a previous generation's history as their own.

As it turns out, the play between history and memory is also a necessarily gender-inflected activity. At about the time my friend was hiding her dolls from the Nazis, David Levinthal was a little boy in California, sending his beloved toy soldiers, cowboys, and Indians into ferocious battle. He, too, was playing Holocaust, but his imagined history was an essentially military one: his bedroom was cluttered with battalions of toy soldiers locked in mortal combat. No women or children here. The little boy's imagination and war narratives were fueled by television images from *Combat, Gunsmoke,* and *Rawhide.* Like other children of his generation, or like all who were blessedly removed from Europe during the war, David Levinthal's memory of the Holocaust was only and always a composite pastiche of television images, toys, and the stories he made up during years of war play. The reality of war and Holocaust was necessarily reduced to the miniature reality of his playthings, the intensely felt reality of his romper-room simulations.

It cannot be surprising, therefore, that when photographer and toy collector David Levinthal began to reexamine his memory of the Holocaust, he found himself reflecting on the toys by which he had first grasped history. But when he began to photograph these toys in 1972, one of his M.F.A. photography teachers at Yale's School of Art asked him, "Why don't you take pictures of the real world, of reality?" Levinthal answered, perhaps a little too honestly, that "These toys *are* my reality!" Rather than forgetting that his relationship to the Holocaust would always be an imagined, make-believe one, he chose to make his vicarious past—as embodied in these simulations—the subject of his photographs.

For when an artist like David Levinthal sets out "to remember" the Holocaust, all he can actually remember are the numberless images passed down to him in books, films, and photographs. When he sets out "to photograph" the Holocaust, therefore, he takes pictures of *his* Holocaust experiences—that is, recirculated images of the Holocaust. Indeed, the visual reality of the Holocaust for Levinthal and his generation is forever only the record of photographs and documentary film. The physical reality of the Holocaust exists now only in its consequences, its effects and simulations: the rest is memory, itself increasingly shaped by the reality of our simulations. This "memory" is not the animate memory of one who was there but is rather as static and inert as the photos themselves, the images already small and toylike.

As a late-twentieth-century photographer, David Levinthal is hardly alone in his fascination with the ready-made simulacrum. "One of my favorite [Eugène Atget] photographs is a shop window full of hats on [mannequin] heads," Levinthal tells us.[1] Like Atget's photographs of mannequins, or Hans Bellmer's surreal photographs of recomposed dolls in process, or Jorge Ribalta's more recent portraiture of sculpted busts, or Laurie Simmons's photographs of mock-domestic doll tableaux, or Cindy Sherman's disturbing mutilated doll images, Levinthal's photographs have always taken the imitations of reality, not reality itself, as their subject.[2] For Levinthal's media-saturated generation, it could even be said that these ready-made simulations have become the primary reality of events to which they refer. Because historical events constantly pass into the ether of time, they remain "present" only in memory, imagination, and their material representations.

The artists of the photoconceptual vanguard have thus turned their interrogating eye to the simulations of reality as relentlessly as a prior generation of photographers once explored what they regarded as a natural and unmediated world. In the process, Levinthal and others continue to reveal the ways the world is constantly packaged and repackaged for us in a commodity culture. By taking as their subject ready-made simulations only, such photographs mock the culture with the reductive banality of its simulations, even as they leave us hungry for the "real thing," for a real world constantly displaced by its media product. In the hands of photoconceptual artists, toys and their reflected images not only evoke memories of childhood and private inner lives but also embody the realities and preoccupations of adult life, as well as larger public issues of history and our vicarious relationship to it through art. Finally, through their "fabricated photography," these artists also ask to what extent reality itself is always a kind of ongoing fabrication—not as a kind of fiction, but more literally as that which is constantly being improvised, moment by moment.[3]

In the case of *Mein Kampf* (1994–1996), the artist's second foray into memory of the wartime, the result is a disturbing and provocative series of oversized Polaroid photographs depicting the artist's dramatically staged tableaux of toy Nazi soldiers and their figurine victims. As Levinthal is quick to clarify, these images do not capture Holocaust history so much as they do the artist's struggle to capture his own hypermediated reality of the Holocaust. Moreover, Levinthal's carefully choreographed and staged photo-tableaux have their own history, their own process, that are as much a part of their significance as the content of the glossy images themselves. In this chapter, I explore the several strata of meaning-making at work in Levinthal's "toyland of Holocaust history." For like much contemporary art, these images were not meant to stand by or for themselves. But rather, they are necessarily part of the artist's larger oeuvre, a life's work dedicated to exploring the fuzzy line between the photograph's traditional function as documentary record of external reality and its more recently acknowledged role in revealing the inner realities of the mind's eye.[4]

The Toy as Cultural Icon

It is true that David Levinthal's photographs have largely "eschewed reality for a world constructed and reinvented in the studio."[5] Yet at the same time, they also examine a particular kind of reality—that of the cultural icon and myth. From the beginning, Levinthal has used toys to examine and break down the mythological icons of popular culture: from *Hitler Moves East* (1977) to *Modern Romance* (1985), from *The Wild West* (1987) to *American Beauties* (1989), the aim has been to photograph toys in ways that estrange their archetypal forms from themselves. In his *Wild West* series, for example, Levinthal dramatically reconverts the simulacra of miniature toy cowboys back into their mythologically proportioned archetypes. Just as the myth of the cowboy has grown bigger than life, the toy miniature reduces the cowboy to smaller than life: and it is this smaller-than-life image that Levinthal then exposes in his large-format Polaroid photographs. In these images, the toys are returned to mythological proportions with an ironic twist, part of an imagined tableau, exaggerated by the imagination itself.

Similarly, his *American Beauties* and *Modern Romance* series take the male-idealized female icon as embodied by erotic Japanese dolls and turns it against itself. At every level, the images remind viewers of women's subjugation at the hands of men: first in the "sexy" little dolls themselves; then in the ominous arrangements of dolls threatened by male figures standing over them; and then again in the photographer's carefully crafted "dark light," a film-noir atmosphere laden with danger and ambiguity.

In all of his toy subjects, men's and women's body types are cast according to prescribed cultural molds: men are square-jawed, finely chiseled, muscular; they are clothed in soldiers' uniforms or cowboy and Indian outfits. The women are always voluptuous, whether blond or dark-haired, their skin shining luminously. They come clothed in long settlers' dresses and bonnets or short skirts; often they are naked. The male figurines are in stiff and aggressive poses, ready to fight. The female figurines are supple and somehow inviting, often lying provocatively or sitting passively, never threatening, except as possible sexual predators. As mini-icons, these toys both reflect and embody the myths of our culture: the self-fulfilling myths of strength and aggressiveness in men, of passive sexuality in women. Because Levinthal's photographs are what he calls "object-driven," inspired by the figures themselves, the subjects of his tableaux and images are not just the toys but the reductive idealizations and cultural myths they embody.

In this way, the photographer reminds us that toys are not antimonuments so much as they are demonumentalizations of their worldly counterparts. As the oversized monument inflates the importance of its subject, turning it into a seemingly natural part of the landscape, as true and enduring as nearby rocks and trees, the toy conversely deflates its subject's pretensions, mocking it with its puniness. Instead of providing grand sites around which the national story accrues, as monuments do, toys play supporting roles in the inner play-lives of children. And instead of playing a role in the public's mind, toys play a role in the private fantasy worlds of the children who hold them. At the same time, however, like monuments, toys are also fixed images, types concretized and meant to stand for all like them.

The Play of Memory

As M.F.A. students at Yale in the early 1970s, David Levinthal and *Doonesbury* cartoonist Garry Trudeau shared a fascination for alternative history-telling, the kind that Art Spiegelman would later characterize as the "*comix*ture of image and narrative." While Levinthal was staging his toy Nazi soldiers in various narrative tableaux and photographing them, Trudeau was planning to tell the fictional story of a German Luftwaffe lieutenant through what he called a "narrative collage" drawing on archival photographs and documents. In such a medium, the comix artist hoped to generate two levels of meaning-making activity. "One was in the narration," Trudeau writes, "in the details of the actions of the subject. The other was in the directed progression of visual elements from one composition to the next. The intentions were to create a sort of sequential montage and to establish cinematic relationships among consecutive images."[6] Working together, Levinthal and Trudeau wed their respective projects to each other in *Hitler Moves East* (1977) to chronicle Operation Barbarossa,

Hitler's invasion of the Soviet Union in June 1941. But instead of using images drawn directly from archival sources, they created their own "archival" images by photographing Levinthal's toys in carefully staged war scenarios, each image inspired by a remembered photograph from their own research.

The result was a stunningly arranged assemblage of what seemed to be action-blurred battle photographs of German Wehrmacht soldiers moving east. Each section of photographs is accompanied by a short but pithy historical narrative telling a different stage of Operation Barbarossa. In the years after its publication, *Hitler Moves East* attained cult status among photographers and graphic artists. Between its faux realism and fluent storytelling, it had come to be regarded as a hybrid form of historical memory, one dependent completely on recycled archival images, shuffled through the artists' media-saturated imaginations. As I thumbed through the pages of *Hitler Moves East,* I kept asking myself, What does it mean to tell the story of Operation Barbarossa in photographs of toys? What am I seeing in these images that remains out of reach to documentary photographs?

At first blush, the photographs take on a documentary hue in their sepia-tinted black-and-white tones. But on further reflection, one realizes that this is only the style of historical documentary. For these images are not about the history of this particular past so much as they are about the artists' media-dependent imagining of such history. What is really being documented here is the artists' own, unabashed imaginations. The powerful sense of the past (not its actuality) is being generated carefully through a measured act of simulation. As a result, we are being moved partly by the sense of documentation and partly by the cunning of the memory-artists. I was seeing not "the past" but rather how Garry Trudeau and David Levinthal have remembered it as passed down to them in photographs and grainy film footage. Theirs was a visual, yet vicarious memory of events, which they turned into a narrative of invented images.

First came their countless hours looking at and handling volumes of archival battle photographs, their sifting through hours of newsreel footage. Then came the hundreds of hours spent arranging these soldiers just so, even planting an indoor lawn to resemble the Ukrainian steppes and mixing explosive charges that would blow their toys sky-high for the sake of a photograph. No doubt, sound effects and the dialogue of dying and wounded soldiers accompanied the entire period of memory-play. All of which simultaneously evoke and reflect the artists' feel for the past, its tactile experience in their hands. What lay behind the commixture of invented photographic images and historical narrative was the free play of memory inspired by the photographs of those who were there.

Nowhere in this project, however, is there the slightest visual reference to the mass murder of Jews. At the same time, it is also clear that much of the power of these images derives from the pathos engendered by our own knowledge of what lay just beyond the border of these photographs. For such images of Nazi soldiers will always be haunted by the actions we know were subsumed by Hitler's move east—such as the mass killing by the S.S. Einsatzgruppen units. What remained just off-stage in *Hitler Moves East* would now be brought into the center of consciousness, both the artist's and viewers', in the photographer's project *Mein Kampf.*

The Artist's Struggle Between History and Memory

Unlike *Hitler Moves East,* which Levinthal claims surprised him in its effect, its raw power, the *Mein Kampf* series of explicitly Holocaust imagery is deliberate, polished, and even a little cold-blooded. Nor is *Mein Kampf* a mere sequel to *Hitler Moves East,* though it does show us quite graphically what Hitler did once he arrived in the east. Rather, *Mein Kampf* embodies the artist's struggle with representing his vicarious experience of the Holocaust. It is David Levinthal's struggle between what he knows and how he has known it, between Holocaust history and how it has been passed down to him in the popular, all-too-mythologized icons of television and photographs. For whether we like it or not, once icons of the Holocaust enter the popular imagination, they also turn mythic, hard and impenetrable.

Still, why *Mein Kampf?* And why the Holocaust? The artist began this series when he found a sparkling new Hitler figurine in an Austrian toy store. "I discovered that there was a man in Germany who had molds from the 30's and who was re-making these figures and hand painting them," Levinthal tells us.[7] But the idea of someone handpainting newly minted armies of toy Hitlers both fascinated and re-pelled the artist: he wanted to know why and what it meant. Levinthal's first impulse was to interrogate the figurine itself, as if it could speak. But what he found lying just beneath his fascination and revulsion with this Hitler figurine was his own preoccu-pation with the Holocaust.

This Hitler figurine struck the artist at first as a kind of golem in miniature, a friendly monster beholden to its maker before running amok, invigorated and em-boldened by its independence. He began thinking that he would do only a series of portraits of Hitler and his Nazi figurines. But before long, it became clear that he could not divorce the pageantry and spectacle of the Nazis, as suggested by these fig-urines, from the terror of the Holocaust. Indeed, through further "visual research," as Levinthal calls it, he found that in films like Leni Riefenstahl's *Triumph of the Will* (1935) it was at least partly this sense of pageantry and spectacle whence the Nazis derived so much of their public power and appeal. For Levinthal now, once associ-ated with the horrible deeds of its makers, such spectacle would always carry with it an ominous, hidden side. To reveal this dark side of the Nazi pageant, Levinthal chose first to simulate it and then juxtapose it to the phantom of its heretofore hidden anti-spectacle: the Holocaust.

For Levinthal, part of the "meaning" in his portraits of the Nazi toys was the process itself, the fashioning of his own miniature spectacles, which involved ex-tended periods of contemplation. Here, moreover, he seemed to replicate the quasi-obsessiveness of the handcrafted toy with his own meticulously crafted tableaux, discovering that the process itself seemed to provide a certain outlet for the artist's Weltschmerz. In this adult working-through, the memory of childhood is always double-edged: it is a happy *and* painful time, when innocence is relentlessly under-cut by experience.

Even his search for such toys has become part of the artist's historical consciousness, part of his own memory of the past. Before he could interrogate Hitler, he first had to capture him from the hands of specialty toy store owners in Vienna. "Do you have anything, um, from the Second World War?" Levinthal asked one such proprietor ingenuously. The Viennese toy store owner was an older man behind the counter, and he studied this American customer warily, his eyes narrowing ever so slightly. "Ja, but they are not for sale." "Oh, but I'd love just to see them," the artist says he answered excitedly. The proprietor disappeared through a door into the back for a moment before returning with several small boxes labeled "Lineol," "Hauser," and "Elastolin." These were what Levinthal had been looking for, toy S.S. soldiers cast from molds designed during the Third Reich. They are hand-painted in a detail that continues to astound the artist, right down to their polished buttons, black jackboots, and death's head insignia. "These are real beauties," Levinthal marveled, "How much are they?" As it turns out, of course, everything has a price, which the artist pays for admission to his vicariously imagined past.

Levinthal insists that these new mini-spectacles are as object-driven as his earlier projects: the little Nazi drummer corp is set before something resembling the Brandenburg Gate; a soldier and dog patrol outside guard tower and wire fence; a woman holding a child whirls away from a German soldier who aims a rifle at her from inches away. But it is also clear that each of these toys has sparked a particular visual association in the artist's mind, the memory of an image, which the artist then brings into physical relief. And because they are meant to evoke, not mime, and to stimulate the imagination but not simulate historical realities, these photographs are shot in what Levinthal terms a "narrative style": what the artist has characterized as "intentionally ambiguous to draw the viewer in so that you make your own story."[8] Or as he elaborates in another interview, "I think I create a window that allows the viewer to come into an image that appears to be more complete than it really is. It becomes complete when the viewer becomes a participant and fills in the missing details."[9] That is, added to the artist's story as he constructed the tableaux are the stories viewers tell themselves about what they see. These pieces depend on narrative for their lives, animated by the stories we tell about them.

Levinthal accomplishes this ambiguity by shooting these tableaux at Polaroid's New York City studio with a 20x24 Land camera, its aperture set wide open, to create an extremely shallow focal plane—hence the blurry fore- and backgrounds. The more ambiguous, underdetermined, and oblique the image, the more it seems to

David Levinthal, Mein Kampf.

invite the viewer's own narrative. The sharper the image, the more repellent it is
of multiple readings, for it crowds out the reader's projected story with the clut-
ter of its own detail. The essential tension in Levinthal's medium is that between
the toy's fixedness and the camera's seeming liquification of its material hardness.
In this way, he turns the traditional assumption of photographic precision against
itself, extending the range of the camera inward to include the mind's eye and
imagination.

Depending on the image, the focal plane in Levinthal's work lies just before or
behind the toy objects, never on them. Rather than concentrating the mind on the
toy object, the focal plane takes us into the space between the object and its once-
worldly referent, into the space between it and us—where the mind is forced to
imagine and thereby collaborate. The indistinct lines don't absorb the eye as sharp
images might; instead the soft focus deflects the mind's eye away from the object and
inward, back into itself. In the seemingly iconic image of guard tower, fence, soldier,

and dog, it is the rich black and blue tints of the sky that absorb the eye, pulling the mind through the figures into the space behind them. This is a kind of reverse reality effect: I stare and realize that the darker and less discernible the dog and soldier are, the more real they become in my mind.

In this regard, such work reminds us of one of the principles of Jochen Gerz's disappearing and invisible countermonuments (discussed in Chapter 5). Rather than embodying the work of memory, Gerz fears, the monument displaces it altogether. An invisible monument, or one that gradually disappears over time, would conversely return the burden of memory to those who come looking for it. "Art, in its conspicuousness, in its recognizability, is an indication of failure," Gerz has said. "If it were truly consumed, no longer visible or conspicuous . . . , it would actually be where it belongs—that is, within the people for whom it was created."[10] In the case of Levinthal's photographs, our eye never rests on the objects but remains suspended somewhere in the space between them and us, between us and our imagination. As a result, the piece of art has come to exist more in us, the viewers, and less on the wall.

What used to be called "soft-focus portraiture," a fountain-of-youth technique by which photographers could obscure the flaws of mortality and the lines of age, has been radically extended by a new generation of painters and photographers to turn the camera into a tool of mimetic doubt and insecurity, not certainty. On one hand, the blurred paintings of Gerhard Richter or Ed

David Levinthal, Mein Kampf.

Ruscha suggest to critics like Donald Kuspit a certain collapse of authoritative meaning in our culture at large.[11] At the same time, such fuzziness also prompts the viewer to work a little harder, if a little less confidently, toward finding meaning, which now exists in the tug-of-war between image and viewer, not in the image or viewer alone. It is a process, a dialogue, in which making meaning, with all its difficulties and uncertainties, becomes as significant as any particular meaning made.

In almost every one of the images from Levinthal's *Mein Kampf* series, many more questions—aesthetic, personal, and historical—are raised than answered: What is the relationship of the artist to events? Does such a medium trivialize memory even as it interrogates it? What of history itself is understood through such images? And what do such images tell us about our relationship to the Holocaust now, fifty years later? Unlike the evocative rawness of *Hitler Moves East,* the cool and studied polish of these images constantly reminds us of their aesthetic intervention between then and now. They are staged to look deliberately staged, choreographed to show their choreography. All rawness is gone, all innocence put to flight. Resonant with our own corrupted memory traces, these photographs show us how far away from events the icons of our culture have taken us.[12]

In one image, for example, a woman cradling a child and whirling away from an Einsatzcommando's professionally aimed bullet explicitly recalls the horrific photograph taken on the eastern front by an S.S. photographer during an Einsatzcommando massacre of Jews. By evoking the photographic image, Levinthal again reminds us that his are images of other images: the artist's photograph of a diorama recapitulates the Nazis' own record of their crimes. Not only are we reminded of the several layers of mediation interposed between the artist's memory and history, but we must also confront the terrible fact that we are now dependent on the murderers for any memory of the victims' last seconds.

In this image's recirculation, we find that this Nazi photograph has in itself become part of the iconic currency of the Holocaust—and has thus taken on a life of its own. Beyond its status as a Nazi artifact, it resonates a conglomerate of axiomatic truisms, so that the image has become emblematic of killers and victims: the woman and child represent the vulnerability and blamelessness of the victims, the generations of Jewish life that would be wiped out in a single blow, a grotesque pietà in which both mother and child are murdered, a certain sacrifice. The paradox in Levinthal's photograph is that such emblems are also rehumanized in their recapitulation. What begins as pure emblem is softened and reanimated in Levinthal's handling of it.

To this day, many people insist that some scenes from the Holocaust cannot ethically be represented. Because no one survived the gas chambers to describe the terror there, its darkness has remained absolute. Other areas on which artists are practically forbidden to tread include the sexuality of victims and the possible sado-sexuality of the killers. This is why some will have trouble assimilating images from *Mein Kampf* of crematoria stuffed with bodies of women in glaringly sexual poses. When I objected to what seemed to be a deliberate eroticization of the murder process and tried to talk Levinthal into eliding from the exhibition several images of naked Japanese dolls with gaudy red nipples, the artist responded that Art Spiegelman had also tried to talk him out of showing those. "But nowhere in the literature have I found anything to suggest an erotic component to the killing process," I said, "only in the imaginations of those who weren't there, like D. M. Thomas in his novel *The White Hotel.*"

To which Levinthal replied that whether or not there was actually a sexual, erotic component to the murder process, it remains certainly—if unfortunately—true that in many of its popular representations, the Holocaust has been eroticized. Because his subject is the ready-made simulation of the Holocaust, he was only showing a Holocaust porno-kitsch already at play in the cultural transformations of these terrible scenes. In popular movies like *Schindler's List* and *Sophie's Choice,* or in novels like *The White Hotel,* for example, Eros and Thanatos are twinned as constituent elements of Holocaust victimization, projected reflexively onto victims by a culture obsessed with both, a culture that has long linked the two as fatally interconnected, a culture that has eventually grown dependent on their union for commercial and entertainment value.[13] Rather than ignoring them, therefore, Levinthal makes the erotic Japanese dolls with their bright red nipples and splayed legs part of his work. He believes, moreover, that both killers and victims understood that part of the dehumanization of the Jews included their sexual degradation in the moments before death.

As women have been objectified in these toys and the Jews were objectified by the Nazis, the victims would here be presented as objectified twice over. Created as sexual objects, the dolls are used to recapitulate not only the relationship between killers and victims but also, if more implicitly, that between contemporary viewers and these very images. Here Levinthal suggests that with every representation of their murder, the Jews are in some sense murdered again and again. Robbed of life by the Nazi gunmen, the victims are robbed of their dignity by the observing photographer

David Levinthal, Mein Kampf.

—and then again with the recirculation of such images. Only now we are the passive bystanders, and not so innocent at that.

The complicated role such images play in the public sphere came into especially sharp relief in a slightly different context a few years ago in Jerusalem. When confronted by leaders of the ultra-Orthodox community in Jerusalem, the curators at Israel's national Holocaust memorial museum, Yad Vashem, refused to remove wall-sized photographs taken by the Nazis of naked Jewish women on their way to the gas chambers at Treblinka (many of them orthodox and so violated unequivocally by the S.S. photographer at the moment). The museum replied that because this degradation, too, was part of the reality of the Holocaust, it had to be shown as part of the historical record—even if it offended the religious community's rigorous sense of modesty. In the eyes of the religious community, however, the humiliation and violation of these women's modesty was as much a part of the crime as their eventual murder. That their modesty would be violated yet again by the viewers now may even suggest not so much a repetition of the crime as an extension of it.

At the same time, despite the curators' stated aim of maintaining the exhibit's historical integrity, the museum may have refused to acknowledge another historical reality: the possibility of their visitors' pornographic gaze. Will we ever know all the reasons why people are transfixed by these images? Is the historical record of past travesties enough to blind us to the possibility of present travesties on the parts of viewers? Can we say with certainty that every museum visitor's gaze is as pure as the curators' historical intent? For the fine line between exhibition and exhibitionistic remains as fragile as it is necessary, even in the hands of scrupulous historians and curators.

At least part of what makes these images so unnerving for viewers is their suggestion that we, as viewers, may be no less complicit in the continuing degradation

David Levinthal, Mein Kampf.

German soldiers examine photographs of a civilian massacre they had conducted a few days before.

of the victim than the original Nazi photographer. In another calculatedly disturbing image in *Mein Kampf,* it is Levinthal's formal design and composition that foists this realization upon viewers, leaving little room in which to escape such conclusions. In this photograph, four women (portrayed by sexy dolls with porcelain white skin) are being shot by two S.S. gunmen. Their rifles aim into a perspectival vortex at the center of the image: we look over the shoulders of both gunmen, right into the center of the V. Three women have their arms up, as if to ward off the bullets, and one woman is already falling down. Only the muzzle of one of the rifles is in focus, though the colors of the bodies are bright and sharp, a swirl of whites, blues, and gun-metal gray, all tinged by red smoke and glare.

From our vicarious but central vantage point, we, too, are implicated in this shooting—as is the photographer, who seems passively to be watching the scene, a participant inspired by the S.S. photographers who recorded but did not prevent similar shootings. Or as Susan Sontag has made so painfully explicit, "Photography is essentially an art of non-intervention. . . . The person who intervenes cannot record; the person who is recording cannot intervene."[14] That is, even as a passive spectator, the photographer plays a role, if by default, in the events he or she would capture: to some extent, every photographer is both choreographer of an event and representer of it. In the case of Levinthal's image, which he has literally choreo-graphed before shooting, such a truism is made palpable. And by forcing us to view the shooting from a vantage point between the two gunmen, the artist has, in effect, made us the implied third gun.

If this relationship among the killers, their own photographs, and ourselves as viewers sounds implausible, consider the chilling sequence of images stored in the Etablissement Cinématographie et Photographie des Armées in Paris. In this series of photographs taken by a German army photographer, about twenty Serbian and Jewish men are rounded up in Nazi-occupied Yugoslavia in a reprisal action. The photographs begin with the men's arrest in the center of town and continue with their transport in the back of a cart to a desolate field in the countryside. Here they are depicted digging their own graves, taking off their clothes, and being shot five at a time. Yet the last photographs in the series are not of the men's bodies or their burial but of the soldiers themselves sitting around in a group, smoking ciga-rettes and viewing photographs of the killing. It is not clear whether their action is being explained for them by a superior or whether curiosity alone compels these soldiers to look at the images of their action. In either case, the German photogra-pher seems to be suggesting in such a sequence that the action in its entirety includ-ed both the shooting of men *and* the photographic representation of their deaths, the killing *and* the killers' subsequent reviewing of their deed in the photographs.[15]

"Can war be beautiful?" Garry Trudeau asks in his Introduction to *Hitler Moves East*. "Or does it only seem that way in the safety of knowing that it is all con-trived and make-believe, that the components are only toys and not really the carri-ers of death?"[16] In these questions, Trudeau wonders also whether simulating is always a kind of play, whether one of the pleasures of mimesis is the safety we feel in being so far removed from real events, a safety that heightens the vicarious thrill of a war imagined. Levinthal would not speak for war itself, but he does acknowledge that like Goya's paintings or Riefenstahl's *Triumph of the Will* or Steven Spielberg's *Schindler's List*, in which the images of killing, Nazi pageantry, and even the Holocaust can be si-multaneously horrible and beautiful, some of his own images from *Mein Kampf*, "par-ticularly those images that deal with the pageantry of the Nazis, [are] seductively beautiful, as were the actual pageants" themselves.[17]

For Levinthal, the question was never whether to show such images but rather how to ask in them: to what extent do we always reobjectify a victim by reproducing images of the victim as victim? How extensively do we participate in this degradation

David Levinthal, Mein Kampf.

by reproducing and then viewing them? To what extent do these images ironize and thereby repudiate such representations? Or how heavily do these images feed on the same prurient energy they purportedly expose? Or as Saul Friedlander has asked, "Is such attention fixed on the past only a gratuitous reverie, the attraction of spectacle, exorcism, or the result of a need to understand; or is it, again and still, an expression of profound fears and, on the part of some, mute yearnings as well?[18] By leaving these questions unanswered, Levinthal confronts us with our own role in the representation of mass murder, the way we cover our eyes and peek through our fingers at the same time.

The line between miming a simulacrum and mimicking it is already a fine and fuzzy one. David Levinthal's work leaves this line as ambiguous as ever. His objects are clearly the myths and icons that our toy culture reifies in its miniatures: the beauty queen, the cowboy, the Indian, the soldier, the great leader. Even in its miniaturization, the type is already mocked somehow—made smaller than life, its idea reduced and made childlike. Yet by reproducing it, by taking the edge off, the artist breathes new life into it, animates it with the stories we tell around such types. Is the myth or icon thus automatically negated in such work? Not necessarily. But our relationship to the myth is now called into question, and the seeming innocence of our preoccupations is now not so innocent, after all.

CHAPTER THREE

Sites Unseen

Shimon Attie's Acts of Remembrance, 1991–1996

"Lieux de mémoire *are created by the interaction between memory and history.* . . .

Without an intent to remember, lieux de mémoire *would be* lieux d'histoire."

—*Pierre Nora,* Realms of Memory

SOME PEOPLE CLAIM INTUITIVELY TO SENSE the invisible aura of past events in historical sites, as if the molecules of such sites still vibrated with the memory of their past. Shimon Attie is not so naive. He knows that this presence of the past is apparent only to those already familiar with a site's history or to those who actually carry a visual memory of this site from another, earlier time. For Attie, memory of a site's past does not emanate from within a place but is more likely the projection of the mind's eye onto a given site. Without the historical consciousness of visitors, these sites remain essentially indifferent to their pasts, altogether amnesiac. They "know" only what we know, "remember" only what we remember.

For by themselves, these sites lack what French intellectual historian Pierre Nora has called "the will to remember." That is, without a deliberate act of remembrance, buildings, streets, or ruins remain little more than inert pieces of the cityscape. Without the will to remember, Nora suggests, the place of memory "created in the play of memory and history. . . becomes indistinguishable from the place of history."[1] If it is true that such places of memory exist "only because of their capacity for metamorphosis," as Nora believes, then here we shall examine the work of an artist as agent of metamorphosis, one whose acts of remembrance transform the sites of history into the sites of memory.

In *Sites Unseen,* Shimon Attie's series of European installations between 1991 and 1996, the artist has done more than simply project his necessarily mediated

Shimon Attie, Joachimstrasse 11a, 1933, 1992. (Writing on the Wall)

memory of a now-lost Jewish past onto otherwise forgetful sites. He has also attempted a simultaneous critique of his own hypermediated relationship to the past. By literally bathing the sites of a now invisible Jewish past in the photographic images of their historical pasts, he simultaneously looks outward and inward for memory: for he hopes that once seen, the images of these projections will always haunt these sites by haunting those who have seen his projections. The sites of a lost Jewish past in Europe would thus retain traces of this past, if now only in the eyes of those who have seen Attie's installations.

When Shimon Attie moved to Berlin in 1991, he found a city haunted by the absence of its murdered and deported Jews. Like many Jewish Americans preoccupied by the Holocaust and steeped in its seemingly ubiquitous images, he saw Jewish ghosts in Europe's every nook and cranny: from the Scheunenviertel in Berlin to the central train station in Dresden; from the canals of Copenhagen to those of Amsterdam; from Cologne's annual art fair to Kraków's Kazimierz neighborhood. For Attie, however, private acts of remembrance in which he alone saw the faces and forms of now absent Jews in their former neighborhoods were not enough. He chose, therefore, to actualize these inner visions, to externalize them, and in so doing to make them part of a larger public's memory. Once thus actualized, he hoped, these images would enter the inner worlds of all who saw them and would continue to haunt the sites even when no longer visible. He hoped that once others

Shimon Attie, Almadtstrasse 43 (formerly Grenadierstrasse 7), Former Hebrew Bookstore, 1930, 1992. (Writing on the Wall, Berlin)

had become witnesses to his memorial projections, the installations themselves would no longer be necessary.

At the same time, *Sites Unseen* was not intended as a series of simple recollective acts, attempts to repair a broken past-continuous. Each installation also recast memory in some way, re-marking its relation to the site even as it explored the site's relation to its past. As a result, each project sustained a certain, yet subtle ambivalence toward itself, even as each mixed the kinds of memory it generated. At each stage, the distance from personal to public memory was measured, as well as the reciprocal exchange between a specific site and its national context, the ways every site resonates with a nation's self-idealizations.

Part photography, part installation, and part performance, the totality of these projects might best be described as an "act of remembrance"—retaining the resonance of actions, staged acts, actors, and acting out. For in equal measure, the projects included the literal actions that brought them into being, made actors of local residents, staged interactions between local residents and their homes, and provided a medium for the artist's own acting out of his obsession with the void left by Europe's absent Jews. Nor should the book you are now holding be mistaken for the "acts of remembrance" it explores, which like the historical events being commemorated are now over. Rather, this book is an after-image in its own right, a reflection on these acts.

In the pages that follow, therefore, I ask what happens between the mind of someone like Attie, immersed in the public iconography of the Holocaust, and the actual sites of history now seemingly oblivious to their pasts. On one hand, Attie the artist is painfully aware that all he knows and remembers of the Holocaust has been passed down to him by others—shaped and filtered by a nation's self-aggrandizing myths, by a popular culture more intent on entertaining than on teaching him. He knows, moreover, that his artwork will inevitably interpose yet another mediating layer between history and memory, another veil of images that might be confused for the history they would recall.

But then, Attie has no alternative. Instead of memory-acts that collapse the distinction between themselves and the past, therefore, he proposes acts of remembrance that expose just this gulf between what happened in the past and how it now gets remembered. Whether it is national myth and self-idealization or the silver screen and its compelling artifice that blurs the distinction between actual past and present memory of it, or whether it is only the muteness of a cityscape that hides its history, Attie makes as his object of memory the distance between then and now, the ways that even his own acts of remembrance cannot but gesture indirectly to what was lost and how we now recall it.

The Writing on the Wall: *Berlin, 1991–1993*

"After finishing art school in San Francisco, I came to Berlin in the summer of 1991," Shimon Attie writes in his introduction to a book for *The Writing on the Wall.* "Walking the streets of the city that summer, I felt myself asking over and over again, Where are all the missing people? What has become of the Jewish culture and community which had once been at home here? I felt the presence of this lost community very strongly, even though so few visible traces of it remained."[2] Strangely enough, it was not the absence of Berlin's lost Jews that Attie felt so strongly but their presence. For in fact, though they may have been invisible to others walking those same streets, Attie's memory and imagination had already begun to repopulate the Scheunenviertel district in Berlin with the Jews of his mind.

After several weeks of photographic research in Berlin's archives, Attie had found dozens of images from the Scheunenviertel of the 1920s and 1930s and was able to pinpoint nearly one-quarter of their precise locations in the current neighborhood just east of Berlin's Alexanderplatz, formerly in the eastern sector of the city. That September, only three months after moving to Berlin, Attie began projecting slides of these photographs onto the same or nearby addresses where they had been taken earlier in the century. "'The Writing on the Wall' grew out of my response to the discrepancy between what I felt and what I did not see," Attie explains. "I wanted to give this invisible past a voice, to bring it to light, if only for some brief moments."[3] And so for the next year, weather permitting, Attie projected these images of Jewish life from the Scheunenviertel before the Holocaust back into present-day Berlin. Each installation ran for one or two evenings, visible to local residents, street traffic and passersby. During these projections, the artist also photographed the installations themselves in time exposures lasting from three to four minutes. The resulting photographs of the installations have been exhibited widely in galleries and museums, works of fine art in their own right, the only remaining traces of the original installations.

But in fact, the artist is all too aware of the difference between the public installations in situ and their reduced and codified standing in a gallery or catalogue. "The point was to intervene in a public space and project right onto those spaces," he

Shimon Attie, Almadtstrasse (formerly Grenadierstrasse and corner of Schendelgasse), Religious Book Salesman, 1930, 1992. (Writing on the Wall)

Shimon Attie, Linienstrasse 137, Police Raid on Former Jewish Residents, 1920, 1992. (Writing on the Wall, Berlin)

Shimon Attie, 107 Joachimstrasse 20, Former Jewish Resident, Theatre, and Torah Reading Room, 1929–31, 1992. (Writing on the Wall, Berlin)

has said. "One can always overlay images in a dark-room or with a computer. But I wanted to touch those spaces."[4] Or one might add, he wanted to "retouch" those spaces the way one retouches photographs. For the photographic process—in literal and metaphorical ways—lies at the heart of this project: as the original archival photographs captured traces of reflected light and dark from the prewar Scheunenviertel, the artist's photographs of the installations would now capture the light of the photographic images themselves as projected onto building walls. The analogue between the mechanical process of photography and the memory of images recorded by the mind's eye is made real here: in both cases, reflected light imprints itself on light-sensitive surfaces, whether film or retina, that bear its traces afterward.

For Attie recognizes at the outset that public spaces, even the dreariest in our day-to-day lives, also reflect meaning and significance back to us. They also become "art" in the eyes of beholders, at once framed and composed by our reflective gaze. Obversely, the projections themselves become inside-out "frames" for all that surrounds them, turning the rock-hard reality of the present into an extension of the past images now draped over it.

Once projected onto the peeling and mottled building facades of this quarter, these archival images seem less the reflections of light than illuminations of figures emerging from the shadows. Attie says he wanted "to peel back the wallpaper of today and reveal the history buried underneath."[5] From the doorways, in particular, former Jewish residents seem to be stepping out of a third dimension. Some, like the resident standing in the doorway at Joachimstrasse 2, are caught unaware by both the original photographer and now, it seems, by us. Others, like the religious book salesman at the corner of what was formerly the corner of Grenadierstrasse and Schendelgasse, seem to have been interrupted by the photographer; the book salesman has turned his head sideways to gaze impassively back at us. Because the streets of the dilapidated Scheunenviertel (called the Finstere Medine, or "dark quarter," by its Yiddish-speaking denizens) are still largely run down, as were many parts of the formerly East Berlin when the wall came down, the projected images added a life to these streets that they appeared otherwise not to have.

If the projected images of Jews going in and out of buildings or sitting in windows or huddled on a corner suggest themselves as a material part of the space they now reinhabited, once photographed, these subjects take on formal qualities that were less apparent in the installations themselves. As works now independent of the installations they represent, the photographs also recompose them, highlighting not only the apparition of a spatial, human dimension created in the installation but also now the iconographic play of signs and symbols. The Hebrew lettering of Yiddish signs mixes with German Gothic lettering in the images, both now strewn together anarchically with painted post–Berlin Wall graffiti—all of it a kind of literary detritus on scarred walls. The projected lettering of Meier Silberberg's kosher butcher shop at Mulackstrasse 32 runs into the taggings of graffiti artists and postunification slogans like "The struggle continues." Even more dramatic in its silence is the photograph of a slide installation from the corner of Joachimstrasse and Auguststrasse: the barely visible head of a Jew in prayer philacteries beneath a white Star of David beams over the doorway of a dark building, itself backlighted by the rosy pink of a sunset. The star stands in stark, formally eloquent contrast to three rows of crucifix-like white windowpanes on the dark building across the street, arrayed like a battle formation of Crusader shields.

Even the human figures of Jews, animated by the play of light and air on textured surfaces, are reformalized in the photographs of the installations, hardened once again into the icons of the so-called *Ost-Juden*. It was the traditionally garbed Jews of eastern Europe, after all, who had moved into this quarter in the 1910s and 1920s, already a netherworld of criminals, prostitutes, and the dispossessed. But it is not this unlikely mixture of the sacred and profane that Attie hopes to capture here. Rather it is a type, "the Jew" of the Germans' minds so long associated with long black caftans, beards, and earlocks that Attie brings back to haunt current residents. Because German Jewry itself was often so well assimilated as to appear effectively invisible, Attie has had to rely on the image of Ost-Juden to make visible the otherwise invisible Jews of Germany—even though they themselves were not representative faces of German Jewry itself.

When these Ost-Juden tried to return to Poland after the first Nazi-inspired pogroms and anti-Jewish boycotts, they found that their Polish papers had been invalidated. As stateless refugees, these Ost-Juden also became Berlin's first true *Luft-menschen,* a type reified in Attie's projection of their images back through the air onto buildings. And it is as both Luftmenschen and as Jewish projections of the Nazi mind that Attie would have these images haunt contemporary Germans. It would be easy to work up sympathy in Germans for all the Jews who were murdered "even though they looked just like us." But it is the idea and treatment of "the other" that concerns Attie in this project. During his stay in Berlin, Attie was fully aware that the more people appeared as "other" in today's Germany, the more likely they were to be persecuted. The tragedy of the Holocaust was not the "mistake" in killing those who looked like everyone else but the hideous rationale that justified killing those who didn't look like us.

Ironically, of course, the "voice" Attie gave these absent Jews was at times also the voice of residents objecting to the project itself. While Attie was installing the *Buchhändler* (bookseller) slide projection, for example, a fifty-year-old man suddenly came running out of the building shouting that his father had bought the building "fair and square" from Mister Jacobs in 1938. "And what happened to this Mr. Jacobs?" Attie asked the man. "Why, of course, he was a multi-millionaire and moved to New York."[6] Of course. All of which was captured by German television crews, who broadcast the incident that night on national news. Attie couldn't have scripted this projection more powerfully. Another resident called the police to complain angrily that Attie's projections of Jews onto his building would make his neighbors think that *he* was Jewish. Make him stop, he pleaded. The residents' response is as much a part of these works as the installations themselves, says Attie. Without these responses, the installations, like the buildings themselves, would have remained inert, inanimate, dead.

Indeed, even though these images may have disappeared from sight as soon as Attie turned off the high-intensity projector, their after-image lived on in the minds of those who had seen them once. From this point on, the images of these Jews "live" only as their subjects lived before them: in the photographs of these installations. These are quite literally photographs of photographs we are seeing here, just as the local burghers now walk their neighborhoods haunted by their memory of Attie's memory-installation. They are now haunted not by the Jews who had once lived here, or even by their absence, but by the images of Jews haunting the artist's mind.

As Michael André Bernstein has made painfully clear, photography is always about loss, about the absence of what was once real in front of the lens: hence the essential melancholia at the heart of the photograph. "To look at a photograph," Bernstein writes, "is to experience a certain sorrow at the sheer fact of loss and separation, curiously mingled with the pleasure of recognizing that what no longer exists, has been, if not restored to us, then at least memorialized for us, fixed in the stasis of an image now forever available to our gaze."[7] Insofar as this bittersweet mixture of sorrow and pleasure necessarily haunts our experience of all photographs, its extremes seem wildly exaggerated in these wall projections. For it's true, they are beautiful and chilling, slightly exhilarating and depressing; they inspire longing *and* fear, hope *and* despair. By keeping the mixture between sorrow and pleasure in balance, they can also keep their potential for redemption in check, never allowing the pain of such loss to be redeemed by the beauty of the image itself.

Shimon Attie, Former Dresden Jewish Citizen. (Trains, Dresden, 1993)

In this way, these installations have served as a somewhat literal metaphor for the artist's projection of his inner desires onto the walls around him. All of us wish we could bring the victims back to life, to repair the terrible wound. But *The Writing on the Wall* is no such reparation or bringing back to life; it is, rather, the reminder of what was *lost,* not what was. At the same time, it is clear in Attie's mind, as he means for it to be in ours, that these projections are simulations, not historical reconstructions. Their immense value lies in showing us not literally what was lost but that loss itself is part of this neighborhood's history, an invisible yet essential feature of its landscape.

Trains: Dresden, 1993

Of all the banal sites of daily life in Germany forever corrupted by their history during World War II, the railways may be the most ineradicably stigmatized in the eyes of Jewish tourists. Not only is this because the image of cattle cars loaded with Jews on their way to (and from) death camps remains so pervasive in the iconography of the Holocaust. But when riding these trains in Germany after the war, many young Jewish travelers can't escape the sense of "having been there before." The sense of traveling the same routes as the victims, watching the same landscape flit by, and hearing the same clackety-clack on the same tracks induces an illusory identification with the victims unlike almost any other experience in Germany.

Like the Scheunenviertel in Berlin, haunted by its now absent Jews, the Dresden train station seemed haunted to Attie by its absence of any sign of the central role train stations played throughout Germany during the Holocaust. These were the sites of collections for deportations, the last places many German Jews ever saw of their homeland, the tracks constituting a literal, material line connecting Germany to the death camps. In keeping with his medium of photographic projections, Attie and his collaborator, Mathias Maile, found photographs of Dresden's former Jewish citizens who either had been deported or had emigrated and then projected them back into the city's central railway station.

This project was in many ways more confrontational than *The Writing on the Wall,* which had more passively chastened local citizens for letting their former neighbors disappear into the ether of time. For in projecting specific faces from Dresden's Jewish community directly onto the trains, tracks and walls of the central station, Attie and Maile linked the photographic memory of the victims directly to their fate: to the literal sites of deportation, of emigration, of German-Jewish leave-taking. After culling some dozen images from family albums of Dresden's tiny Jewish community, Attie converted them into high-contrast black-and-white slides. For two weeks beginning on the ninth of November 1993 (the anniversary of Kristallnacht), images of handsome, smartly dressed young and middle-aged men and women shone brightly from the rafters of the station; other images of sad-eyed Jews peered up at travelers from the tracks or stared down rebukingly from the walls or confronted travelers face to face from the sides of trains. The familiar daily routine of travel was estranged and disrupted by these immense black-and-white projections; weekend holidays commenced on a decidedly melancholy, less festive note. For a few moments every day, postwar Germans were haunted by the vicarious memory of an American Jew. Now they, too, were forced to see and remember what the Jewish traveler cannot put out of his or her mind: that on this platform, on these tracks, the Jews whose faces I see began to die.

In a similar installation in Hamburg, Attie projected images without the benefit of explaining captions. But when a curious passerby asked him whether these were the pictures of the German Railway founders, he decided to mount large posters that made the source of these images explicitly clear. With this lesson in mind, he repeated the process in Dresden. He had wanted the rebuke of memory to come from within contemporary travelers as the significance of these images dawned on them—now trapped in this conflation of time and space. The more he had to explain, he felt, the less successful and more coercively didactic the project became. But as word of the memorial projections spread, his accompanying captions became less necessary; and in the end, as tens of thousands of travelers saw and thereby internalized these images, the projections themselves became unnecessary altogether.

Portraits of Exile: Copenhagen, June–July 1995

An epitaph written in water is no epitaph at all, as John Keats realized when he penned his own to read: "Here lies one whose name is writ in water." Unlike the nameless tombstone bearing these words and marking Keats's grave in Rome's Protestant cemetery, however, all traces of Denmark's extraordinary rescue of its Jews were erased by the very water that bore them to safe haven in Sweden. The water that made their rescue possible, and covered their tracks so well, also made a landscape of commemorative traces of this rescue impossible. As a memorial medium, in fact, water is more like fleeting time in its ephemerality than like a fixed landscape in its stasis, and so more emblematic of memory itself—always taking the shape of the vessel into which it is poured.

In the memorial and historical culture of Denmark, water is also much more. It was not only the road to rescue for Denmark's Jews during the Nazi occupation in October 1943, but it has always constituted Copenhagen's historical and economic raison d'être as ancient seaport, quite literally the capital's historical lifesource. With these thoughts in mind Shimon Attie chose the Børsgraven Canal in Copenhagen as his installation site for *Portraits of Exile*—a commemoration of the fiftieth anniversary of Denmark's liberation from the Nazis. This was not to be merely a self-congratulatory celebration of the war's end in the monolithic image of Denmark's heroic rescue of the Jews, however. For unlike the images of Jews projected back onto the buildings of the Scheunenviertel in Berlin, which seemed to an-

Shimon Attie, Installation Shot. *On lightbox in foreground: present-day refugee from the former Yugoslavia with Danish entry stamp on passport.* (Portraits of Exile, Copenhagen)

imate otherwise inert surfaces, it was the somewhat stock and myth-hardened imagery of heroism itself that Attie animated—and thus dissolved—in the watery medium of Copenhagen's canals.

Here he installed a row of nine light boxes, each approximately six feet by five feet, about thirty-three feet apart, and submerged nearly three feet below the water's surface some fifteen feet from the bank of the canal. Eight of these light boxes were mounted with the transparency of a photograph depicting either the face of a Danish Jew rescued to Sweden or the face of a present-day refugee living in Denmark. One light box in the middle of the series was mounted with the transparent image of a sea map charting the straits between Denmark and Sweden. Visible by night and day, these backlighted faces stared up eerily, stirring with life as the water rippled over them. From a distance, the images seemed to float on the surface as orbs of light, a trail of stepping stones leading out to sea.

Shimon Attie, in foreground: Danish Jew rescued to Sweden in October 1943 with yellow star.
(Portraits of Exile, Copenhagen)

But the spectacle itself might have blinded viewers to details apparent only on closer inspection. When the wind and tides were perfectly still, and the water's surface took on a mirrorlike sheen, other layers of these images came into view just beyond the surface reflection of one's face. Each image was of a different refugee, each overlaid with a different sign of exile: a portrait of a Danish Jewish man overlaid onto an image of a yellow Jewish star; another of a Danish Jewish woman overlaid onto a sea map; other faces of rescued Danish Jews overlaid onto images of a fishing boat and a commercial freighter used in the rescue. The middle image of the sea map was itself overlaid by two boats, one with Jews on their way to Sweden, the other with present-day refugees coming to Denmark.

At this point, the narrative created in this sequence of images began to generate a decidedly double-edged memorial message, fraught with pride and shame. For the next portrait of a Bosnian Moslem refugee in turban was followed by a Bosnian woman overlaid by an image of the Flotel Europa moored one canal away—a notoriously overcrowded floating hotel ship crammed with refugees awaiting political asylum in Denmark, some of them for years. The last two images consisted of the face of a Yugoslav man seemingly textured by an overlaid sea map and a Yugoslav woman whose face was blotched by the image of a passport entry stamp. Placed in the center of a topographical triad composed of the Danish foreign ministry, the parliament, and the National Bank of Denmark, these portraits of exile seemed simultaneously to shine as commemorative and warning lights to the government.

This mixed memorial message was intended not to refute Denmark's reigning self-idealization as a perennial haven of refuge but only to pierce the self-congratulatory side of this myth that blinds it to other, conflicting historical realities. Nor were such images juxtaposed to imply equivalence between refugees but to heighten a troubling contrast: where almost all Danish Jews were saved, not all Bosnians have found refuge, many more murdered at home than given safe haven in Denmark or other European countries. At the same time, the artist showed how every national commemoration necessarily occludes as much history as it recalls. For even this greatest of mass rescues during the Holocaust, once mythologized as part of the national character, has overshadowed another, less well known fact of this era: that Denmark had refused to grant asylum to thousands of Jews attempting to flee Nazi Germany before the war.

Such a fact does not diminish the brilliance of Denmark's national heroism but only complicates it, thereby making it less mythlike, more real. Public memory here is as fraught and contradictory, as complex and multisided, as the history being commemorated. In its mixed message, such an installation may even suggest that it is the memory of a mixed past that actually impels a nation toward new acts of rescue. For the national memory of heroism, like the heroic act itself, stems from a mixture of motives—high, low, and ambivalent.

Brick by Brick: *Cologne, November 1995*

The physical sites of history are not the only potential sites of memory. In Attie's eyes, even the designs of household objects can recall the times of their origin and, by extension, the households from which they have been torn. Pieces of Bauhaus or Art Deco furniture come to stand as icons of an era that point beyond themselves to the dark age they passed through and to the owners—both killers and victims—they may have survived. Having reanimated public sites in Berlin and Dresden with images of their forgotten pasts, the artist now turned his gaze into the more private, even intimate sanctum of the household, its objects transformed into accusing sites of memory.

In *Brick by Brick,* an installation just outside the doors of the Cologne Art Fair in November 1995, Attie projected images of simple household objects dating from turn-of-the-century Germany onto the massive brick columns of the Rheinhalle. Projected so that they seemed almost to be materializing from within the brick columns, images of a Singer sewing machine, a late nineteenth-century commode, a Bauhaus menorah, a Bauhaus dining room table, an overstuffed armchair, and four other similarly aged objects confronted patrons of ART COLOGNE as they left the exhibit hall. Though this particular crowd of collectors and connoisseurs would have recognized the general period of these objects' origins, neither they nor the artist could know the provenance of any given piece—gleaned by the artist from antique stores as well as from Bauhaus and other catalogues. But this ambiguity was partly the point, for it was into this area of uncertainty that the artist projected his preoccupations, assigning not a precise provenance but a generic, possible provenance to these and all pieces like them.

At the same time, this was a site-specific installation. For as Attie and his collaborator, Mathias Maile, made clear in a handbill passed out to visitors at the fair, the Kölner Messegebaüde (Cologne Fair Building) had its own dark, if multilayered and unacknowledged past. Built in 1923, the Cologne Fair Building had hosted its share of fairs, it was true, but after the Nazis came to power in 1933, it also served as an examination center for German army draftees as well as a great hall for the ideological reeducation of German schoolteachers. After launching the war in 1939, the Nazi government took control of the fair building and turned it first into a prisoner-of-war camp and then, in 1940, into a gathering and deportation site for Sinti and Roma. Still later it served as a transfer station for Jews about to be deported to the east through the neighboring Deutz-Tief train station.

In fact, because the Nazis had taken over all such exhibition halls in Germany by this time, the fate of the Cologne Fair Building was no more ignoble than that of any other public hall in Germany. Rather, what had made this fair building special in Attie's eyes were the ways another part of its history seemed to find some continuity in the art fair itself. For some reason, the Cologne Art Fair, arguably the most prestigious of its kind in Germany today, opens every year on November ninth or tenth, the anniversary of Kristallnacht in 1938. Even more significant for Attie, however, was the building's use during the war as a storehouse for confiscated furniture and other household belongings of Jews who had been either forced to emigrate or deported to concentration camps. As the hall's stores filled up, Nazi Party officials would hold auctions open to party members whose households had been damaged by Allied bombings. As a chilling illustration, Attie photocopied an announcement for one such auction, Gothic script and all, as part of his handbill:

Auction
Attention, Bombing Victims!
On Monday, the 21st of December 1942 and following days, I will hold an auction at the Cologne-Deutz Fair (South Hall) from 9:00 A.M. to 3:00 P.M. Bedroom, men's Bedroom, all kinds of wardrobes, tables, down beds, couches, sofas, teawagon, upright clock, table clock . . . .[8]

The list of objects included all the furnishings typical of any middle- or upper middle-class German Jewish home. The rest of the handbill described how beginning in 1942, a slave labor camp was installed on the Cologne fairgrounds in the form of a so-called worker education camp. And finally, at the end of 1942, a satellite camp of Buchen-wald composed of "SS Construction Crew III" was established on the fairgrounds, supplying some one thousand slave-laborers to the nearby Rhenish factories.

Thus greeted by this "counter-fair" on their way out of ART COLOGNE, patrons were forced to reconsider this site as something more than an exhibition hall for con-

*Shimon Attie,
on column in
foreground:
sewing
machine.*
(Brick by
Brick,
Cologne,
1995)

*Shimon Attie,
on column:
briefcase.*
(Brick by
Brick, Cologne,
1995)

temporary art. On display at the fair, but not for sale, Attie's installation redefined the hall as nexus of history, commerce, and memory. In a way, the art fair's organizers had foisted this link on Attie by scheduling its opening every year on the anniversary of Kristallnacht. Once inspired, however, Attie pursued the question that might logically follow "What happened to all the Jews of Germany?" That is, "What happened to all their household belongings and personal effects?" Further implied questions include not only "Where were you during the war?" but also "To whom did that table belong before the war? Is it an ill-gotten gain, a Nazi-sanctioned piece of war booty? Or was it passed down innocently from one generation to the next?" Instead of suggesting answers, the artist let such questions float in the space of the art fair, between his installation and the bustling art patrons. Contemporary German collectors were now confronted uneasily with the possibility that these objects had even been distributed among their own households.

What makes such an installation so subversive is the way it plants the seeds of doubt in every such piece: the more authentic it is, the more it might remind its current owner of its possible provenance. Even perfectly "innocent" pieces might now echo with the voices of the dead, and by their very design, such pieces begin to accuse their owners. In effect, the provenance of antiques from this era makes them not only valuable but historical. In *Brick by Brick*, the artist has thus stigmatized an entire generation of household objects and, in so doing, has transformed each piece from mere memento into an accusing memento mori.

The Neighbor Next Door: Amsterdam, December 1995

Like the people of other nations, the Dutch tend to remember their World War II past as it congeals around a few well-chosen images: in their case, of course, Anne Frank constitutes the central memorial icon. But as a remarkably self-critical generation of new historians in Holland has already made clear, the Dutch self-idealization in the image of Anne Frank has always been double-edged: she reminds the Dutch both that they helped hide her family from the Nazis and that they betrayed her. As these historians are quick to point out, despite the national mythology of the "sheltering Dutch," a higher percentage of its Jews—over 80 percent—was murdered during the Holocaust than any other nation's except for Poland's.[9]

Indeed, the memorial canonization of Anne Frank in Holland is not a simple matter of national self-aggrandizement but has much more to do with the deeply mixed Dutch self-perception as traditional refuge on one hand and as a nation of by-standers and collaborators on the other. As a young girl, Anne Frank exemplifies the blamelessness of Jews killed for no reason other than being Jews; by extension, she represents for the Dutch their own, uninvited violation by the Nazis. At the same time, she reminds the Dutch that even though they harbored her, in the end they also betrayed her as well as another hundred thousand Dutch Jews. By reflecting back to the Dutch their mixed record of resistance and neutrality, victimization and collaboration, Anne Frank has effectively become an archetype for Holland's war memory.[10]

In keeping with Holland's capacity for self-critique, Attie's Amsterdam installation, *The Neighbor Next Door,* attempted to remind the Dutch of the essential gulf between the historical record and their national memory of the Holocaust, the essential double-sidedness of "the neighbor next door." At the same time, he hoped to suggest that for the estimated one hundred thousand illegal immigrants hiding in Holland today, the myth of "the neighbor next door" lives on in decidedly mixed fashion, as they find economic refuge in a land that needs but does not necessarily want them. It now reflects their contemporary reality, as well, as they peek from behind closed curtains or look over their shoulders on the way to or from illegal jobs.

For one week in the middle of December 1995, Attie mounted sixteen-millimeter film projectors inside the windows of three different apartments along Prinsengracht, the canal-street in central Amsterdam along which Anne Frank's family and an estimated 155 other groups hid during World War II. From 5:00 P.M. to 1:00 A.M. each day, Attie beamed onto the street short film loops from footage shot clandestinely from nearby windows by those in hiding during the Nazi occupation. Even in darkness, the grainy film footage appeared shadowy and fleeting. In one ten-second loop projected from Prinsengracht 572, the stiff, gray figures of a Nazi funeral cortege filed into view on its way to bury a Dutch Nazi collaborator assassinated by the resistance; at Prinsengracht 468, wet cobblestones flickered silently with the images of a military band decked out in the insignia of the Dutch Nazi Party, marching in an endless six-second loop. Only the images of passing German soldiers giving the "Heil, Hitler" salute flitting across the sidewalk in front of Prinsengracht 514 had been from film shot by Nazi propagandists, now mocked by the robotic repetition of the loop itself.

In these projections, Attie hoped to convey how the world looked *from* the hiding place, as opposed to how the hiding place looked to the outside world through free Dutch eyes. In addition, he tried to try to show how hiding was experienced by those who hid: already a kind of internment, for some the first of many incarcera-

Shimon Attie, Passing Nazi Drum Corps at Prinsengracht 468. (The Neighbor Next Door, Amsterdam, 1995)

tions on the way to concentration camps and death. Here the national image of sheltering was being turned inside-out, the lens turned back on those for whom the "neighbor next door" had become more a self-aggrandizing image than a reality. The image of the sheltered was now displaced by moving images of what the sheltered saw: Dutch bystanders, collaborators, and Nazis. By reanimating the past of those supposedly rescued, Attie could reiterate the national myth even as he unlocked its hold on the past.

The Walk of Fame: Kraków, June–July 1996

In his Kraków project, *The Walk of Fame,* Attie suggests that art itself can check the excesses of art, that instead of blurring the line further between history and its later representations, art can redraw this line and that, through parody, it can discourage a society from unwittingly displacing history as it happened with history as it appears in the movies. He was inspired, he says, not by the ways Steven Spielberg's film *Schindler's List* might have passed itself off as history but rather by the potential confusion in tourists' minds wrought by an officially sanctioned tour in Kraków called "Retracing 'Schindler's List.'"[11]

In this tour, organized by Franciszek Palowski, a Polish journalist who had interviewed Spielberg for Polish television and later wrote a book on the filming of *Schindler's List,* tourists are invited to visit the sites of film-making in and around Kraków in order to learn more of the actual history of Schindler's list and its telling in cinema. As a guide, Palowski is careful to distinguish between the sites of history and the sites where Spielberg chose to film this history. Nevertheless, Attie fears that the mere possibility of such a tour throws "authentic historical sites, events and individuals into open competition with their celluloid copies in determining our understanding of history."[12] It is one thing to add the history of the film to the history of events, another to displace the history of events with the history of the film.

Moreover, Attie worries that "as actual history becomes conflated with cinematic fiction, it becomes more and more difficult to distinguish between the two."[13] In fact, underlying Attie's misgivings here seems to be not just the confusion in mind wrought by such a tour but the ways that such a tour is, in many ways, more appealing to tourists in the thrall of celebrity history than history itself. For when all is said and done, tourists may indeed prefer visiting the sites of *their* cinematic experience of the Holocaust to seeing the sites of *others'* actual Holocaust experiences. After all, their only "real" experience of the Holocaust is the "reel" experience of the movie. Having survived the film, in effect, they return as vicarious pilgrims to the cinematic sites, just as survivors of the camps return to the sites of their actual suffering. If the movie becomes our history of the Holocaust, then the movie sets become the places where "history is made." And once we are invited to visit the sites of filming as if they were the places where "history is made," it is too short a step toward confusing the history made in this film for history itself.

In some ways, this dilemma even parallels the impossible problem the director himself faced as he prepared on-site filming of *Schindler's List*. When Spielberg approached Polish authorities with the request to film scenes on their original sites at Auschwitz and Birkenau, he was initially granted permission; after all, other films such as *Triumph of the Spirit* and the television miniseries *The Winds of War* had been filmed in situ at Auschwitz, with significant economic benefits for the local population. The director seemed convinced at this point that a "true story" filmed at its historical location would somehow be perceived as more true than if filmed off-site. But in the years between these earlier films and Spielberg's project, an international council had been appointed to protect memory at Auschwitz from just this kind of incursion. Unbeknownst to Spielberg but well known to the new commission, fake gas chambers and papier-mâché chimneys had already been left behind at Auschwitz-Birkenau by the other film crews, infecting the ruins of gas chamber complexes there with a terrible fiction. When word got out that Spielberg had been granted permission to film at Auschwitz-Birkenau, council members protested vigorously, and the council immediately rescinded permission. After delicate negotiations, Kalman Sultanik intervened with national authorities on behalf of the International Auschwitz Council, and Spielberg was invited to film nearby, though not on the site of the concentration camp. On film, of course, Spielberg's movie sets are at least as convincing as the authentic site could ever have been without a major overhaul short of complete reconstruction of the camp—which would have violated the integrity of the memorial as it stands.

Because he is not a documentary filmmaker, Spielberg did not need to hew to original sites of history for his fictional account any more than the novelist needs to rely on notarized testimony for dialogue. The aim was never to film authentic sites but to make the sites he filmed look authentic: this is what filmmakers do, and Spielberg did it brilliantly. In addition to building his own concentration camp set near the real one, Spielberg found a plethora of authentic-looking old squares and buildings in which to shoot his Kraków ghetto scenes. As its residents know well and its tourists happily discover, Kraków's great charm as a tourist center stems from the fact that it has never been bombed or otherwise damaged in Poland's many wars and occupations. Only new buildings made the authentic center of the Jewish ghetto at Zgoda Square unfit for shooting sequences that had actually taken place there. These scenes were shot instead on Szeroka Street, the center of the former Jewish district in Kazimierz.

We also learn from "Retracing 'Schindler's List'" that because the ghetto scenes at Zgoda Square in the Podgórze district were filmed in Kazimierz across the river, Spielberg had to reverse the direction of the march of ghetto Jews, so that they flowed over the bridge *into* his filmic ghetto in Kazimierz and not out of Kazimierz over the Vistula River into Podgórze, as they had originally. Also of cultural interest here is the plot of land Spielberg chose for his gargantuan movie set of the Płaszow concentration camp: the site of the former Jewish cemetery on Jerozolimska (Jerusalem) Street in Podgórze.

As late as April 1995, Attie's plan for an installation in Kraków looked entirely different. In a project then entitled *Routes of Silence,* the artist had hoped to mount slide projectors on the trams in Kraków that still run through what had been the Jewish ghetto there during the war, beaming images of the old ghetto back onto the present sites. In addition, he had planned to affix light boxes along the route to show "images from the ghetto, as well as images relating to Poland's postcommunist struggle to be assimilated into the West and the challenges the country faces today with both old and new forms of racism."[15] But on his arrival in Kraków, he found the situation on the ground to be much more interesting, and more complicated, than his critique of Poland's wartime memory might have allowed. Though his original plan had been supported by both the city of Kraków and the local Goethe Institute, once the artist heard of "Retracing 'Schindler's List,'" his project evolved from a critique of Poland's wartime memory into a critique of the dangers implicit in over-mediation itself. Unable to bear the confusion of movie and historical sites, Attie abandoned his own preconceived project and embarked on an alternative installation, one he hoped would expose the fascination for the filmic at the expense of the historical. As a result, the "Walk of Fame" may be as much an overall critique of Holocaust-by-mediation as it is of a specific displacement of historical by cinematic reality.

To this end, Attie installed twenty-four simulated five-point terrazzo stars, copies of the famous stars lining Hollywood Boulevard's "Walk of Fame," on Szeroka

Shimon Attie, J. H. Borenstein. (The Walk of Fame, Kraków, 1996)

Street, where Spielberg had constructed his ghetto movie-set: what Attie calls "ground zero" for the conflation of movie history and historical fact. Instead of recalling the movie stars enshrined so famously on Hollywood Boulevard, however, Attie substituted the names of Jews who had actually been on Oscar Schindler's list, abbreviating the first names so as not to offend the memory of actual victims. By remembering victims as if they were worth remembering solely because they had now become Hollywood stars, Attie parodically repeated this flow of history into celebrity, mocking it and thereby hoping to expose its insidiousness.

At the same time, Attie takes pains to explain that he did not direct this project against the individuals who survived Schindler's list and the celebrity it has brought some of them; nor did he make Spielberg's film a target of his counter-memorial installation. Rather, in his words, "its intention was to highlight and critically reflect the larger problematic eclipsing of historical fact by cinematic fiction," by which the unfurling movie's reel is mistaken for the real.[16] On display in Kraków during the months of June and July 1995, these purple stars were embedded into the square in front of the Old Synagogue and Jewish Museum, each with a small motion picture camera and a name like H. Blumentrucht or J. H. Borenstein. Riven by cracks that seemed continuous with the surrounding stones, they appeared old, worn, and

permanently part of the square. Instead of the memorial icon of a yellow star, these survivors were commemorated with the purple terrazzo stars of Hollywood celebrities, an echo of that moment at the end of *Schindler's List* when the actual survivors appeared with the stars who "played" them.

As an artist, Shimon Attie is all too aware of his own dependence on the art of others for his knowledge of the Holocaust. As a Jewish American born after the war, he knows the Holocaust only by indirection, by the efforts of survivors, historians, and artists to pass down their knowledge to him. But although he acknowledges this necessarily vicarious relationship to Holocaust history, he is still nettled by the possible consequences of what might be called the overmediation of events. He fears, rightly, that a generation after the Holocaust could still come to mistake *their* hypermediated experiences of the Holocaust for the Holocaust itself, that events will come to be displaced altogether by their representations.

This is, he acknowledges, a conundrum. For because these representations of the Holocaust *are* all that those removed from events will ever know of the genocide, what is to keep art from usurping the authority of historical actuality? Moreover, if artists and filmmakers insist on keeping the boundaries between their art and actual events as fuzzy as possible, all toward the aesthetic (but not necessarily historical) end of making their art seem as convincing and entertaining as possible, then what is to save the next generation from losing the ability to discriminate between what they know, how they know it, and what actually happened? Instead of a simple answer to this, the next generation's defining preoccupation, Shimon Attie has offered a series of installations that work through the dilemma itself, that examine the role we ourselves play in the gaping space between a site and its past, between its history and our memory of it.

CHAPTER FOUR

Memory, Countermemory,
and the End of the Monument

Horst Hoheisel, Micha Ullman, Rachel Whiteread,
and Renata Stih and Frieder Schnock

"The sunken fountain is not the memorial at all. It is only history turned into a
pedestal, an invitation to passersby who stand upon it to search for the memorial in
their own heads. For only there is the memorial to be found."
—Horst Hoheisel, "Rathaus Platz Wunde"

AMONG THE HUNDREDS OF SUBMISSIONS IN the 1995 competition for a German national "memorial to the murdered Jews of Europe," one seemed an especially uncanny embodiment of the impossible questions at the heart of Germany's memorial process. Artist Horst Hoheisel, already well known for his negative-form monument in Kassel, proposed a simple, if provocative antisolution to the memorial competition: blow up the Brandenburger Tor, grind its stone into dust, sprinkle the remains over its former site, and cover the entire memorial area with granite plates. How better to remember a destroyed people than by a destroyed monument?

Rather than commemorating the destruction of a people with the construction of yet another edifice, Hoheisel would mark one destruction with another destruction. Rather than filling in the void left by a murdered people with a positive form, the artist would carve out an empty space in Berlin by which to recall a now absent people. Rather than concretizing and thereby displacing the memory of Europe's murdered Jews, the artist would open a place in the landscape to be filled with the memory of those who come to remember Europe's murdered Jews. A landmark

RAVENSBRÜCK

Horst Hoheisel, Blow Up the Brandenburger Tor. *Proposal for the 1995 competition for "Berlin's Memorial for the Murdered Jews of Europe."*

celebrating Prussian might and crowned by a chariot-borne Quadriga, the Roman goddess of peace, would be demolished to make room for the memory of Jewish victims of German might and peacelessness. In fact, perhaps no single emblem better represents the conflicted, self-abnegating motives for memory in Germany today than the vanishing monument.[1]

Of course, such a memorial undoing will never be sanctioned by the German government, and this, too, is part of the artist's point. Hoheisel's proposed destruction of the Brandenburg Gate participates in the competition for a national Holocaust memorial, even as its radicalism precludes the possibility of its execution. At least part of its polemic, therefore, is directed against actually building any winning design, against ever finishing the monument at all. Here he seems to suggest that the surest engagement with Holocaust memory in Germany may actually lie in its perpetual irresolution, that only an unfinished memorial process can guarantee the life of memory. For it may be the *finished* monument that completes memory itself, puts a cap on memory-work, and draws a bottom line underneath an era that must always haunt Germany. Better a thousand years of Holocaust memorial competitions in Germany than any single "final solution" to Germany's memorial problem.[2]

Like other cultural and aesthetic forms in Europe and North America, the monument—in both idea and practice—has undergone a radical transformation over the course of the twentieth century. As intersection between public art and political memory, the monument has necessarily reflected the aesthetic and political revolutions, as well as the wider crises of representation, following all of the century's major upheavals—including both World Wars I and II, the Vietnam War, the rise and fall of communist regimes in the former Soviet Union and its Eastern European satellites. In every case, the monument reflects both its sociohistorical and its aesthetic context: artists working in eras of cubism, expressionism, socialist realism, earthworks, minimalism, or conceptual art remain answerable to the needs of both art and official history. The result has been a metamorphosis of the monument from the heroic, self-aggrandizing figurative icons of the late nineteenth century celebrating national ideals and triumphs to the antiheroic, often ironic, and self-effacing conceptual installations that mark the national ambivalence and uncertainty of late twentieth-century postmodernism.

Horst Hoheisel, Blow Up the Brandenburger Tor. *Proposal for the 1995 competition for "Berlin's Memorial for the Murdered Jews of Europe."*

In fact, the monument as both institution and concept had already come under withering attack well before the turn of the century. "Away with the monuments!" Friedrich Nietzsche declared in his blistering attack on a nineteenth-century German historicism that oppressed the living with stultified versions of the past, what Nietzsche called "monumental history."[3] To which, a chorus of artists and cultural historians have since added their voices. "The notion of a modern monument is veritably a contradiction in terms," Lewis Mumford wrote in the 1930s. "If it is a monument it is not modern, and if it is modern,   it cannot be a monument."[4] Believing that modern architecture invites the perpetuation of life itself, encourages renewal and change, and scorns the illusion of permanence, Mumford wrote, "Stone gives a false sense of continuity, a deceptive assurance of life."[5] Indeed, he went on to suggest that traditionally it seems to have been the least effectual of regimes that chose to compensate their paucity of achievement in self-aggrandizing stone and mortar.

More recently, the German historian Martin Broszat suggested that in their references to history, monuments may not remember events so much as bury them altogether beneath layers of national myth and explanation. As cultural reifications, in this view, monuments reduce or, in Broszat's words, "coarsen" historical understanding as much as they generate it.[6] In another vein, art historian Rosalind Krauss finds that the modernist period produces monuments unable to refer to anything beyond themselves as pure marker or base. After Krauss, critics have asked whether an abstract, self-referential monument can ever commemorate events outside of itself or whether it only motions endlessly to its own gesture to the past.[7]

Still others have argued that rather than preserving public memory, the monument displaces it altogether, supplanting a community's memory-work with its own material form. "The less memory is experienced from the inside," Pierre Nora warns, "the more it exists through its exterior scaffolding and outward signs."[8] In fact, Andreas Huyssen has even suggested that in a contemporary age of mass memory production and consumption, there seems to be an inverse proportion between the memorialization of the past and its contemplation and study.[9]

It is as if once we assign monumental form to memory, we have to some degree divested ourselves of the obligation to remember. In the eyes of modern critics and artists, the traditional monument's essential stiffness and grandiose pretensions to permanence thus doom it to an archaic, premodern status. Even worse, by insisting that its meaning is as fixed as its place in the landscape, the monument seems oblivious to the essential mutability in all cultural artifacts, the ways the significance in all art evolves over time. In this way, monuments have long sought to provide a naturalizing locus for memory, in which a state's triumphs and martyrs, its ideals and founding myths are cast as naturally true as the landscape in which they stand. These are the monument's sustaining illusions, the principles of its seeming longevity and power. But in fact, as several generations of artists—modern and postmodern alike—have made scathingly clear, neither the monument nor its meaning is everlasting. Both a monument and its significance are constructed in particular times and places, contingent on the political, historical, and aesthetic realities of the moment.

The early modernist ambivalence toward the monument hardened into outright hostility in the wake of World War I. Both artists and some governments shared a general distaste for the ways the monument seemed formally to recapitulate the archaic values of a past world now discredited by the slaughter of the war. A new generation of cubists and expressionists, in particular, rejected traditional mimetic and heroic evocations of events, contending that any such remembrance would elevate and mythologize events. In their view, yet another classically proportioned Prometheus would have falsely glorified and thereby redeemed the horrible suffering they were called upon to mourn. The traditional aim of war monuments had been to valorize the suffering in such a way as to justify, even redeem, it historically. But for these artists, such monuments would have been tantamount to betraying not only their experience of the Great War but also their new reasons for art's existence after the war: to challenge the world's realities, not affirm them.

As Albert Elsen has noted, modern and avant-garde sculptors between the wars in Europe were thus rarely invited to commemorate either the victories or losses, battles or war dead of World War I.[10] And if figurative statuary were demanded of them, then only antiheroic figures would do, as exemplified in the pathetic heroes of German sculptor Wilhelm Lehmbrück's *Fallen Man* and *Seated Youth* (both 1917). As true to the artists' interwar vision as such work may have been, however, neither public nor state seemed ready to abide memorial edifices built on foundations of doubt instead of valor. The pathetic hero was thus condemned by emerging totalitarian regimes in Germany and Russia as defeatist for seeming to embody all that was worth forgetting—not remembering—in the war. Moreover, between the Nazi abhorrence of abstract art—or what it called *entartete Kunst* (decadent art)—and the officially mandated socialist realism of the Soviet Union, the traditional figurative monument even enjoyed something of a revival in totalitarian societies. Indeed, only the figurative statuary of officially sanctioned artists, like Germany's Arno Breker, or styles like the Soviet Union's socialist realism, could be trusted to embody the Nazi ideals of "Aryan race" or the Communist Party's vision of a heroic proletariat. In its consort with two of this century's most egregiously totalitarian regimes, the monument's credibility as public art was thus eroded further still.

Fifty-five years after the defeat of the Nazi regime, contemporary artists in Germany still have difficulty separating the monument there from its fascist past. German memory-artists are heirs to a double-edged postwar legacy: a deep distrust of monumental forms in light of their systematic exploitation by the Nazis and a profound desire to distinguish their generation from that of the killers through memory.[11] In their eyes, the didactic logic of monuments—their demagogical rigidity and certainty of history—continues to recall too closely traits associated with fascism itself. How else would totalitarian regimes commemorate themselves except through totalitarian art like the monument? Conversely, how better to celebrate the fall of totalitarian regimes than by celebrating the fall of their monuments? A monument against fascism, therefore, would have to be monument against itself: against the traditionally didactic function of monuments, against their tendency to displace the past they would have us contemplate—and finally, against the authoritarian propensity in monumental spaces that reduces viewers to passive spectators.

As I have suggested in the Introduction, one of the most intriguing results of Germany's memorial conundrum has been the advent of what I would call its "countermonuments": memorial spaces conceived to challenge the very premise of the monument. For a new generation of German artists, the possibility that memory of events so grave might be reduced to exhibitions of public artistry or cheap pathos remains intolerable. They contemptuously reject the traditional forms and reasons for public memorial art, those spaces that either console viewers or redeem such tragic events, or indulge in a facile kind of *Wiedergutmachung* or purport to mend the memory of a murdered people. Instead of searing memory into public consciousness, they fear, conventional memorials seal memory off from awareness altogether; instead of embodying memory, they find that memorials may only displace memory. These artists fear rightly that to the extent that we encourage monuments to do our memory-work for us, we become that much more forgetful. They believe, in effect, that the initial impulse to memorialize events like the Holocaust may actually spring from an opposite and equal desire to forget them.

In the pages that follow, I would like both to recall a couple of the countermonuments I have discussed at much greater length elsewhere and to add several more recent installations to the discussion. In this way, I might both refine and adumbrate the concept of countermonuments in Germany, the ways they have begun to constitute something akin to a "national form" that pits itself squarely against recent attempts to build a national "memorial to the murdered Jews of Europe" in the center of the country's reunited capital, Berlin. As before, I find that the ongoing debate in Germany has been especially instructive in my own considerations of the monument's future in this decidedly antiredemptory age.

Horst Hoheisel's Negative Forms and Memorial Spielerei

Some ten years before Horst Hoheisel proposed blowing up the Brandenburg Gate in Berlin, the city of Kassel had invited artists to consider ways of rescuing one of its own destroyed monuments—the "Aschrott Brunnen." This forty-foot-high neo-Gothic pyramid fountain, surrounded by a reflecting pool set in the main square in front of city hall, was built in 1908. It was designed by the city hall's architect, Karl Roth, and funded by a local Jewish entrepreneur, Sigmund Aschrott. But as a gift from a Jew to the city, it was condemned by the Nazis as the "Jews' Fountain" and so was demolished during the night of 8–9 April 1939 by local Nazis, its pieces carted away by city work crews over the next few days. Within weeks, all but the sandstone base had been cleared away, leaving only a great, empty basin in the center of the square. Two years later, 463 Kassel Jews were deported from the central train station to Riga, followed in the next year by another 3,000, all murdered. In 1943 the city filled in the fountain's basin with soil and planted it over in flowers; local burghers then dubbed it "Aschrott's Grave."

During the growing prosperity of the 1960s, the town turned Aschrott's Grave back into a fountain, sans pyramid. But by then, only a few of the city's old-timers could recall that its name had ever been Aschrott's anything. When asked what had happened to the original fountain, they replied that to their best recollection, it had been destroyed by English bombers during the war. In response to this kind of fading memory, the Society for the Rescue of Historical Monuments proposed in 1984 that some form of the fountain and its history be restored—and that it recall all the founders of the city, especially Sigmund Aschrott.

In his proposal for "restoration," Horst Hoheisel decided that neither a preservation of its remnants nor its mere reconstruction would do. For Hoheisel, even the

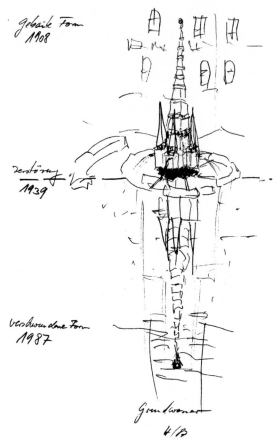

gebäude Form
1908

zerstörung
1939

verschwundene Form
1987

Grundwasser
4/B

„Platz – Wunde Aschrottbrunnen"

Horst Hoheisel, artist's sketch of the Aschrott-Brunnen Memorial, Kassel, 1987.

fragment was a decorative lie, suggesting itself as the remnant of a destruction no one knew much about. Its pure reconstruction would have been no less offensive: not only would self-congratulatory overtones of Wiedergutmachung betray an irreparable violence, but the artist feared that a reconstructed fountain would only encourage the public to forget what had happened to the original. In the best tradition of the countermonument, therefore, Hoheisel proposed a "negative-form" monument to mark what had once been the Aschrott Fountain in Kassel's City Hall Square.

On being awarded the project, Hoheisel described both the concept and the form underlying his negative-form monument:

I have designed the new fountain as a mirror image of the old one, sunk beneath the old place in order to rescue the history of this place as a wound and as an open question, to penetrate the consciousness of the Kassel citizens so that such things never happen again.

That's why I rebuilt the fountain sculpture as a hollow concrete form after the old plans and for a few weeks displayed it as a resurrected shape at City Hall Square before sinking it, mirror-like,

Horst Hoheisel, model for the Aschrott-Brunnen Memorial, Kassel, 1987.

12 meters deep into the ground water.

    The pyramid will be turned into a funnel into whose darkness water runs down. From the "architektonischen Spielerei," as City Hall architect Karl Roth called his fountain, a hole emerges which deep down in the water creates an image reflecting back the entire shape of the fountain.[12]

How does one remember an absence? In this case, by reproducing it. Quite literally, the negative space of the absent monument now constitutes its phantom shape in the ground. The very absence of the monument is now preserved in its precisely duplicated negative space. In this way, the monument's reconstruction remains as illusory as memory itself, a reflection on dark waters, a phantasmagoric play of light and image. Taken a step further, Hoheisel's inverted pyramid might also combine with the remembered shape of its predecessor to form the two interlocking triangles of the Jewish star—present only in the memory of its absence.

    In his conceptual formulations, Hoheisel invokes the play of other, darker associations as well, linking the monument to both the town's Jewish past and a traditional anti-Semitic libel. "The tip of the sculpture points like a thorn down into the water," the artist writes. "Through coming into touch with the ground water, the history of the Aschrott Fountain continues not over but under the city." As an emblem of the Holocaust, the history of the Aschrott Fountain becomes the subterranean history of the city. In Hoheisel's figure, the groundwater of German history may well be poisoned—not by the Jews but by the Germans themselves in their murder of the Jews. By sinking his inverted pyramid into the depths in this way, Hoheisel means to tap this very history. "From the depth of the place," he says, "I have attempted to bring the history of the Aschrott Fountain back up to the surface."

Of course, on a visit to City Hall Square in Kassel, none of this is immediately evident. During construction, before being lowered upside down into the ground, the starkly white negative-form sat upright in the square, a ghostly reminder of the original, now absent monument. Where there had been an almost forgotten fountain, there is now a bronze tablet with the fountain's image and an inscription detailing what had been there and why it was lost. As we enter the square, we watch as water fills narrow canals at our feet before rushing into a great underground hollow, which grows louder and louder until we finally stand over the "Aschrott-Brunnen." Only the sound of gushing water suggests the depth of an otherwise invisible memorial, an inverted palimpsest that demands the visitor's reflection. Through an iron grate and thick glass windows we peer into the depths. "With the running water," Hoheisel suggests, "our thoughts can be drawn into the depths of history, and there perhaps we will encounter feelings of loss, of a disturbed place, of lost form."

In fact, as the only standing figures on this flat square, our thoughts rooted in the rushing fountain beneath our feet, we realize that we have become the memorial. "The sunken fountain is not the memorial at all," Hoheisel says. "It is only history turned into a pedestal, an invitation to passersby who stand upon it to search for the memorial in their own heads. For only there is the memorial to be found." Hoheisel has left

Horst Hoheisel, negative-form, Aschrott-Brunnen Monument, Kassel, 1987.

Neo-Nazis demonstrate at the Aschrott-Brunnen Monument, Kassel, 1997.

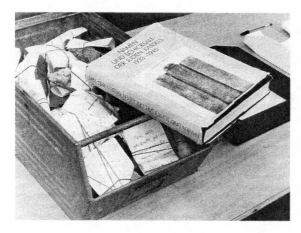

*Horst Hoheisel, Denk-Stein-Sammlung
Memorial Project, Kassel, 1988–1995.*

nothing but the visitors themselves standing in remembrance, left to look inward for memory.

Neo-Nazi demonstrators protesting an exhibition critical of the Wehrmacht when it came to Kassel in June 1998 were granted permission by the mayor to hold their protest in the Aschrott-Brunnen plaza, in front of Kassel's city hall. Here they stood atop the original fountain's foundation stones that had been salvaged by Hoheisel to mark the perimeter of the original fountain. Skin-headed and tattooed, wearing black shirts and fatigues, the neo-Nazis waved black flags and taunted a crowd of counter-protesters who had assembled outside police barricades surrounding the neo-Nazis. In a press release, Hoheisel recounted the history of the site, from the donation of the fountain to Kassel by Sigmund Aschrott, to its demolition at the hands of the Nazis in April 1939, to the memorial's dedication in 1987, and finally to the neo-Nazis' demonstration there in June 1998. For Hoheisel, the neo-Nazis' "reclamation" of the site, their triumphal striding atop the ruins of the fountain that their predecessors had destroyed in 1939, seemed to bear out his dark hope that this would become a negative center of gravity around which all memory—wanted and unwanted—would now congeal.

By this time, Hoheisel had initiated several other memorial projects, including another in Kassel. One more pedagogically inclined project turned to the next generation. With permission from local public schools, the artist visited the classrooms of Kassel with a book, a stone, and a piece of paper. The book was a copy of *Namen und Schicksale der Juden Kassels* (The names and fates of Kassel's Jews), a memorial book for Kassel's destroyed Jewish community. In his classroom visits, Hoheisel told students the story of Kassel's vanished Jews, how they had once thrived there, lived in the very houses where these schoolchildren now lived, how they had sat at these same classroom desks. He then asked all the children who knew any Jews to raise their hands. When no hands appeared, Hoheisel would read the story of one of Kassel's deported Jews from his memory book. At the end of his reading, Hoheisel invited each student to research the life of one of Kassel's deported Jews: where they had lived and how, who were their families, how old they were, what they had looked like. He asked them to visit formerly Jewish neighborhoods and get to know the German neighbors of Kassel's deported Jews.

After this, students were asked to write short narratives describing the lives and deaths of their subjects, wrap these narratives around cobblestones, and deposit them in one of the archival bins the artist had provided at every school. After several dozen such classroom visits, the bins had begun to overflow and new ones were furnished. In time, all of these bins were transported to Kassel's Hauptbahnhof, where they were stacked on the rail platform whence Kassel's Jews were deported. It is now a permanent installation, what the artist calls his *Denk-Stein Sammlung* (memorial stone archive).

This memorial cairn—a witness-pile of stones—marks both the site of deportation and the community's education about its murdered Jews, their absence now marked by the evolving memorial. Combining narrative and stone in this way,

Horst Hoheisel, Denk-Stein-Sammlung Memorial Project, installed at train station, Kassel, 1988–1995.

Temporary memorial at Buchenwald built by former inmates, May 1945.

the artist and students have thus adopted the most Jewish of memorial forms as their own—thereby enlarging their memorial lexicon to include that of the absent people they would now recall. After all, only they are now left to write the epitaph of the missing Jews, known and emblematized primarily by the void they have left behind.

Similarly, when invited by the director of the Buchenwald Museum, Volkhard Knigge, shortly after its postreunification revisions to memorialize the first monument to liberation erected by the camp's former inmates

Horst Hoheisel, "Warm memorial" to commemorate the former inmates' memorial at Buchenwald, 1995.

in April 1945, Hoheisel proposed not a resurrection of the original monument but a "living" alternative. In collaboration with architect Andreas Knitz, the artist designed a concrete slab with the names of fifty-one national groups victimized here and engraved with the initials K.L.B. (Konzentrationslager Buchenwald) that had marked the prisoners' original wooden memorial obelisk. And as that obelisk had been constructed out of the pieces of barracks torn down by their former inmates—that is, enlivened by the prisoners' own hands—Hoheisel built into his memorial slab of concrete a radiant heating system to bring it to a constant 98.6 degrees Fahrenheit (36.5 degrees Celsius) that might suggest the body heat of those whose memory it would now enshrine. Visitors almost always kneel to touch the slab, something they would not do if it were cold stone, and they are touched in turn by the human warmth embodied here. Dedicated in April 1995, on the fiftieth anniversary of the prisoners' own memorial (which lasted only two months), this warm memorial reminds visitors of the memory of actual victims that has preceded their own, subsequent memory of this time. In winter, with snow covering the rest of the ground, this slab is always clear, an all-season marker for the site of the prisoners' original attempt to commemorate the crimes against them.

Horst Hoheisel, "Warm memorial" at Buchenwald, detail, 1995.

Horst Hoheisel and Henning Langenheim, "Arbeit macht frei" projection onto the Brandenburger Tor, 27 January 1996.

Christian Boltanski, Micha Ullman, Rachel Whiteread

While taking a walk in Berlin's former Jewish Quarter, the artist Christian Boltanski found himself drawn curiously to the occasional gaps and vacant lots between buildings. On inquiring, he found that the building at Grosse Hamburgerstrasse 15 and 16 had been destroyed by Allied bombings in 1945 and never rebuilt. In a project he mounted for the exhibition *Die Endlichkeit der Freiheit* in October 1990 called *Missing House,* the artist thus set to work retracing all the lives of people who had lived in this "missing house" between 1930 and 1945—both the Jewish Germans who had been deported and the non-Jewish Germans who had been given their homes.[13]

Boltanski found family photographs and letters, children's drawings, rationing tickets, and other fragments of these lives, photocopied them, and put them all together with maps of the neighborhood in archival boxes. At this point, he had nameplates hung on the white-plastered wall of the building next door to identify the now missing inhabitants, Jews and non-Jews—leaving the lot empty. The *Missing House* project became emblematic for Boltanski of the missing Jews who had once inhabited it; as its void invited him to fill it with memory, he hoped it would incite others to memory as well.

In two other installations, one realized and the other as yet only proposed, artists Micha Ullman and Rachel Whiteread have also turned to both bookish themes and negative spaces in order to represent the void left behind by the "people of the book." To commemorate the infamous Nazi book-burning of 10 May 1933, the city of Berlin invited Micha Ullman, an Israeli-born conceptual and installation artist, to design a monument for Berlin's Bebelplatz. Today the cobblestone expanse of the Bebelplatz is still empty of all forms except for the figures of people who stand there and peer down through a ground-level window into the ghostly white, underground room of empty bookshelves Ullman has installed. A steel tablet set into the stones simply recalls that this was the site of some of the most notorious book-burnings and quotes Heinrich Heine's famously prescient words, "Where books are burned, so one day will people be burned as well." But the shelves are still empty, unreplenished, and it is the absence of both people and books that is marked here in yet one more empty memorial pocket.

Indeed, the English sculptor Rachel Whiteread has proposed casting the very spaces between and around books as the memorial figure by which Austria's missing Jews would be recalled in Vienna's Judenplatz. In a competition initiated by Nazi-hunter Simon Wiesenthal in 1996, a distinguished jury of experts appointed by the city chose a brilliant, if abstract and controversial, design by the Turner Award–winning British artist Rachel Whiteread. Her winning proposal for Vienna's official Holocaust memorial—the positive cast of the space around books in an anonymous library, the interior turned inside-out—thus extends her sculptural predilection for solidifying the spaces over, under, and around everyday objects, even as it makes the book itself her central memorial motif. But even here, it is not the book per se that constitutes her now displaced object of memory but the literal space between the book and us. For as others have already noted, Whiteread's work since 1988 has made brilliantly palpable the notion that materiality can also be an index of absence: whether it is the ghostly apparition of the filled-in space of a now demolished row house in London (*House* launched Whiteread to international prominence) or the proposed cast of the empty space between the book leaves and the wall in a full-size library, Whiteread makes the absence of an original object her work's defining pre-

occupation.[14] Like other artists of her generation, Rachel Whiteread is concerned less with the Holocaust's images of destruction and more with the terrible void this destruction left behind.

Given this thematic edge in her work, it is not surprising that Whiteread was one of nine artists and architects initially invited to submit proposals for a Holocaust memorial in Vienna. Other invitees included the Russian installation artist Ilya Kabakov, Israeli architect Zvi Hecker, and the American architect Peter Eisenman. As proposed, Whiteread's cast of a library turned inside-out measures approximately 33 feet by 23 feet, is 13 feet high, and resembles a solid white cube. Its outer surface would consist entirely of the roughly textured negative space next to the edges of book leaves. On the front wall facing onto the square there would be a double-wing door, also cast inside out and inaccessible. In its formalization of absence on one hand and of books on the other, it found an enthusiastic reception among a jury looking for a design that "would combine dignity with reserve and spark an esthetic dialogue with the past in a place that is replete with history."[15] Despite

Above, below, and facing page: Micha Ullman, "Bibliotek" memorial to the Nazi book-burnings, Bebelplatz, Berlin, 1996.

the jury's unanimous decision to award Whiteread's design first place and to begin its realization immediately, the aesthetic dialogue it very successfully sparked in this place so "replete with history" eventually paralyzed the entire memorial process.

For like many such sites in Vienna, the Judenplatz was layered with the invisible memory of numerous anti-Semitic persecutions—a synagogue was torched here in a pogrom in 1421, and hundreds of Jews died in the autos-da-fé that followed. Though Whiteread's design had left room at the site for a window into the archaeological excavation of this buried past, the shopkeepers on the Judenplatz preferred that these digs into an ancient past also be left to stand for the more recent murder of Austrian Jews as well. And although their anti-Whiteread petition of two thousand names refers only to the lost parking and potential for lost revenue they fear this "giant colossus" will cause, they may also have feared the loss of their own Christian memory of this past. For to date, the sole memorial to this medieval massacre was to be found in a Catholic mural and inscription on a baroque facade overlooking the site of the lost synagogue. Alongside an image of Christ being baptized in the River Jordan, an inscription in Latin reads: "The flame of hate arose in 1421, raged through the entire city, and punished the terrible crimes of the Hebrew dogs."

Rachel Whiteread, scale model of the Judenplatz Holocaust Memorial, Vienna, 1997.

In the end, the reintroduction into this square of a specifically Jewish narrative may have been just as undesirable for the local Viennese as the loss of parking places.

In fact, unlike Germany's near obsession with its Nazi past, Austria's relation to its wartime past has remained decorously submerged, politely out of sight. Austria was a country that had (with the tacit encouragement of its American and Soviet occupiers) practically founded itself on the self-serving myth that it was Hitler's first victim. That some 50 percent of the Nazi S.S. was composed of Austrians or that Hitler himself was Austrian-born was never denied. But these facts also never found a place in Austria's carefully constructed postwar persona. In a city that seemed to have little national reason for remembering the murder of its Jews, the entire memorial project was soon engulfed by aesthetic and political Sturm und Drang, and the vociferous arguments against the winning design brought the process to a halt. Maligned and demoralized, Whiteread soon lost her stomach for the

Rachel Whiteread,
model for the
Judenplatz with
inserted Holocaust
Memorial,
Vienna, 1997.

fight and was resigned, she told me, to the likelihood that her memorial would never be built.

But then suddenly, in early 1998, the city of Vienna announced that a compromise had been found that would allow Whiteread's memorial to be built after all. By moving the great cube three feet within the plaza itself, the city found that there would be room for both the excavations of the pogrom of 1421 and the new memorial to Vienna's more recently murdered Jews. Nonetheless, the debate in Austria has remained curiously displaced and sublimated. Lost in the discussion were the words one of the jurors and a curator at New York's Museum of Modern Art, Robert Storrs, had used to describe what made Whiteread's work so appropriate in the first place. "Rather than a tomb or cenotaph," Storrs wrote,

> Whiteread's work is the solid shape of an intangible absence — of a gap in a nation's identity, and a hollow at a city's heart. Using an aesthetic language that speaks simultaneously to tradition and to the future, Whiteread in this way respectfully symbolizes a world whose irrevocable disappearance can never be wholly grasped by those who did not experience it, but whose most lasting monuments are the books written by Austrian Jews before, during and in the aftermath of the catastrophe brought down on them.

Renata Stih and Frieder Schnock, Memorial to the Deported Jewish Citizens of the Bayerische Viertel, Bayerische Platz, Berlin, 1993.

Renata Stih and Frieder Schnock, "At the Bayerische Platz, Jews may sit only on yellow park benches." Part of the memorial installation at the Bayerische Platz, Berlin, 1993.

Juden dürfen am Bayerischen Platz nur die gelb markierten Sitzbänke benutzen.

Rather than monumentalizing only the moment of destruction itself, Whiteread's design would recall that which made the "people of the book" a people: their shared relationship to the past through the book. For it was this shared relationship to a remembered past through the book that bound Jews together, and it was the book that provided the site for this relationship.

Though Whiteread is not Jewish, she has—in good Jewish fashion—cast not a human form but a sign of humanity, gesturing silently to the acts of reading, writing, and memory that had once constituted this people as a people. If it is really true that Vienna has chosen to go ahead with Whiteread's allusive and rigorously intellectual design, then the city and its Jewish community must both be congratulated: the Jewish community for the courage and audacity of its aesthetic convictions, and the city for finally bringing boldly to the surface its previously subterranean shame.

Renata Stih and Frieder Schnock

As did the American artist Shimon Attie during his stay in Berlin, the Berlin artists Renata Stih and Frieder Schnock find their city essentially haunted by its own lying beauty, its most placid and charming neighborhoods seemingly oblivious to the all-too-orderly destruction of its Jewish community during the war. Tree-lined and with its nineteenth-century buildings relatively unscathed by Allied bombs

Renata Stih and Frieder Schnock, Memorial to the Deported Jewish Citizens of the Bayerische Viertel, Bayerische Platz, Berlin, 1993.

Arischen und nichtarischen Kindern wird das Spielen miteinander untersagt.

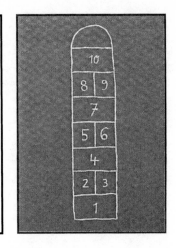

during the war, the Bayerische Viertel (Bavarian Quarter) of Berlin's Schöneberg district is particularly peaceful these days and off the tourist track. It had also been home to some sixteen thousand German Jews before the war, many of them professional and well-to-do, including at different times Albert Einstein and Hannah Arendt. But with nary a sign of the war's destruction in evidence, nothing in the neighborhood after the war pointed to the absence of its escaped, deported, and murdered Jewish denizens.

Haunted precisely by this absence of signs, and skeptical of the traditional memorial's tendency to gather what they thought should be pervasive memory into a single spot, Stih and Schnock won a competition in 1993 for a memorial to the neighborhood's murdered Jews with a proposal to mount eighty signposts on the corners, streets, and sidewalks in and around the Bayerische Platz. Each would include a simple image of an everyday object on one side and a short text on the other, excerpted from Germany's anti-Jewish laws of the 1930s and 1940s. On one side of such a sign, pedestrians would see, for example, a hand-drawn sidewalk hopscotch pattern, and on the other its accompanying text: "Ärischen und nichtärischen Kindern wird das Spielen miteinander untersagt" (1938; Aryan and non-Aryan children are not allowed to play together). Or a simple red park bench on a green lawn: "Juden dürfen am Bayerischen Platz nur die gelb markierten Sitzbänke benutzen" (1939; On the Bavarian Place, Jews may sit only on yellow park benches). Or a pair of swimtrunks: "Berliner Bademanstalten und Schwimmbäder dürfen von Juden nicht betreten werden" (3.12.1938; Baths and swimming pools in Berlin are closed to Jews). A black-and-white rotary telephone dial: "Telefonanschlusse von Juden werden von der Post gekundigt" (29.7. 1940; Telephone lines to Jewish households will be cut off).[17]

With the approval of the Berlin Senate, which had sponsored the memorial competition, the artists put their signs up on lampposts throughout the quarter without announcement, provoking a flurry of complaints and calls to the police that neo-Nazis had invaded the neighborhood with anti-Semitic signs. Thus reassured that the public had taken notice, the artists pointed out that these same laws had been posted and announced no less publicly at the time—but had provoked no such response by Germans then. At least part of the artists' point was that the laws then were no less public than the memory of them was now. Indeed, one sign with the image of a file even reminds local residents that "all files dealing with anti-Semitic activities [were] to be destroyed" (16.2.1945); and another image of interlocking Olympic rings recalls that "anti-Semitic signs in Berlin [were] temporarily removed for the 1936 Olympic Games." That is, for the artists, even the absence of signs was an extension of the crime itself. Stih and Schnock recognize here that the Nazi persecution of the Jews was designed to be, after all, a self-consuming Holocaust, a self-effacing crime.

The only "signs" of Jewish life in this once Jewish neighborhood are now the posted laws that paved the way for the Jews' deportation and murder. As part of the cityscape, these images and texts would "infiltrate the daily lives of Berliners," Stih has explained, no less than the publicly posted laws curtailed the daily lives of Jews between 1933 and 1945. And by posting these signs separately, forcing pedestrians to happen

Renata Stih and Frieder Schnock,
Memorial to the Deported Jewish Citizens
of the Bayerische Viertel, Bayerische Platz,
Berlin, 1993.

Die in Berlin aufgestellten judenfeindlichen Schilder werden 1936 während der Olympischen Spiele vorübergehend entfernt.

Renata Stih and Frieder Schnock, Memorial to the Deported Jewish Citizens of the Bayerische Viertel, Bayerische Platz, Berlin, 1993.

upon them one or two at a time, the artists can show that the laws incrementally "removed Jews from the social realm," from the protection of law. These "places of remembrance" would remind local citizens that the murder of the neighborhood's Jews did not happen overnight, or in one fell swoop, but over time—and with the tacit acknowledgment of their neighbors. Where past citizens once navigated their lives according to these laws, present citizens would now navigate their lives according to the memory of such laws.

In keeping with their vision of decentralized memory, of integrating memory of the Holocaust into the rhythms of everyday life, Stih and Schnock proposed an audacious "nonmonument" for the 1995 international competition for Germany's national memorial to Europe's murdered Jews. Taking as their premise the essential impossibility and undesirability of a "final memorial" to commemorate the Nazis' "final solution" to the Jewish question, they submitted a design called *Bus Stop—The Non-Monument*. Rather than filling the designated space of nearly five acres for the national memorial between the Brandenburger Tor and Potsdamer Platz in Berlin, they would keep it desolate as a reminder of the destruction brought upon Berlin by the Nazis and turn it into an open-air bus terminal for coaches departing to and returning from regularly scheduled visits to several dozen concentration camps and other sites of destruction throughout Europe. "There is not one single bus stop in central Berlin from which you can take buses to the places listed in this schedule," the artists tell us in a foreword to their précis for the project.[18] Therefore, they call for a single place whence visitors can board a bright red bus at a regularly scheduled time for a nonstop trip both to such well-known sites as Auschwitz, Treblinka, and Dachau and to the lesser known massacre sites in the east, such as Vitebsk and Trawniki. A central steel-and-glass waiting hall flanking the 426-foot-long boarding platform would provide travelers with computer-generated histories and bibliographies of all the sites listed at the terminal, a kind of memorial travel office that would extol history and memory over the usual forgetfulness, the attempt at forced amnesia, that drives leisure vacations. Buses would leave hourly for sites within Berlin and daily for sites outside the city. Not so much a "central memorial" as a "centrifugal" memorial, *Bus Stop* would thus send visitors out in all directions into a European-wide matrix of memorial sites.

With twenty-eight buses making local Berlin runs every hour and another sixty or so branching out daily for sites throughout Germany and Europe, this would also be, quite literally, a mobile memorial that paints its matrix of routes with memory. By becoming such a part of everyday life in Berlin, these red buses emblazoned with destinations like Buchenwald and Sobibor would, the artists hope, remind every-

Renata Stih and Frieder Schnock, Bus Stop—The Non-Monument. *Proposal for the 1995 competition for Berlin's "Memorial for the Murdered Jews of Europe."*

one of the "thorough integration of the terror machinery [itself] within everyday life in Germany from 1933 to 1945."[19] At night the rows of parked and waiting buses, with their destinations illuminated, would become a kind of "light-sculpture" that dissolves at the break of day into a moving mass to reflect what Bernd Nicolai has called "the busy banality of horror."[20]

Possibly the most popularly acclaimed of all entries in the 1995 competition, *Bus Stop* placed eleventh among the 528 submissions from around the world. The competition's organizers, intent on concentrating memory of Europe's murdered Jews into a single site in Berlin, felt that *Bus Stop* dispersed memory too far and wide, implicitly spreading the blame for the murder onto the regimes of conquered nations during the war. In response, the artists self-published a 128-page *Fahrplan*, or timetable, of actual departure times of buses, trains, and planes in the public transportation sector for all the sites in their original memorial plan. Unlike a conventional timetable, however, Stih and Schnock added concise histories of the sites themselves to accompany the hours of departure and return. The schedule to Lodz tells us both how to get there *and* how many Jews lived there before the war, how the ghetto there was established, when it was liquidated, how the deported Jews were murdered, and who did the killing. Similar histories accompany schedules to Lublin, Stutthof, Riga, Drancy, Babi Yar, and the other ninety or so destinations, including dozens in Germany alone.

Like other countermemorials, *Bus Stop* would, in effect, return the burden of memory to visitors themselves by forcing visitors into an active role. Though the bus rides might recall the deportations themselves, these would be deportations not to actual history but to memory itself. Indeed, the ride to and from the sites of destruction would constitute the memory-act, thereby reminding visitors that memory can be a kind of transport through space in an ongoing present moment, as well as a transport through time itself. In this way, the memorial remains a process, not an answer, a place that provides time for memorial reflection, contemplation, and learning between departing and arriving.

For an American watching Germany's memorial culture come to terms with the Holocaust, the conceptual torment implied by the countermonument holds immense appeal. As provocative and difficult as these monuments may be, no other memorial form seems to embody so well both the German memorial dilemma and the limitations of the traditional monument. The most important "space of memory" for these artists has not been the space in the ground or above it but the space between the memorial and the viewer, between the viewer and his or her own memory:

the place of the memorial in the viewer's mind, heart, and conscience. To this end, they have attempted to embody the ambiguity and difficulty of Holocaust memorialization in Germany in conceptual, sculptural, and architectural forms that would return the burden of memory to those who come looking for it. Rather than creating self-contained sites of memory, detached from our daily lives, these artists would force both visitors and local citizens to look within themselves for memory, at their actions and motives for memory within these spaces. In the cases of disappearing, invisible, and other countermonuments, they have attempted to build into these spaces the capacity for changing memory, places where every new generation will find its own significance in this past.

In the end, the countermonument reminds us that the best German memorial to the fascist era and its victims may not be a single memorial at all—but simply the never-to-be-resolved debate over which kind of memory to preserve, how to do it, in whose name, and to what end. That is, what are the consequences of such memory? How do Germans respond to current persecutions of foreigners in their midst in light of their memory of the Third Reich and its crimes? Instead of a fixed sculptural or architectural icon for Holocaust memory in Germany, the debate itself—perpetually unresolved amid ever-changing conditions—might now be enshrined.

The status of monuments in the twentieth century remains double-edged and is fraught with an essential tension: outside of those nations with totalitarian pasts, the public and governmental hunger for traditional, self-aggrandizing monuments is matched only by the contemporary artists' skepticism of the monument. As a result, even as monuments continue to be commissioned and designed by governments and public agencies eager to assign singular meaning to complicated events and people, artists increasingly plant in them the seeds of self-doubt and impermanence. The state's need for monuments is acknowledged, even as the traditional forms and functions of monuments are increasingly challenged. Monuments at the end of the twentieth century are thus born resisting the very premises of their birth. Thus, the monument has increasingly become the site of contested and competing meanings, more likely the site of cultural conflict than one of shared national values and ideals.

CHAPTER FIVE

Memory Against Itself in Germany Today

Jochen Gerz's Countermonuments

"When it comes to fascism, Germans tend to be speechless. But here, you see, they have been offered a blank slate on which to vent their feelings."
—Jochen Gerz, Art News

"What we did not want was an enormous pedestal with something on it presuming to tell people what they ought to think."
—Jochen Gerz and Esther Shalev-Gerz, Galeries Magazine

EXIT / Dachau

"FACED WITH GERMANY'S PAST, A NUMBER of people my age, even those too young to remember events, or born after the war, have always been aware of not knowing exactly how to behave," the artist Jochen Gerz has said. "They exercise a sort of sublime repression of the past. Hence my idea of repressing the work of art. Since Freud's teachings, it is well known that things we have repressed continue to haunt us. My intention is to turn this relation to the past into a public event."[1] Not only has the Berlin-born Gerz succeeded in making Germany's fraught relations with its past a painfully public event. In half a dozen memorial projects and installations between 1972 and 1998, he has also opened a new generation's eyes to the essential incapacity in conventional public institutions like the museum or the monument to serve as wholly adequate sites for Germany's tortured memory of

Jochen Gerz, EXIT / Materialien zum Dachau-Projeckt. *Installation in Bochum, 1974.*

the Holocaust. For Gerz, "this relation" between the Germans and their past necessarily includes the relation between Germans and their memorial sites. After Gerz's work over the past twenty-five years, neither relation has been quite the same.

In fact, perhaps the first truly countermemorial installation in Germany was mounted by Jochen Gerz for Sammlung Kunstmuseum in Bochum in 1972. In *EXIT / Materialien zum Dachau Projekt*, Gerz built a long hall with twenty tables in two rows of ten, each with a chair underneath and a dimly lit lightbulb dangling overhead. On each table he anchored a photo album, handcrafted by the artist, with images he had taken at the Dachau museum earlier that year. Without explicit directions, visitors to the installation would seat themselves at the tables and begin to leaf through the photographs in the albums. Because the albums were bound in freshly cut wooden covers and the chairs themselves were newly fashioned of unsanded wood, splinters were rife in both hands and seat.

Each album opened with a photograph of an EXIT sign from the museum, and from invisible speakers overhead, visitors heard the recorded sounds of someone running with plodding, feverish footsteps and out-of-breath panting. Accompanying these sounds were the rapid clacking of a typewriter, with its bell and sound of the carriage return. In this continuous sound loop of running away, of panting, and of typing, visitors seemed to be hearing an ongoing escape from the place they had just sat down to visit, as if they had begun their tour of Dachau by looking for a way out.

The albums continued with photographs of a sign with "Gedenkstatten Ord-nung"—memorial site regulations—telling visitors how to behave in the museum and concentration camp rooms: no smoking, no dogs, no baby strollers, no litter, no touching, no straying from the path; the museum is open from nine until five. Images of further signs from everywhere on the grounds of the former camp follow: do not damage exhibitions, do not write on the walls; exhibits not recommended for children under thirteen; and again, no smoking. Then follows a photograph of cushioned benches in the museum with the imprints of visitors' buttocks left behind. Then a train schedule, photographs of a fire alarm, a fire extinguisher, a telephone with a blank space for a fire department number. Other signs over doorways read: no entry, no exit. The lock on a toilet door is turned part way and reads on either side "besetzt" and "frei," occupied and free.

Toward the end of the album, the vicarious memory-tourist came upon images of the museum's guestbooks, wherein the responses from the museum's prior visitors became part of later visitors' experiences. But even here, Gerz's photographs showed that the terms of the visitors' responses were strictly enforced: there were spaces only for the visitor's age, profession, and nationality—just as might have been found on the concentration camp prisoners' own identity cards. "Do you find the documentation in this museum instructive?" asks the questionnaire. "Yes or no." "What do you consider negative/positive in this presentation?" "Do you have any suggestions?" A photograph of a visitor meticulously answering the questions follows.

Though he includes a handful of photographs showing the larger grounds of the concentration camp, the object of Gerz's tourist photographs from Dachau was not the well-groomed roll-call area, the various memorial shrines, guard towers, or barbed wire; nor as it turns out was his object even the memory of what happened at Dachau between 1933 and 1945. What Gerz would now remember to us about his visit was his sense of the seemingly ubiquitious signs that dictated his own memorial experience at Dachau. His was not memory of the past but the experience of the present moment as explicitly controlled and shaped by the museum—and it was this experience he was attempting to show in his installation.

Neither was this only about Gerz's own experience as a postwar tourist at Dachau nor even about the "memory" he found there. Rather, Gerz wanted to show the uncanny resemblance between the language of "administering memory" at the Dachau museum and the language that once administered the concentration camp itself. It was as if the Nazis' efforts to control the lives of former inmates had become both the latent content *and* the method of the museum's exhibition of the past.[2] As his text for the project also makes clear, *EXIT / Dachau* is more than a critique of this museum alone; it challenges the capacity of all museums to dictate the terms by which we remember. Nor would he go so far as to overstate the parallel between the maintenance of order in an operating concentration camp and its subsequent memorial. But in this project, Jochen Gerz was the first artist to critique the Holocaust memorial museum as a formal, if ironic extension of the authoritarian regime it would commemorate.[3]

For Gerz, there was no escape from the rules governing memory. His aim was to explore this liminal plane between us and the museum site *as constituted in* the memorial's rules. Here he grasped earlier than any of his counterparts the significance of our relationship to the site of memory for "our memory." The grounds for this relationship were not just the declared regulations of the museum but, as Gerz suggests, the undeclared regulations implicit in any memorial installation that necessarily govern our experiences in their spaces. Through the repetitive photographs of the outward signs regulating our experience, he gestures to the concentration camp memorial's entire world of unstated though no less powerful rules for remembrance: its veneration of the object, of the hallowed ground in telling the story of itself.

In fact, Gerz may even be suggesting that what we finally "learn" from such museums may be less about history than how to comport ourselves in its vicinity. We learn both the rules of the memorial and the facts of history, but in tandem, and in ways that mutually shape each other. For better or for worse, Gerz seems to be saying, we cannot know this history outside of the ways it is shaped for us in the museum. In this installation, he hoped to draw attention to the ways our experience in the museum shapes the history we've come to remember, so that we may never mistake one for the other, even as we cannot know one outside of the other. In the process, he issued an implicit challenge to the museum to distinguish itself ever further from the legacy it would now preserve.

During this same year, 1972, as Gerz was working through his relationship to the past as mediated for him by official institutions like the museum, he began to explore art forms that might be immune to the museum altogether. Trained in language, literature, and Sinology, Gerz was fascinated with the possibilities of art forms

Gedenkstätten-Ordnung

Die KZ-Gedenkstätte Dachau ist geöffnet täglich
von 9.00 Uhr bis 17.00 Uhr

Es wird gebeten, die Würde des Ortes zu achten,
die Gedenkstätte nur in entsprechender Kleidung
zu besuchen und jeden Lärm zu vermeiden

Nicht gestattet ist:

1. Das Rauchen in den Gebäuden

2. Das Mitbringen von Hunden

3. Das Mitführen anderer Fahrzeuge als Krankenroll-
stühle und Kinderwagen

4. Das Beschädigen irgendwelcher Gegenstände,
insbesondere das Beschreiben von Wänden und
Einrichtungsgegenständen

5. Jegliche Verunreinigung

6. Das Verlassen der Wege

7. Die Verbreitung von Druckschriften und
dergleichen

8. Das Betreiben von Handel und Werbung jeglicher
Art, sowie das Veranstalten von Sammlungen

9. Der Zutritt von Kindern unter 12 Jahren ohne
Begleitung Erwachsener

10. Das Fotografieren und Filmen zu gewerblichen
Zwecken ohne Erlaubnis der Verwaltung

Nicht geräumte und nicht gestreute Wege sind
dem Verkehr nicht freigegeben; für Unfälle wird
nicht gehaftet

Bayerische Verwaltung
der Staatlichen Schlösser, Gärten und Seen

Jochen Gerz, "Memorial Site Rules" at the Dachau Memorial Museum, EXIT / Materialien zum
Dachau-Projeckt.

that could exist outside of their own materiality, a kind of action-art that would leave no material traces. Here he explored ways to enact a visual form that echoed the manner in which spoken words could leave behind meaning and memory of themselves but no other trace. In a video performance *Crier jusqu'à l'épuisement* (To cry until exhaustion, 1972), for example, Gerz stood outdoors on a small outcropping of rock in Blanc-Mesnil, just north of Paris, and screamed into the air as long and as loud as he could. Two hundred feet away a video camera and microphone recorded Gerz as he screamed "Hallo!" at the top of his lungs for twenty-five minutes until his voice was worn to a barely audible whisper. He continued screaming, but no sound could be heard on the video for the remainder of the video performance. The scream continued, but now the only sound of it was a recording he had previously taped of a similar scream, which had been playing in tandem with his live scream—now a silent scream and a reproduction.

In two other photo installations from the same year, Gerz worked through related issues of aesthetic competence and ineffectuality in the face of the world's larger realities. In *To Warm the Earth,* Gerz assembled ten photographs of himself sprawled on large, empty patches of plowed earth, in which he appears to be hugging or holding the ground. But because these photographs are shot from a considerable distance, the artist's body is little more than a black clump on a vast and desolate landscape. The idea of this little figure thus warming the earth is both touching and even comically absurd when we recall, as the art critic Roald Nasgaard aptly reminds us, how the German title to this work (*anfassen, erwarmen*) conjures up "an *anfasser* or pot holder, made here (in a rereading of the images) to grasp onto an earth that is too cold to handle."[4] In yet another installation, Gerz was similarly defeated in his attempt to mime his own photographic reproduction. Here he stood for two hours on a Parisian street beside a life-sized photograph of his head and shoulders taken only two hours before in the exact spot. Viewers stopped to compare the real with the photograph and inevitably found the real person—now exhausted and drooping—the inferior work.

In a similarly inspired performance in 1974, entitled *Leben* (Life), Gerz spent seven hours writing the word *Leben* in chalk on the floor of the Bochum museum, over and over again, until the scrawled word covered the entire gallery floor. On a wall of the gallery opposite the room's entrance he mounted a printed text explaining the significance of his work. When the "show" opened, viewers entered the room, whose walls were empty except for a text across the hall. As visitors walked over the floor to read the text, Gerz's chalk handwriting was eventually scuffed off the floor by their shoes, erased in the visitors' pursuit of its meaning.

Along these lines, his contribution to the Documenta exhibition of 1977 in Kassel took place not within the confines of the exhibition hall itself, or even in the town of Kassel. In *Die Transsib. Prospekt* (The trans-Sib. prospect), Gerz traveled ten thousand miles on the Trans-Siberian Express, from Moscow to Khabarovsk and back, with his carriage windows closed and covered. For sixteen days, he traveled in a sealed train car, oblivious to the passing countryside. He kept no record of the trip and brought back no artifacts or other traces of the journey—except for sixteen slates on which he had imprinted his feet, once on each day of the trip. The journey would exist only in his mind and in the minds of those who came to Documenta, where they would see only the sixteen footprinted slates.

Like other performance artists of the day, Gerz made his process the artwork itself, building into it its own expiration. Because the process itself could not be exhibited, its art remained outside the museum's reach. To "see" the work, viewers would have to imagine it, thereby initiating their own art process. His work would now exist in those who had seen it, not in institutions dedicated to "preserving"— and thereby reshaping—it. The moment the process ceased, so technically did the artwork itself. The traces left behind in images, installations, and exhibitions would, in their seemingly banal gestures, point out the insufficiency of the preservation when compared to the act itself and the life of this act in the minds of those who may have seen it transpire.

Gerz thus came to be widely regarded as one of Europe's most provocative artists of "erasure" and self-abnegation, his primary objective being the exploration of what he has called "the no-man's land between the real and its reproduction."[5] In Gerz's poetry, this would be the moment just before or after language; in his photographs they are the spaces along the edges, what is just out of the image. Or as his installation of 1974 would have it, in which a microphone located in the center of the gallery transmitted the sounds produced there to a loudspeaker in the same room, "the memorial day for 29 May 1974 is the same day."

The Monument Vanishes: Harburg-Hamburg

Within a year of meeting the Israeli sculptor and performance artist Esther Shalev on a trip he made to Israel in 1983, Jochen Gerz was one of six artists invited to propose a design in Hamburg for a "Monument Against Fascism, War, and Violence—and for Peace and Human Rights." When Gerz first broached his invitation

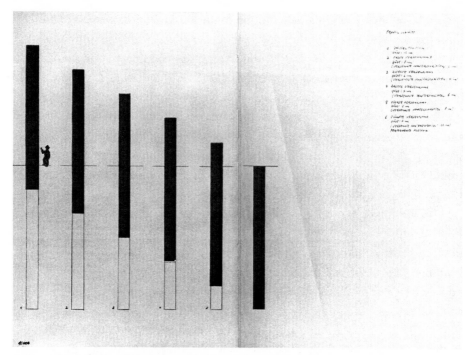

Jochen Gerz and Esther Shalev-Gerz, artists' sketch for the disappearing Harburg Monument Against Fascism and for Peace, 1985.

to propose a design for this monument, Shalev replied by gesturing out her window to Israel's own monument-dotted landscape, "What do we need with another monument? We have too many already. What we need is one that disappears."[6] Here she agreed to work with Gerz toward finding a form that challenged the monument's traditional illusions of permanence, its authoritarian rigidity. The resulting collaboration between Gerz and Shalev would thus combine a traditional Jewish skepticism of material icons and a postwar German suspicion of monumental forms.

With these conditions in mind, Jochen Gerz and Esther Shalev-Gerz, now married, designed their countermonument "Against Fascism, War, and Violence— and for Peace and Human Rights." The artists' first concern was how to commemorate such worthy sentiments without ameliorating memory altogether. That is, how would their monument put such memory in place without usurping the commu-

Facing page: The Harburg Monument Against War and Fascism and for Peace at its unveiling, 1986.

nity's will to remember? Their second reservation was how to build an antifascist monument without resorting to what they regarded as the fascist tendencies in all monuments. "What we did not want," they declared, "was an enormous pedestal with something on it presuming to tell people what they ought to think."[7] Theirs would be a self-abnegating monument, literally self-effacing.

So when the city of Hamburg offered them a sun-dappled park setting in the center of town, they rejected it in favor of what they termed a "normal, uglyish place." Their countermonument would not be refuge in memory, tucked away from the hard edges of urban life, but rather one more eyesore among others on a blighted cityscape. They chose the commercial center of Harburg, a somewhat dingy suburb of Hamburg located thirty minutes by subway across the river and populated with a mix of Turkish *Gästarbeiter* (guest workers) and blue-collar German families. Set in a pedestrian shopping mall, their countermonument would rise sullenly amid red brick and glass shop windows: package-laden shoppers could like it or hate it, but they could not avoid it.

Unveiled in Harburg in 1986, this forty-foot-high, three-foot-square pillar was made of hollow aluminum plated with a thin layer of soft, dark lead. A temporary inscription near its base read—and thereby created constituencies in—German, French, English, Russian, Hebrew, Arabic, and Turkish:

> We invite the citizens of Harburg, and visitors to the town, to add their names here to ours. In doing so, we commit ourselves to re-main vigilant. As more and more names cover this 12 meter tall lead column, it will gradually be lowered into the ground. One day it will have disappeared completely, and the site of the Harburg monument against fascism will be empty. In the end, it is only we ourselves who can rise up against injustice.

A steel-pointed stylus with which to score the soft lead was attached at each corner by a length of cable. As five-foot sections were covered with memorial graffiti, the monument was lowered into the ground, into a chamber as deep as the column was high. The more actively visitors participated, the faster they covered each section with their names, the sooner the monument disappeared. After several lowerings over the next seven years, the monument itself vanished on 10 November 1993 with its last sinking. Nothing is left but the top surface of the monument, now covered with a burial stone inscribed to "Harburg's Monument Against Fascism." In effect, the vanishing monument has returned the burden of memory to visitors: now all that stands here are the memory-tourists, forced to rise and to remember for themselves.[8]

With audacious simplicity, the Gerzes' countermonument thus flouted any number of cherished memorial conventions: its aim was not to console but to provoke, not to remain fixed but to change, not to be everlasting but to disappear, not to be ignored by its passersby but to demand interaction, not to remain pristine but to invite its own violation and desanctification, not to accept graciously the burden of memory but to throw it back at the town's feet. By defining itself in opposition to the traditional memorial's task, the Gerzes' Harburg monument illustrated concisely the possibilities and limitations of all memorials everywhere. In this way, it functioned as a "counterindex" to the ways time, memory, and current history intersect at any memorial site.

How better to remember forever a vanished people than by the perpetually unfinished, ever-vanishing monument? As if in mocking homage to Jochen Gerz's national forebears who had planned the Holocaust as a self-consuming set of events —that is, intended to destroy all traces of itself, all memory of its victims—the Gerzes designed a self-consuming memorial that would leave behind only the rememberer and the memory of a memorial. As the self-destroying sculpture of Jean Tinguely and others challenged the very notion of sculpture, the vanishing monument similarly challenged the idea of monumentality and its implied corollary, permanence.[9]

Citizens add their names to Harburg's disappearing monument, 1986.

Although self-effacing sculpture and monuments share a few of the same aesthetic and political motivations, each also has its own reasons for vanishing. Artists like Tinguely created self-destroying sculpture in order to preempt the work's automatic commodification by a voracious art market. At the same time, and by extension, these artists hoped such works would thereby remain purely public and that, by vanishing, they would leave the public in a position to examine itself as part of the piece's performance. "The viewer, in effect, [becomes] the subject of the work," as Douglas Crimp has observed. Or, in Michael North's elaboration of this principle, "the public *becomes* the sculpture."[10]

The Gerzes' countermonument took this insight several steps further. "Art, in its conspicuousness, in its recognizability, is an indication of failure," Jochen Gerz has said. "If it were truly consumed, no longer visible or conspicuous, if there were only a few manifestations of art left, it would actually be where it belongs—that is, within the people for whom it was created."[11] The countermonument was direct heir to Gerz's thesis on art and being, his ambivalence toward art's materiality. For Gerz, it seemed, once the art object stimulates in the viewer a particular complex of ideas,

Graffiti scrawl on Harburg's disappearing monument, 1989.

Graffiti scrawl on Harburg's disappearing monument, 1989.

emotions, and responses that then come to exist in the viewer independently of further contact with the piece of art, it can wither away, its task accomplished.

By extension, once the monument moves its viewers to memory, it also becomes unnecessary and so may disappear. As a result, Gerz suggests, "We will one day reach the point where anti-Fascist memorials will no longer be necessary, when vigilance will be kept alive by the invisible pictures of remembrance."[12] "Invisible pictures," in this case, would correspond to our internalized images of the memorial itself, now locked into the mind's eye as a source of perpetual memory. All that remains, then, is the memory of the monument, an after-image projected onto the landscape by the rememberer. The best memorial, in the Gerzes' view, may be no monument at all, but only the memory of an absent monument.

The Gerzes are highly regarded in Europe as poets and photographers and as conceptual and performance artists. Much of their conceptual art conflates photographs and poetry, overlaying image with word. In their performances, they aspire simultaneously to be "the painter, medium, paintbrush, and not just witness to a work."[13] In their countermonument, the artists attempted a "performative piece" that initiated a dynamic relationship among artists, work, and viewer, in which none emerged singularly dominant. In its egalitarian conception, the countermonument would not just commemorate the antifascist impulse but enact it, breaking down the hierarchical relationship between art object and its audience. By inviting its own violation, the monument humbled itself in the eyes of beholders accustomed to maintaining a respectful, decorous distance. It forced viewers to desanctify the memorial, demystify it, and become its equal. The Harburg monument denaturalized what the Gerzes felt was an artificial distance between artist and public generated by the holy glorification of art. Ultimately, such a monument would undermine its own authority by inviting and then incorporating the authority of passersby.

In fact, in this exchange among artist, art object, and viewer, the sense of a single authority, a single signatory, dissolves altogether: that the work was never really self-possessing and autonomous is now made palpable to viewers. The artist provides the screen, passersby add their names and graffiti to it, which causes the artist to sink the monument into the ground and open up space for a fresh exchange. It is a progressive relationship that eventually consumes itself, leaving only the unobjectified memory of such an exchange. In its abstract form, this monument claims not to prescribe—dictate, the artists might say—a specific object of memory. Rather, it more passively accommodates all memory and response, as the blank-sided obelisk always has. It remains the obligation of passersby to enter into the art: it makes artist-rememberers and self-memorializers out of every signatory. By inviting viewers to commemorate themselves, the countermonument reminds them that to some extent all any monument can do is provide a trace of its makers, not of memory itself.

The Gerzes' monument was a visual pun intended: as the monument would rise up symbolically against fascism before disappearing, it calls upon us to rise up literally in its stead. It reminds us that all monuments can ever do is rise up symbolically against injustice, that the practical outcome of any artist's hard work is dissipated in its symbolic gesture. The Gerzes suggest here that it is precisely this impotence of the symbolic stand that they abhor in art, the invitation to vicarious resistance, the sublimation of response in a fossilized object. In contrast, they hoped that the countermonument would incite viewers, move them beyond vicarious response to the actual, beyond symbolic gesture to action.

From the beginning, the artists had intended their work to torment—not reassure—its neighbors. They have likened it, for example, to a great black knife in the back of Germany, slowly being plunged in, each thrust solemnly commemorated by the community, a self-mutilation, a kind of topographical hara-kiri.[14] The countermonument objectifies for the artists not only the Germans' secret desire that all these monuments just hurry up and disappear but also the urge to strike back at such memory, to sever it from the national body like a wounded limb. In particular, the Gerzes took mischievous, gleeful delight in the spectacle of a German city's ritual burial of an antifascist monument it just spent $144,000 to make—enough, in the words of Hamburg's disgruntled mayor, to repave ninety-seven yards of *Autobahn*. Indeed, the fanfare and celebration of its unveiling in 1986 were repeated in all subsequent lowerings, each attended by eager city politicians, invited dignitaries, and local media. That so many Germans would turn out in such good faith to cheer the destruction of a monument against fascism exemplified, in the artists' eyes, the essential paradox in any people's attempt to commemorate its misdeeds.

At every sinking, the artists attempted to divine a little more of the local reaction. "What kind of monument disappears?" some citizens wanted to know. "Is it art when we write all over it?" asked teenagers. At one point, the Gerzes went from shop to shop to gather impressions, which varied from satisfaction at the attention the monument had generated in their commercial district to other, less encouraging responses. "They ought to blow it up," said one. Another chimed in, "It's not so bad

The Harburg monument after its seventh lowering, 1992.

Memory Against Itself

The Harburg monument disappears, 10 November 1993.

| 10. Oktober 1986 | 1. September 1987 | 23. Oktober 1988 | 6. September 1989 | 22. Februar 1990 |
| Einweihung | 1. Absenkung | 2. Absenkung | 3. Absenkung | 4. Absenkung |

Harburg's disappearing monument.

as far as chimneys go, but there ought to be some smoke coming out of it."[15] The Gerzes found that even resentment is a form of memory.

In their original conception, the Gerzes had hoped for row upon row of neatly inscribed names, a visual echo of the war memorials of another age. This black column of self-inscribed names might thus remind all visitors of their own mortality, not to mention the monument's. Execution did not follow design, however, and even the artists were taken aback by what they found after a couple of months: an illegible scribble of names scratched over names, all covered over in a spaghetti scrawl, what Gerz likened to a painting by Mark Tobey. People had come at night to scrape over all the names, even to pry the lead plating off its base. There were hearts with "Jürgen liebt Kirsten" written inside, Stars of David, and funny faces daubed in paint and marker pen. Inevitably, swastikas began to appear. How better to remember what happened than by the Nazis' own sign? After all, Jochen insists, "a swastika is also a signature." In fact, when city authorities warned of the possibility of vandalism, the Gerzes had replied, "Why not give that phenomenon free rein and allow the monument to document the social temperament in that way?"[16]

The town's citizens were not as philosophical, however, and began to condemn the monument as a trap for graffiti. It was almost as if the monument, covered over in this scrawl, taunted visitors in its ugliness. But what repelled critics more was

4. Dezember 1990 27. September 1991 27. November 1992 10. November 1993
5. Absenkung   6. Absenkung   7. Absenkung   letzte Absenkung

not clear. Was it the monument's unsightly form or the grotesque sentiments it captured and then reflected back to the community? As a social mirror, it became doubly troubling in that it reminded the community of what happened then and, even worse, how they responded now to the memory of this past. To those members of the community who deplored the ease with which this work was violated, the local newspaper answered succinctly: "The filth brings us closer to the truth than would any list of well-meaning signatures. The inscriptions, a conglomerate of approval, hatred, anger and stupidity, are like a fingerprint of our city applied to the column."[17] The countermonument accomplished what all monuments must: it reflected back to the people—and thus codified—their own memorial projections and preoccupations.

Today, all that remains of the Harburg monument against fascism and for peace is an empty clearing marked by a tablet. The pillar itself is visible in a glass-enclosed chamber below, and visitors mill around to read the memorial's texts, which remain behind. They have, as the Gerzes had hoped, become the memorial for which they searched. In this way, the memorial has not only returned the burden of memory to those who come looking for it but has changed the way a generation of artists and the public have come to regard the very idea of the memorial. This became apparent not only in the somewhat monumental piles of articles written about the memorial but in the dozens of "countermemorial" projects that became the standard for subsequent Holocaust memorial competitions in Germany.

The Invisible Monument: Saarbrücken

In keeping with the bookish, iconoclastic side of Jewish tradition, the first "memorials" to the Holocaust period came not in stone, glass, or steel—but in narrative. The *Yizker Bikher* (memorial books) recalled both the lives and the destruction of European Jewish communities according to the most ancient of Jewish memorial media: the book. Indeed, as the preface to one of these books suggests, "Whenever we pick up the book we will feel we are standing next to [the victims'] grave, because even that the murderers denied them."[18] The shtetl scribes hoped that when read, the *Yizker Bikher* would turn the site of reading into memorial space. In response to what has been called "the missing gravestone syndrome," the first sites of memory created by survivors were thus interior spaces, imagined gravesites.[19]

In his next memorial installation at Saarbrücken, Jochen Gerz seems to have recapitulated not only this missing gravestone syndrome but also the notion of the memorial *as* an interior space. Celebrated in Germany for his hand in Harburg's vanishing monument, Gerz was appointed in April 1990 as a guest professor at the School of Fine Arts in Saarbrücken. In a studio class he devoted to conceptual monuments, Gerz invited his students to participate in a clandestine memory-project, what he regarded as a kind of guerrilla memorial action. The class agreed enthusiastically, swore themselves to secrecy, and listened as Gerz described his plan: Under the cover of night, eight students would steal into the great cobblestone square leading to the Saarbrücker Schloss, former home of the Gestapo during Hitler's Reich. The castle and square, after all, had also been where the Nazis brought the Jews of Saarbrücken on Kristallnacht in 1938 to publicly humiliate them; and it was from this square that the town's remaining Jews had been deported to Gurs in southern France on 22 October 1940.

Gerz continued: Carrying book bags laden with cobblestones removed from other parts of the city, the students would spread themselves across the square, sit in pairs, swill beer, and yell at each other in raucous voices, pretending to have a party. All the while, in fact, they would stealthily pry loose some seventy cobblestones from the square and replace them with the like-sized stones they had brought along, each embedded underneath with a nail so that they could be located later with a metal detector. Within days, this part of the memorial-mission had been accomplished as planned.[20]

Meanwhile, other members of the class had been assigned to research the names and locations of every former Jewish cemetery in Germany—more than two

Jochen Gerz, Place of the Invisible Memorial — 2,146 Stones Against Racism, *Saarbrücken, 1997.*

thousand of them—now abandoned, destroyed, or vanished. When their classmates returned from their beer party, their bags heavy with cobblestones, all set to work engraving the names of missing Jewish cemeteries on the stones, one by one. The night after they finished, the memory-guerrillas returned the stones to their original places, each inscribed and dated. But in a twist wholly consistent with the Gerzes' previous countermonument, the stones were replaced face down, leaving no trace of the entire operation. The memorial would be invisible, itself only a memory, out of sight and therefore, Gerz hoped, *in mind.*

Yet as Gerz also realized, because the memorial was no longer visible, public memory would depend on knowledge of the memorial-action becoming public. Toward this end, Gerz wrote Oskar Lafontaine, minister-president of the Saarland and vice president of the German Social Democratic Party, apprising him of the deed and asking him for parliamentary assistance to continue the operation. Lafontaine responded with 10,000 German marks from a special arts fund and a warning that the entire project was patently illegal. The public, however, had now become part of the memorial. For once the newspapers got wind of the project, a tremendous furor broke out over the reported vandalization of the square; editorials asked whether yet another monument like this was necessary; some even wondered whether the whole thing had been a conceptual hoax designed merely to provoke a memorial storm.

As visitors flocked to the square looking for the seventy stones out of more than eight thousand, they, too, began to wonder "where they stood" vis-à-vis the memorial: Were they standing on it? In it? Was it really there at all? On searching for memory, Gerz hoped, they would realize that the memory was already in them. This would be an interior memorial: as the only

Jochen Gerz, Place of the Invisible Memorial—2,146 Stones Against Racism, *detail of stone.*

Jochen Gerz, Place of the Invisible Memorial —2,146 Stones Against Racism, *Saarbrücken, 1997.*

Memory Against Itself   143

standing forms in the square, the visitors would become the memorials for which they searched.

Where the politicians stood was less equivocal. As Jochen Gerz rose to address the Saarbrücken Stadtverband to explain his project, the entire Christian Democratic Union contingent stood up and walked out. The rest of the parliament remained and voted the memorial into public existence. Indeed, they even voted to rename the plaza "Square of the Invisible Monument," its name becoming the only visible sign of the memorial itself. Whether the operation had ever really taken place, the power of suggestion had planted the memorial where it would do the most good: not in the center of town but in the center of the public's mind. In effect, Jochen Gerz's *2,146 Stones Against Racism* returns the burden of memory to those who come looking for it.

In the catalogue Gerz compiled for this invisible memorial, the artist deepened his project further by including an implicit challenge to his own reliance on absence as thematic motif for the memory Germany's missing Jews. In her catalogue essay, cultural historian Irit Rogoff suggests that in this project, as well as in subsequent installations, Gerz's object of commemoration here is not history at all but the visitor's insatiable desire to repair and fill in the now-absent event with their knowledge of it.[21] In another essay, Rogoff elaborates: "If the task of commemoration is in part one of attaining redemption then its language is one of resolution. There is an entire vocabulary which stands in for our desire for such resolution: to heal, to make amends, to work through, to commemorate, to pay respects, to lay to rest."[22] But at the same time, she wonders whether the contemporary obsession with absence also reflects the not-so-benign desire on the part of Germans to assign a reductive unity to Jewish victims that did not exist when they were alive. As the Jews had been ascribed monolithically evil characteristics by their killers, Rogoff wonders now whether contemporary German mourners have begun to substitute one monolithic understanding for another. In neither case are victims recalled in their multiple, variegated, and individual human lives—but only as blocks for the projections of the Germans' limited grasp of their victims.

Questions Are the Monument in Bremen, Biron, and Berlin

Based largely on his work in Harburg and Saarbrücken, Jochen Gerz was awarded the Roland Prize for Art in the Public Realm in November 1990. With this award came a commission to realize a project of the artist's choosing somewhere in the public spaces of Bremen. Gerz gratefully accepted the prize, but then, instead of submitting a proposal for a new public art work in Bremen, he created a questionnaire that he then called a public sculpture. "Imagine the traditional situation," Gerz explained in the first of six public seminars held on the occasion of his prize.

> The senate says: "We want you to do a public work." In the Renaissance, the princes knew where a socle for a sculpture should be placed. Today the politician comes with the taxpayers' money. I asked the cultural senator about his wishes concerning a sculpture. After thinking intensively, he felt ill at ease and said he couldn't speak for the others. This shows that today one can't pose such questions any more. Three years later I asked the people themselves what they wanted. *It's not a question of developing a form, but of telling ourselves what our standpoint is.*[23]

Over the next five years, Gerz initiated a series of questionnaires to different groups of Bremen citizens, including the entire mailing lists of the two largest contemporary art museums in Bremen and a local gallery, students from the art academy, a local factory, readers of the regional edition of the daily newspaper, *taz,* and the students and faculty at the University of Bremen. All told, 232 out of 50,000 invited citizens responded first to three general questions: What topic should the work address? Do you believe that your ideas can be realized in a work of art? Would you like to participate in the artwork? The artist then presided over a series of six public seminars in which he thematized and evaluated the answers of each of the six responding groups to these questions, according to what he felt were the respondents' preoccupying issues—ecology, racism, politics, social criticism, and art. The public work, in this case, would truly be the interested public's work. Those who took time to respond—that is, to visit—these questions, to attend the public seminars and share in the answers of others would both constitute the work's public and, in Gerz's view, the work itself.

Because the seminars were conducted in question-and-answer format (participants and the artist asking each other questions), they became extensions of the original questionnaire, an ongoing dialogue between artist and public. With the asking and the answering, the inner changes of mind, and the understanding that would come with hearing others' answers, the process remained animate as long as it was not reduced to a single space in the city, Gerz suggested. No material object could adequately substitute for the process or represent it afterward. Nevertheless, if one had to imagine a public space that would not be the "end of the road and whose goal is not to possess an object," one example might be The Bridge.[24] "It stands alone," he said. "It has elements of: 'from-to . . .', 'before-after', or 'between.' Beneath it is the flowing water. Again and again there is the quality of being unfinished, the quality of being en route." Therefore, he announced, if citizens wanted some public "sign" of the process itself, one that would not put an end to the process of questioning just what should constitute "public art," he would place it on a bridge, a text that would read:

> When you look out on the water, you can see yourself and at the same time you are the image that leaves you, like a bird its trembling bush. Perhaps forever. The Bremen Questionnaire is a sculpture developed from the images of all those who imagined it. All of them are the authors. Thus, something came to be which should be many things, since all the answers were different. They show the fear of dictatorship, the desire to protect the earth, and anger about the language of politics. Many are suspicious of the arts, too. "We have invented empty spaces, only to fill them up . . . ." The Bremen Questionnaire is dedicated to its authors, and to everyone who stops here and sees something that doesn't exist.[25]

Today the text and names of its "authors" are inscribed into a triangular section jutting out of the pedestrian walkway on the Burgermeister-Schmidt Bridge in Bremen. Water flows beneath, and traffic moves noisily nearby. Against this literal flowing motion beneath and above it, the text is implacably still. It is a signpost pointing toward the questions still being asked and answered by the citizens of Bremen, but in its stasis it shows why it could not be the public work in and of itself.

Even as the public "sculpture of the Bremen Questionnaire" was unfolding, the ancient village of Biron in France's Dordogne, was inviting Gerz to design a replacement for the town's central monument to its war dead. Having lived for most of his life in Paris, Gerz and his work were well known to the adviser for the visual arts of Aquitaine, who recommended the artist to the town for its project. But after researching this village of 133 inhabitants, its medieval architecture, its chateau, and stone escarpments, Gerz surprised the town's officials by proposing to restore the former obelisk to the town's war dead in its original stone and color. In Gerzian fashion, however, he would not stop with the inanimate obelisk. To its stone face, he would now add enamel squares with the engraved answers to what he called the "secret question" he would put to each and every one of the town's inhabitants: "For what would you risk your life?"[26]

In March 1996, with the assistance of students from the Art College of Bordeaux, Gerz interviewed each of the town's citizens individually and recorded their answers, which he then had inscribed anonymously on 127 enamel plates. These red plates were mounted on the obelisk, its pedestal, and the surrounding stone base, and the monument was dedicated in July 1996. Yet because this was, in Gerz's words, to be "The Living Monument of Biron," he has also designated a local citizen to ask this "secret question" in confidential interviews with all future adults of the town when they turn eighteen. These answers, too, will be added to the obelisk over time, so that the "memory" of past dead becomes an ongoing, unfinishable work in progress. In putting such a question at the heart of the monument and then allowing new answers to change the monument's surface over time, this memorial process challenges the very certainty of both the obelisk's form and the reasons for remembering in the first place. Every generation will thus renew the memorial in the image of its own preoccupations, grasping the deaths of forebears in its own, imagined reasons for dying.

Born in Berlin in 1940, Jochen Gerz has said that one of his own earliest memories stems from the day in 1944 when his family home was hit by a bomb. Literally struck dumb by the sight of his home destroyed, "he watched the fir-trees in the garden gently topple—'They fell so slowly and burned like candles. Everything was so quiet.'"[27] Reportedly, he lost his voice entirely for the next year and spoke again only on his fifth birthday. When, fifty-three years later, Gerz became one of twenty-five artists invited to propose a design for Germany's national "memorial for murdered Jews of Europe" in Berlin, he responded by codifying the question that seems to have been on his lips since he was four: "Warum?" Why?

Given his preference for contingent and open-ended questions over the monumentally definitive and stultifying answer, the question at the heart of Gerz's proposed design for Berlin cannot come as a surprise. "The question 'Why did it happen?' is central to the Memorial Monument," Gerz has written, "since it embodies the point of departure for reflection and life after the Shoah."[28] Like his memorial proposals in Biron and Bremen, this design does not pretend to embody memory itself so much as it does the "point of departure" for memory in those who come to visit it. His design would accomplish this by dividing the massive five-acre site into two parts: three-quarters of the square would be paved in stones engraved with visitors' answers to the question posed atop thirty-nine evenly spaced, brushed steel light-poles, approximately fifty-two feet high, in fiber-optic cable in the thirty-nine languages of the Jewish victims from throughout Europe: "Warum?" The other quarter of the memorial site would be devoted to a building Gerz calls "the Ear," which would pose the same question aloud and invite visitors to respond in writing and to each other in conversation, discussion, and debate. In this way, Gerz says, the building "prepares visitors for their role as 'authors' and points them toward their own contributions."[29]

Gerz estimates that there would be room in the site for some 165,000 replies, each cut one and a half inches deep by a computerized writing device into the stone.

The script of the answers (each averaging around 120 letter-characters) would be so small that subsequent visitors would have to bend over to read it. The inscription process itself would take place in situ, as a "physical event— a form of atonement or 'working through,'" in Gerz's words, which would remain always unfinished and ongoing. On the opening of the memorial, he says, it would be important to note the blank slate of memory waiting to be filled in. As the entire space is eventually filled in, new space would be created by replacing the earliest responses with new ones. Memory and the answers it generates would be as ephemeral as the passing generations themselves.

Jochen Gerz, The Secret Question: The Living Monument of Biron, 1996.

For Gerz's proposal, "the Ear" building was designed by the Iranian architect Nasrine Seraji and would include three large rooms, one each for memory, answers, and silence. As administered by a foundation established by the Bundestag, the first room, Memory, would serve as the first European repository for Steven Spielberg's Shoah Oral History Foundation, where visitors would view and hear the video testimonies of Holocaust survivors gathered by the foundation. In the second room, Answers, visitors would meet with each other to attempt answers to the question, "Why did it happen?" Here resident scholars of the Holocaust would volunteer to serve as facilitators for such answers, and archives holding the thousands of answers offered by other visitors would be available on shelves for reading and yet further discussion. From the room of Answers, visitors would go into a circular room at the center of "the Ear," where it would be so dark that visitors would be unable to gauge the room's dimensions or to know who else was in the room. Except for a bench around the room's circumference, the room would be empty. Gradually visitors would be able to make out a round spot of sky above, as filtered through a translucent window in the ceiling. The only sound would be a work by American composer La Monte Young, "eternal e," which consists of a single tone that can be heard by the human ear only in faint waves. "Listeners [would] not know if what they are hearing is an existing composition or unique music they are imagining and composing themselves," Gerz has explained. In effect, he concludes, "The third room is a mirror in which one sees nothing—neither the testimonials of others, nor one's own recollections. It is a space of meditation. Imageless. Art's contribution after Auschwitz."[30]

Like Gerz's other memorial proposals, his design for Berlin's "memorial for Europe's murdered Jews" aims to make room for memory not within the landscape so much as within visitors themselves. But unlike the elegant, if laconic simplicity of his previous countermonumental forms, this proposal's formal execution seemed to embody too literally the project's extremely complicated and multiple conceptual aims, all of them seemingly brought into physical relief at once. Conceptually, each part of this design speaks volumes about what memorials can and cannot accomplish: its question returns the burden of memory-work to its visitors; its engraved stones make visitors' responses part of the installation and mark the multiplicity of memory and understanding, thereby refusing to collectivize memory into singular meaning; its plaza evolves over time to reflect changing memory and preoccupations, thus keeping memory animate and alive. In all of its elements, this plan replicates precisely those parts of his other works that make them so important and engaging.

This said, however, the Findungskommission appointed to choose a winning design, of which I was part, also concluded that the formal design seemed to have outsmarted itself, beginning with the question "Why?" Echoed from pylon to pylon in all the languages of the victims, "Why?" seemed here to be answered perpetually by further asking "Why?" The question seemed unending in and of itself, an invitation to mystification, not just asked here, but codified as unanswerable. Whereas "What happened?" and "How did it happen?" can be answered historically, "Why?" seemed to invite metaphysical, philosophical, even religious speculation. And although there is nothing intrinsically wrong with such speculation, the only answers to "Why?" built into European, Christian religious traditions tend to be self-justifying, even redemptory. "Why?" "Because it was God's way." Or, "Because of humankind's innate evil." In *If This Is Man,* Primo Levi asks a guard at Auschwitz why he has just struck an inmate friend of his for no apparent reason. The guard's answer strikes Levi as paradigmatic: "Hier ist kein warum." Here there is no why. It is an inappropriate question to ask—of the guard then or of ourselves now, Levi implies, because it also invites us to make judgments based on our moral universe outside the camps. When asked on the historical level, such a question can be answered only by the perpetrators themselves, whose answer must also be self-justifying. Only those who perpetrated the crime can answer "why" they did it, and in these answers we receive the Nazis' rationale for the crime itself, in which Jews remain submerged in the Nazis' worldview—as subhuman, parasitic contaminators of German racial purity and culture. Why did the Nazis kill the Jews? Only the Nazis can tell. The rest of us should not be put in a position to provide a rationale for the Nazis. And even if this is part of Gerz's aim, the implied silence after such a question may also begin sound like the silence of the victims themselves, made to answer somehow for their own murder.

Beyond the mystifying question, the Findungskommission also resisted the formal execution of the memorial itself. The steel pylons with the fiber-optic light and "Warum" in thirty-nine languages were meant to challenge the more traditional (cold and authoritarian) stone and mortar. But here we found an unintentional but clear visual reference to a trade pavilion with flagpoles, each with a national language instead of colors at the top. Even the "earlike" document house, where visitors would answer the question among themselves, seemed too literal a reference to the ear. Indeed, where the brilliance of Gerz's other works seemed to come precisely in their succinct abstraction, here the concrete references—even when unintended—seemed to reduce the concepts underlying them to mere space, material, and object.

Although the memorial's commissioners named Gerz's proposal as one of four finalists, and sympathy for its conceptual aims was uniformly high, organizers finally concluded that its brilliant concept was not matched by formal execution of design. This memorial, perhaps the most important to Gerz of all his projects, would remain unbuilt. By the end of the competition, however, it was also clear that in his previous work, Jochen Gerz had single-handedly defined the countermemorial, whose very precepts had been codified in the Berlin memorial's précis. In fact, it could also be said that without Gerz's earlier brilliant critiques of the memorial—as found in the Dachau project, at Harburg, and at Saarbrücken—this memorial competition in Berlin could not have been conceived as it was. Only in its open invitation to challenge the memorial's traditional redemptory and consoling aims was this project's premise acceptable to a new generation of artists in the first place. For this reason alone, Jochen Gerz might always be regarded as co-creator of Germany's national memorial for Europe's murdered Jews—whether he actually designed it or not.

CHAPTER SIX

Daniel Libeskind's Jewish Museum in Berlin

The Uncanny Arts of Memorial Architecture

"[According to Schelling], the uncanny [is] something which ought to have remained hidden but has come to light."

—Sigmund Freud, "The Uncanny"

HOW DOES A CITY "HOUSE" THE MEMORY of a people no longer at "home" there? How does a city like Berlin invite a people like the Jews back into its official past after having driven them so murderously from it? Such questions may suggest their own, uncanny answers: A "Jewish Museum" in the capital city of a nation that not so long ago voided itself of Jews, making them alien strangers in a land they had considered "home," will not by definition be *heimlich* but must be regarded as *unheimlich*—or, as our translation would have it, uncanny. The dilemma facing the designer of such a museum thus becomes: How then to embody this sense of *unheimlichkeit*, or uncanniness, in a medium like architecture, which has its own long tradition of *heimlichkeit*, or homeliness? Moreover, can the construction of a contemporary architecture remain entirely distinct from, even oblivious to, the history it shelters? Is its spatial existence ever really independent of its contents?

In their initial conception of what they then regarded as a Jewish Museum "extension" to the Berlin Museum, city planners hoped to recognize both the role Jews had once played as co-creators of Berlin's history and culture and that the city was fundamentally haunted by its Jewish absence. At the same time, the very notion of an "autonomous" Jewish Museum struck them as problematic: the museum wanted to show the importance and far-reaching effect of Jewish culture on the city's

history, to give it the prominence it deserved. But many also feared dividing German from Jewish history, inadvertently recapitulating the Nazis' segregation of Jewish culture from German. This would have been to reimpose a distinct line between the history and cultures of two people—Germans and Jews—whose fates had been inextricably mingled for centuries in Berlin. From the beginning, planners realized that this would be no mere reintroduction of Jewish memory into Berlin's civic landscape but an excavation of long-suppressed memory.

Freud may have described such a phenomenon best: "This uncanny is in reality nothing new or alien, but something which is familiar and old-established in the mind and which has become alienated from it only through the process of repression. . . . The uncanny [is] something which ought to have remained hidden but has come to light."[1] Thus would Berlin's Jewish Museum generate its own sense of a disquieting return, the sudden revelation of a previously buried past. Indeed, if the very idea of the uncanny arises, as Freud suggests, from the transformation of something that once seemed familiar and homely into something strange and "unhomely," then how better to describe the larger plight of Jewish memory in Germany today? Moreover, if "unhomeliness" for Freud was, as Anthony Vidler suggests, "the fundamental propensity of the familiar to turn on its owners, suddenly to become defamiliarized, derealized, as if in a dream," then how better to describe contemporary Germany's relationship with its Jewish past?[2] At least part of the uncanniness in such a project stems from the sense that at any moment the "familiar alien" will burst forth, even when it never does, thus leaving one always ill at ease, even a little frightened with anticipation—hence the constant, free-floating anxiety that seems to accompany every act of Jewish memorialization in Germany today.

After Anthony Vidler's magnificent reading of the "architectural uncanny," I would also approach what I am calling an "uncanny memorial architecture" as "a metaphor for a fundamentally unlivable modern condition."[3] But rather than looking for uncanny memory per se, or uncanny memorials or architecture, we might (after Vidler) look only for those uncanny qualities in memorial architecture. In fact, what literary critic Robin Lydenberg aptly sees in "uncanny narrative" might be also applied here to a particular kind of uncanny memorial architecture: the stabilizing function of architecture, by which the familiar is made to appear part of a naturally ordered landscape, will be subverted by the antithetical effects of the unfamiliar.[4] It is a memorial architecture that invites us into its seemingly hospitable environs only to estrange itself from us immediately on entering.

By extension, the memorial uncanny might be regarded as that which is necessarily antiredemptive. It is that memory of historical events which never domesticates such events, never makes us at home with them, never brings them into the reassuring house of redemptory meaning. It is to leave such events unredeemable yet still memorable, unjustifiable yet still graspable in their causes and effects.

In designing a museum for such memory, the architect is charged with housing memory that is neither at home with itself nor necessarily housable at all. It is memory redolent with images of the formerly familiar but that now seems to defamiliarize and estrange the present moment and the site of its former home. Whether found in Shimon Attie's estrangement of contemporary sites with the images of their past or Renata Stih and Frieder Schnock's reintroduction of anti-Jewish laws into formerly Jewish neighborhoods emptied of Jews by these very laws, such memory marks the fraught relationship between present-day Germany and its Jewish past.

In the pages that follow, I would like to tell the story of architect Daniel Libeskind's extraordinary response to the nearly paralyzing dilemma Berlin faces in trying to reintegrate its lost Jewish past. Because this story is necessarily part of a larger history of the Jewish Museum in Berlin, I begin with a brief history of this museum's genesis in prewar Berlin in order to situate the museum's place in the mind of Libeskind himself. From here I follow with the city planners' more contemporary conceptualization of the museum and its impossible questions and then conclude with Libeskind's nearly impossible-to-build architectural response. The aim here will not be merely to explain Libeskind's startling design but to show how as a process it articulates the dilemma Germany faces whenever it attempts to formalize the self-inflicted void at its center—the void of its lost and murdered Jews.

The Jewish Museum and the Berlin Museum

As is often the case with community museums, the origins of the Jewish Museum in Berlin were inauspicious, even quaint. A Dresden jeweler by the name of Albert Wolf (1841–1907) bequeathed a small art collection (consisting mostly of coins, medallions, and portraits) to the Jewish community in Berlin. In the years that followed, the community's senior librarian, Moritz Stern, continued to develop the collection, showing it between 1917 and 1930 in three exhibition rooms located in the massive synagogue complex at 31 Oranienburger Strasse as the "Art Collection of the Jewish Community in Berlin." Meanwhile, encouraged by this gift and the warm reception of a series of exhibitions on "Jewish art" that showed in London and Berlin in 1908, a private collector from Berlin, Salli Kirschstein, initiated efforts to found a Society for the Friends of the Jewish Museum.

When Karl Schwarz took over the collection in 1928, it numbered some 20 paintings and 227 ceremonial objects. A year later, Schwarz and Kirschstein finally founded the Jewish Museum Society, and Schwarz oversaw an acquisitions campaign that increased the collection's holding to 80 paintings and 348 ceremonial objects. At this point, the proclaimed goal of the society was "to propagate interest in Jewish art and culture, and with the help of funding and gifts from the circle of members, to transform the art collection into a Jewish Museum."[5] From the beginning, Berlin's Jewish Museum thus conceived of itself as a place where Jewish art and culture, from the beginnings of Jewish history to the art of the present day, would be exhibited. In the words of an earlier chronicler, Hermann Simon, "Every cultural manifestation of Judaism would be given equal consideration," and collections would not be defined according to religious criteria only. This would become a permanent home for the "living presentation of Jewish art and cultural history."[6]

Indeed, it was with catastrophic timing that Berlin's first Jewish Museum opened in January 1933, one week before Adolph Hitler was installed as chancellor. Housed in refurbished exhibition halls at the Oranienburger Strasse complex already home to the synagogue there, as well as to the Jewish community center and library, Berlin's first Jewish Museum opened quite deliberately in the face of the Nazi rise to power with an exhibition of work by artists of the Berlin Seccesionists, led by the German Jewish artist Max Liebermann.[7] It is almost as if the museum had hoped to establish the institutional fact of an inextricably linked German-Jewish culture, each a permutation of the other, as a kind of challenge to the Nazis' assumption of an essential hostility between German and Jewish cultures.

Yet even here, the very notion of what constituted a "Jewish Museum" would be a matter of contention for the community: Would the museum show art on Jewish religious themes by both Jewish and non-Jewish artists? Or would it show anything by Jewish artists? The question of what constituted "Jewish art" had been broached. Indeed, from its origins onward, questions of "Jewishness," "Germanness," and even "Europeanness" in art exhibited by the museum began to undercut the case for something called a "Jewish Museum" in Berlin. So when the museum opened with a show of Max Liebermann's work in 1933, the very idea of a taxonomy of religious communities and their art seemed an affront to the most assimilated of Berlin's Jews. The Jewish art historian and director of the Berlin Library of Arts, Curt Glaser, attacked both the idea of a "Jewish Museum" in Berlin and the presumption that

Liebermann's work was, by dint of his Jewish birth only, somehow essentially Jewish —even though there was nothing thematically Jewish in the work itself. Such a show, Glaser wrote at the time, "leads to a split, which is totally undesirable and from an academic point of view in no way justifiable. Liebermann, for example, is a European. He is a German, a Berlin artist. The fact that he belongs to a Jewish family is totally irrelevant with regards to the form and essence of his art."[8] Thus was an integrationist model for the Jewish Museum in Berlin first proposed and first challenged within days of the Museum's official opening.[9]

In spite of constant pressure by the Nazis over the next five years, the Jewish Museum mounted several more exhibitions of German Jewish artists and their milieu. But with the advent of the Nuremberg laws defining "the Jew" as essentially "un-German," the Nazis suddenly forbade all but Jews to visit the museum, and all but Jewish artists to exhibit there. With this sleight of legislative hand, the Nazis thus transformed the institutional "fact" of an inextricably linked German-Jewish culture into a segregated ghetto of art and culture by Jews for Jews. Moreover, as "Jewish art," all that was shown there was officially classified as *entartete*, or decadent. Just as the Nazis would eventually collect Jewish artifacts to exhibit in a planned museum "to the extinct Jewish race," they turned the Jewish Museum into a museum for *entartete Kunst*.

Whether assimilated to Nazi law or not, like the other Jewish institutions in its complex on Oranienburger Strasse and across the Reich, the Jewish Museum was first damaged, then plundered during the pogrom on Kristallnacht, 10 November 1938. Its new director, Franz Landsberger, was arrested and sent to Sachsenhausen before eventually emigrating to England and the United States. Nazi authorities dismantled the museum and confiscated its collection of art and artifacts. Some four hundred paintings from the collection were eventually found in the cellars of the former Ministry for Culture of the Reich on Schluterstrasse after the war. According to the museum's chroniclers, Martina Weinland and Kurt Winkler, the cache of paintings was seized by the JRSO (Jewish Relief Organization) and handed over to the Bezalel National Museum in Jerusalem, which later became the Israel Museum.[10]

Meanwhile, Berlin's Märkische Museum, which had been established in 1876 to tell the story of the city's rise from a provincial hub to the capital of a reunified German Reich in 1876, continued to thrive. Like the exhibitions of any official institution, those at the Märkische Museum reflected the kinds of self-understanding dominant in any given era—from the Weimar period to the Nazi Reich, from postwar Berlin to the Communist takeover of the east. But when the Berlin Wall was erected in August 1961, West Berliners suddenly found themselves cut off from the Märkische Museum, now located behind the wall in the east. Hoping to preserve the memory of a single, unified Berlin as bulwark against its permanent division and unwilling to cede control of the city's "official history" to the party apparatchiks of the east, a citizens' committee proposed a Berlin Museum for the western sector, which the Berlin Senate approved and founded in 1962.

Thus founded in direct response to the violent rending of the city by the Berlin Wall, the Berlin Museum moved from one improvised home to another in the western sector of the city. Only in 1969 did it find a permanent home under the roof of what had been the "Colliegenhaus"—a baroque administrative building designed and built by Philipp Gerlach for the "Soldier King" Friedrich Wilhelm I in 1735—located on Lindenstrasse in what had once been the center of Southern Friedrichstadt. Gutted and nearly destroyed during Allied bombing raids during the war, the Colliegenhaus had been carefully restored during the 1960s and would now provide some 27,000 square feet of exhibition space for the new Berlin Museum. The aim of the museum would be to represent and document both the cultural and historical legacies of the city—through an ever-growing collection of art, maps, artifacts, plans, models, and urban designs—all to show the long evolution of Berlin from a regional Prussian outpost to capital of the German Reich between 1876 and 1945. But due to a chronic lack of space, a large part of its holdings—including its departments of theatrical history and Judaica, among others—had been more or less permanently consigned to the museological purgatory of storage and scattered in depots throughout the city.

Even as the Berlin Museum searched for a permanent home during the 1960s, Heinz Galinski, then head of West Berlin's Jewish community, publicly declared that the city was also obligated to build a Jewish Museum to replace the one destroyed by the Nazis in 1938. All but the main building of the Oranienburger Strasse synagogue complex had been damaged beyond repair during the war and demolished in 1958, so the museum could not be rebuilt in its original site. Moreover, because that complex had been located in the eastern sector of the city, it would be as inaccessible to the west as the Märkische Museum. According to social historian Robin Ostow, Galinski told the Berlin *Stadtverwaltung* that he didn't want a mere replication of the ghetto at the higher level of a cultural institution. Rather, he wanted the history of Berlin's Jews to be exhibited in the Berlin Museum as part of the city's history.[11] Here the laudable, if nearly impossible to execute "integrationist model" of Jewish and Berlin history once again found its voice.

With this mandate added to its own, the Berlin Museum began to collect materials and artifacts on Jewish history for what its curators hoped would be an autonomous Jewish department within the Berlin Museum. In 1971, two years after opening in the Colliegenhaus on Lindenstrasse, the Berlin Museum mounted its first exhibition devoted to Jewish life in Berlin, a gigantic show entitled "Contribution and Fate: 300 Years of the Jewish Community in Berlin, 1671–1971." Though it focused primarily on famous Jewish Berliners from the 1920s and seemed to embody an intense nostalgia for the "heile Welt" (holy world) of pre-Nazi Germany, according to Robin Ostow, this exhibit also inspired public discussion around the need for an autonomous Jewish Museum within the Berlin Museum.

Four years later, in 1975, the Berlin Senate established a Jewish "department" within the Berlin Museum. In consultation with Heinz Galinski, the Senate announced that "close association with the Berlin Museum in the shape of one of its departments protects the Jewish Museum from isolation and conveys an interwoven relationship with the whole [of] Berlin cultural history."[12] At this point, the Society for a Jewish Museum was established with Galinski as its chair, its express mandate to promote the Jewish Museum "as a department of the Berlin Museum." But by this time, Frankfurt had already built an independent Jewish Museum, and a Berlin citizens' group calling itself Friends of the Jewish Museum continued to agitate for a separate building for the Jewish Museum in Berlin. And once again, the debate was joined around an irresolvable paradox, articulated here in a 1985 op-ed article in *Die Welt:* "Nowhere else was the image of the successful German-Jewish symbiosis regarded with more conviction than in pre-1933 Berlin; yet Berlin was also the chief starting point for the years of terror, 1933 to 1945. The history of Berlin will always be interwoven with the history of the Berlin Jews."[13] The writer of this article concludes that because an autonomous Jewish Museum could never compensate for the terrible loss of Berlin's Jewish community, the "establishment of a Jewish museum in the Berlin of today is neither meaningful nor necessary."[14] His solution, like the Senate's and Galinski's, would be to locate the remaining Jewish collections in the Berlin Museum proper, to reintegrate them into Berlin's story of itself.

Between 1982 and 1987, the debate around the Jewish Museum assumed two parallel tracks: one over whether to locate the museum outside the Berlin Museum, the other over where it would be sited *if* it were located outside the Berlin Museum. Various groups proposed and opposed a number of venues, including the Moritzplatz and Hollmannstrasse; others, like the Ephraim Palais, became politically and logistically untenable. In 1986, while various sites for the Jewish Museum were being debated, even the Prinz-Albrecht Palais was suggested to the Society for a Jewish Museum, to which the society responded indignantly: "Should this of all palaces become a symbol of Berlin Judaism? The culture of the murdered in the house of the murderers? No more needs to be said."[15] Indeed, no more was said on locating the Jewish Museum in the former Berlin home of the Nazi Party.

In November 1986, the Jewish Museum Department of the Berlin Museum was moved temporarily to the Martin Gropius Bau, where it could exhibit a portion of its holdings. The status of its new home was best described by Volker Hassemer, senator for culture, at its opening. "The new display rooms [at the Gropius Bau] are a milestone in the gradual process to reconstruct and extend the Jewish department of the Berlin Museum," he said, before continuing,

> They remain, nonetheless—and this must be stated quite frankly to the public—a temporary solution on the path to the ideal solution desired by us all. That is, a Jewish department as a recognizable component of the Berlin Museum. . . . We must make it quite clear that the creators and the products of this culture were not something "exotic," not something alienated from this city and its cultural life, but that they were and still are a part of its history. . . . In view of this obligation . . . , I am convinced it is both correct and justified not to develop the Jewish department of the Berlin Museum as the core of an independent Jewish museum in Berlin, but as an independent department within the Berlin Museum.[16]

This view was corroborated by Hans-Peter Herz, Chair of the Society for a Jewish Museum, who also stated plainly, "We do not want a special museum for the Berlin Jews, but a Jewish department within the Berlin Museum."[17]

In 1988, the Senate agreed to approve financing for a "Jewish Museum Department" that would remain administratively under the roof of the Berlin Museum but would have its own, autonomous building. A prestigious international competition was called in December 1988 for a building design that would both "extend" the Berlin Museum and give the "Jewish Museum Department" its own space. But because this was also a time when city planners were extremely sensitive to the destructive divisiveness of the Berlin Wall itself, which the Berlin Museum had been founded to overcome, they remained wary of any kind of spatial demarcation between the Museum and its "Jewish Museum Department"—hence, the unwieldy name with which they hoped to finesse the connection between the two: "Extension of the Berlin Museum with the Jewish Museum Department."

According to planners, the Jewish wing would be both autonomous and integrative, the difficulty being to link a museum of civic history with the altogether uncivil treatment of that city's Jews. The questions such a museum raises are as daunting as they are potentially paralyzing: How to do this in a form that would not suggest reconciliation and continuity? How to reunite Berlin and its Jewish part without suggesting a seamless rapprochement? How to show Jewish history and culture as part of German history without subsuming it altogether? How to show Jewish culture as part of *and* separate from German culture without recirculating all the old canards of "a people apart"?

Rather than skirt these impossible questions, the planners confronted them unflinchingly in an extraordinary conceptual brief for the competition that put the questions at the heart of the design process. According to the text by Rolf Bothe (then director of the Berlin Museum) and Vera Bendt (then director of the Jewish Department of the Berlin Museum), a Jewish museum in Berlin would have to comprise three primary areas of consideration: (1) the Jewish religion, customs, and ritual objects; (2) history of the Jewish community in Germany, its rise and terrible destruction at the hands of the Nazis; and (3) the lives and works of Jews who left their mark on the face and the history of Berlin over the centuries.[18] But in elaborating these areas, the authors of the conceptual brief also challenged potential designers to acknowledge the terrible void that made this museum necessary. If part of the aim here had been the reinscription of Jewish memory and the memory of the Jews' murder into Berlin's otherwise indifferent civic culture, another part would be to reveal the absence in postwar German culture that demanded this reinscription.

Most notably, in describing the history of Berlin's Jewish community, the authors made clear that not only were the city's history and Jews' history inseparable but that nothing (not even this museum) could redeem the expulsion and murder of Berlin's Jews—"a fate whose terrible significance should not be lost through any form of atonement or even through the otherwise effective healing power of time. *Nothing in Berlin's history ever changed the city more than the persecution, expulsion, and murder of its own Jewish citizens. This change worked inwardly, affecting the very heart of the city.*"[19] In thus suggesting that the murder of Berlin's Jews was the single greatest influence on the shape of this city, the planners also seem to imply that the new Jewish extension of the Berlin Museum may even constitute the hidden center of Berlin's civic culture, a focal point for Berlin's historical self-understanding.

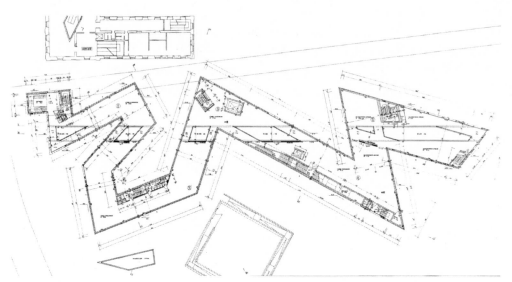

Daniel Libeskind, architect's first-floor plan sketch, The Jewish Museum Extension to the Berlin Museum, 1988.

As the wall had instantly transformed Berlin into a divided city, a visible reminder of both World War II and the newer Cold War between eastern and western Europe, the other great shaper of Berlin's cultural landscape was now evident only by its absence. The planners' description of the ways the Jews have left their mark on the face of Berlin history reinforced the centrality of this museum for understanding Berlin's history. "The history of the Jews of Berlin is so closely tied up with the history of the city that it is virtually impossible to separate the two; i.e., an autonomous Jewish Museum is necessary but almost inconceivable without the history of Berlin, in the same way as, conversely, a Berlin Museum of urban history would lose all meaning if it did not take its Jewish citizens into consideration."[20] With this in mind, the aim of the museum would be to show that Jewish history is part of and separate from German history, a balancing act demanding almost impossible discretion, diplomacy, and tact.

Daniel Libeskind's Uncanny Design

Guided by this conceptual brief, city planners issued an open invitation to all architects of the Federal Republic of Germany in December 1988. In addition, they invited another twelve architects from outside Germany, among them the American architect Daniel Libeskind, then living in Milan. Born in Lodz in 1946 to the survivors of a Polish-Jewish family almost decimated in the Holocaust, Libeskind had long wrestled with many of the brief's questions, finding them nearly insoluble at the architectural level. Trained first as a virtuoso keyboardist who came to the United States with violinist Yitzhak Perlman in 1960 on an American-Israeli Cultural Foundation Fellowship, Libeskind gave up music when, in his words, there was no more technique to learn. From there he turned to architecture and its seemingly inexhaustible reserve of technique. He studied at Cooper Union in New York under the tutelage of John Hejduk and Peter Eisenman, two of the founders and practitioners of "deconstructivist architecture." Thus, in his design for a Jewish Museum in Berlin, Libeskind proposed not so much a solution to the planners' conceptual conundrum as he did its architectural articulation. The drawings he submitted to the committee in mid-1989 have come to be regarded as masterpieces of process art as well as architectural design.

Of the 165 designs submitted from around the world for the competition that closed in June 1989, Daniel Libeskind's struck the jury as the most brilliant and complex, possibly as unbuildable. It was awarded first prize and thereby became the first work of Libeskind's to be commissioned.[21] Where the other finalists had concerned themselves primarily with the technical feat of reconciling this building to its surroundings in a way that met the building authority's criteria and with establishing a separate but equal parity between the Berlin Museum and its Jewish Museum Department, Libeskind had devoted himself to the spatial enactment of a philosophical problem. As architectural critic Kurt Forster had once described another design in this vein, this would be "all process rather than product."[22] And as an example of process architecture, according to Libeskind, this building "is always on the verge of Becoming—no longer suggestive of a final solution."[23] In its series of complex trajectories, irregular linear structures, fragments, and displacements, this building is also on the verge of unbecoming—a breaking down of architectural assumptions, conventions, and expectations.

His drawings for the museum thus look more like the sketches of the museum's ruins, a house whose wings have been scrambled and reshaped by the jolt of genocide. It is a devastated site that would now enshrine its broken forms. In this work, Libeskind asks, If architecture can be representative of historical meaning, can it also represent unmeaning and the search for meaning? The result is an extended building broken in several places. The straight void-line running through the plan violates every space through which it passes, turning otherwise uniform rooms and halls into misshapen anomalies, some too small to hold anything, others so oblique as to estrange anything housed within them. The original design also included inclining walls, at angles too sharp for hanging exhibitions.

From Libeskind's earliest conceptual brief onward, the essential drama of mutually exclusive aims and irreconcilable means was given full, unapologetic play. For him, the impossible questions mattered the most: How to give voice to an absent Jewish culture without presuming to speak for it? How to bridge an open wound without mending it? How to house under a single roof a panoply of essential oppositions and contradictions?[24] He thus allowed his drawings to work through the essential paradoxes at the heart of his project: how to give a void form without filling it in? How to give architectural form to the formless and to challenge the very attempt to house such memory?

Before beginning, Libeskind replaced the very name of the project—"Extension of the Berlin Museum with the Jewish Museum Department"—with his own more poetic rendition, "Between the Lines." "I call it [Between the Lines] because it is a project about two lines of thinking, organization, and relationship," Libeskind says. "One is a straight line, but broken into many fragments; the other is a tortuous line, but continuing indefinitely. These two lines develop architecturally and programmatically through a limited but definite dialogue. They also fall apart, become disengaged, and are seen as separated. In this way, they expose a void that runs through this museum and through ar-

Daniel Libeskind, scale model of The Jewish Museum Extension to the Berlin Museum on a backdrop of Berlin Holocaust victims' names, 1988.

chitecture, a discontinuous void."[25] Through a twisting and jagged lightening bolt of a building, Libeskind has run a straight-cut void, slicing through it and even extending outside of it: an empty, unused space bisecting the entire building. According to Libeskind, "The new extension is conceived as an emblem where the not visible has made itself apparent as a void, an invisible. . . . The idea is very simple: to build the museum around a void that runs through it, a void that is to be experienced by the public."[26] As he makes clear, this void is indeed the building's structural rib, its main axis, a central bearing wall that bears only its absence.

Libeskind does not want to suggest that this void was imposed on Berlin from outside; it was, he implies, one created in Berlin from within. It was not the bombing of Berlin that created the void, but the vacuum and inner collapse of moral will that allowed Berlin to void itself of Jews. According to Libeskind, this void will also represent a space empty of Jews that echoes an inner space empty of the love and values that might have saved Berlin's Jews. At the same time, according to Vera Bendt, his zigzag line can suggest the broken backbone of Berlin society.[27]

Indeed, it is not the building itself that constitutes his architecture but the spaces inside the building, the voids and absence embodied by empty spaces: that which is constituted by those spaces between the lines of his drawings. By building voids into the heart of his design, Libeskind thus highlights the spaces between walls as the primary element of his architecture. The walls themselves are important only insofar as they lend shape to these spaces and define their borders. It is the void "between the lines" that Libeskind seeks to capture here, a void so real, so palpable, and so elemental to Jewish history in Berlin as to be its focal point after the Holocaust— a negative center of gravity around which Jewish memory now assembles.[28]

As becomes clear, this design is also descended from a stage in Libeskind's work characterized by Peter Eisenman as the "not-architectural"—specifically as represented in his earlier series of drawings, *Chamber Works* (1983).[29] For the sake of an actual museum, it is almost as if Libeskind has allowed his not-architectural drawings to evolve into buildability, as a last stage of not-architecture, that stage before it becomes architecture. This design contains all of the signs of not-architecture—just before it edges into the buildable. As such, of course, his design blurs the lines between drawing, sculpture, and architecture.

In this context, Eisenman also describes Libeskind's early efforts at Cooper Union as attempts "to set elements free from their function in both tectonic and formal senses—from the causality of function and form."[30] Indeed, as we see from a glance at his earlier series entitled *Micromegas*, Libeskind's preoccupation with absences, voids, and silences predates by several years his design for the Jewish Museum. In this series of drawings from 1978, Libeskind attempts to sever the connection altogether between form and function. If until then architecture had taught that form was function, he hoped to show that form could be much more than merely functional—by being much less. Here he has exploded geometrical shapes into their components, rearranging them in ways to show affinities and dissimilarities between their parts and other shapes.

Unable to disregard the musical compositions of Anton Weber, Arnold Schoenberg, and John Cage already so deeply embedded in his consciousness, Libeskind had also embarked on a series called *Chamber Works* in 1983, subtitled *Meditations on a Theme from Heraclitus*. Music, art, architecture, and history all formed the interstices of these compositions. In these drawings, a complex of lines gives way to empty space, which comes into view as the subject of these drawings, which are meant only to circumscribe spaces, to show spaces as contained by lines. In *Chamber Works*, the last in these experimental series, Eisenman finds that Libeskind leaves only traces of the journey of his process behind. Though as traces these, too, seem almost to evaporate, so that by the end of this series there is a gradual collapse of structure back into the elemental line, thin and drawn out, more space than ink, which is almost gone. In his 1988 work *Line of Fire*, Libeskind takes this single line, folds, and breaks it—and thereby transforms it from not-architecture to the buildable.

As Kurt Forster points out, Libeskind's 1989 design for the Jewish Museum descends not only from *Line of Fire* but from a myriad of sources—poetic, artistic, musical, and architectural: from Paul Klee's enigmatic sketches of Berlin as a site of "Destruction and Hope" to architect Jakob G. Tscernikow's studies of multiple fold and intercalated shapes in his *Foundations of Modern Architecture* (1930) to Paul Celan's "Gesprach im Gerbirg" (1959). In its compressed and zigzagging folds, as Forster shows, Libeskind's design echoes both exercises and disruptions of architecture and art from before the war. Forster thus highlights the striking parallels between Paul Klee's post–World War I sketches and Libeskind's own idiosyncratic site-location map of Berlin.[31]

Before designing the physical building, Libeskind began by situating the museum in what might be called his own metaphysical map of Berlin, constituted not so much by urban topography as it was by the former residences of its composers, writers, and poets—that is, the cultural matrix of their lives in Berlin. In Libeskind's words, "Great figures in the drama of Berlin who have acted as bearers of a great hope and anguish are traced into the lineaments of this museum. . . . Tragic premonition

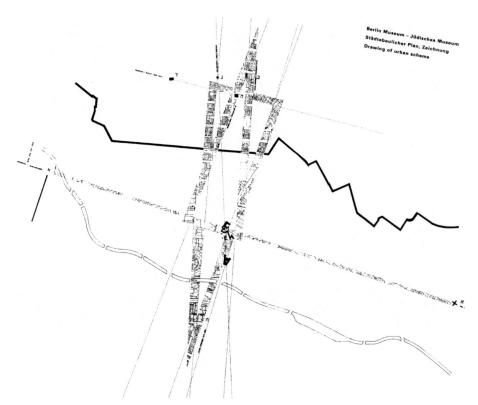

Daniel Libeskind, architect's sketch of a distorted Star of David overlaid onto a map of Berlin, based on the addresses of Berlin's great cultural figures, 1988.

(Kleist), sublimated assimilation (Varnhagen), inadequate ideology (Benjamin), mad science (Hoffmann), displaced understanding (Schleiermacher), inaudible music (Schoenberg), last words (Celan): these constitute the critical dimensions which this work as discourse seeks to transgress."[32] All were transgressors of the received order, and out of these transgressions, culture was born. In Libeskind's view, the only true extension of the culture Berlin's Jews helped to generate would also have to transgress it.

In his preliminary sketch of the city, therefore, Libeskind traces what he calls Berlin's cultural Jewish topography, "an invisible matrix or anamnesis of connections in relationship" between Germans and Jews. "I felt that certain people and particular certain writers, scientists, composers, artists and poets formed the link between Jewish tradition and German culture," Libeskind has said. "So I found this connection and I plotted an irrational matrix which was in the form of a system of squared

Daniel Libeskind, realistic zinc model of The Jewish Museum Extension to the Berlin Museum, 1989.

triangles which would yield some reference to the emblematics of a compressed and distorted star: the yellow star that was so frequently worn on this very site."[33] He then searched out the addresses of where these writers lived and eventually connected the streets of Rachel Varnhagen to Friedrich Schleiermacher, or of Paul Celan to Mies van der Rohe—all toward plotting a particular urban and cultural constellation of what he calls "Universal History." In this way, Libeskind would thus anchor his building in Berlin's cultural topography, a palimpsest for contemporary Berlin's landscape.

Little of which, it must be said, was readily apparent to jurors on their first encounter with Libeskind's proposal. Indeed, as one juror admitted, this was not a case of "love at first sight." The group had to work hard to decipher Libeskind's complex series of multilayered drawings: a daunting maze of lines broken and reconnected, interpenetrations, self-enclosed wedges, superimposed overlaps. But as the jurors did, the difficulty of the project itself began to come into view along with its articulation in Libeskind's brief. On peeling away each layer from the one under it, jurors found that the project's deeper concept came into startling relief. It was almost as if the true dilemma at the heart of their project was not apparent to them until revealed in Libeskind's design. The further they probed, the richer and more complex the design's significance became until only it seemed to embody—in all of its difficulty—the essential challenge of the project itself.

At the same time, there was some concern among jurors that in the face of such a stupendously monumental piece of architecture, one that wears its significance and symbolic import openly and unashamedly, the contents of the museum would wither in comparison. As a work of art in its own right, worried the museum's

The Jewish Museum Extension to the Berlin Museum.

director, Rolf Bothe, "The museum building might seem to make its contents sub-ordinate and insignificant."[34] Indeed, given the early design, which included walls slanted at angles too oblique for mounting and corners too tight for installations, this museum seemed to forbid showing much else beside itself: it would be its own content. Others worried that such a radical design would in the end generate just too much resistance among traditional preservationists and urban planners. Was it wise, they wondered, to choose a design that might not actually get built?

But Klaus Humpert found that by not making an attempt at urban repair and ignoring the street lines and leaving the baroque building untouched, Libeskind's design answered the problem precisely by leaving it unresolved. In effect, he found the building authority's mandate of urban repair at odds with his mandate to show the link and the separation, the ruptured link. The result is an unrepaired urban landscape, an irreparable harm represented as just that: irreparable. Even the juror with the greatest stake in the IBA's mandate of urban repair, architect Josef Paul Kleihues, found the design irresistibly appropriate to this particular task. It is one thing to restore the architectural integrity of the city and another to enforce architectural integrity on a site dedicated to the memory of integrity's rupture. Architectural integrity in this case would mean exposing the impossibility of an architectural recuperation of a city's moral integrity.

In a very real sense, Libeskind revealed to the jurors what this process and problematic really were about. Where they had conceived "The Jewish Museum" as an "extension" to the Berlin Museum, Libeskind literally showed them the interpenetration between Berlin history and the history of the Jews in Berlin. The president of Berlin's Jewish community, Heinz Galinski, for example, had envisioned a kind of "museum within a museum," something that suggested a neat demarcation in which neither history would seem to have much to do with the other. "The Jewish Museum should focus inwardly on Berlin history, yet outwardly appear as a independent unit," Galinski wrote. "Libeskind has submitted a design that proposes a totally different solution. Libeskind's idea of the contextual and architectonic interpenetration of Berlin history with the history of the Jews in Berlin is so unique that I felt compelled to give this design my complete approval although this meant relinquishing ideas I had previously held." He requested that it be built without delay. For in his words, "No future visitor will be able to look around the Jewish Museum without taking in the history of Berlin; nor will anyone be able to visit the Berlin Museum without experiencing the history of Berlin's Jewish citizens in the past and the present."[35]

Only the mayor of Kreuzberg, the district of Berlin in which the museum would be built, continued to resist the design. In his words, "A design was expected that would relate to the proportions of the existing building, fit in inconspicuously into the green ribbon and leave space for the mundane needs of the local people for green spaces and playgrounds."[36] For both the mayor and the borough's official architect, Libeskind's provocative vision seemed to be at direct odds with their desire to preserve the green spaces and playgrounds there. This was to be a pleasant place for the people to come relax and it seems, to forget their troubles, both present and past. But in the end, even city-architect Franziska Eichstadt-Böhlig agreed that perhaps it was time to "face up to the interpenetration of German and Jewish history after having repressed it for forty years."[37]

Other doubts centered on Libeskind himself. Falkk Jaeger, an architectural critic and guest of the commission who sat in on deliberations, reminded the jurors that to this point, Libeskind had never actually built anything, even though he had won several prestigious design competitions. In Jaeger's eyes, Libeskind was not so much a practicing architect as he was an architectural philosopher and poet. His buildings, according to Jaeger, were extremely complex structures consisting equally of "beams, axes, fragments, imagination and fantasies, which can usually never be built." At the same time, Jaeger continued, "this building-sculpture, which seems to lie beside the existing building like a petrified flash of lightening, cannot be called deconstructivist." Which is to say, it was eminently buildable, even as it would retain signs of fragments and voids. It is a working through, a form of mourning that reaches its climax "in the experience of a melancholy which has been made material." In this way, the critic believes this to be a *Gesamtkunstwerk* (total artwork) that need not fulfill any other function to justify its existence. Whatever is finally housed here, no matter what it is, Jaeger concludes, will thus never be conventional, never boring.[38]

Inside the Museum: Voids and Broken Narrative

After accepting Libeskind's museum design in the summer of 1989, the Berlin Senate allotted some 87 million German marks (nearly 50 million U.S. dollars) for its construction. In 1990, Libeskind submitted a cost analysis for his design (170 million marks) that nearly doubled the government's allotted budget. But even his revised budget of 115 million marks was deemed politically unthinkable at a time when the breaching of the Berlin wall had forced all to begin focusing on the looming, unimaginable costs of reunification. All government building plans were put on hold as

Exterior view of the untempered zinc facade of The Jewish Museum Extension to the Berlin Museum during construction, 1997.

Berlin and Germany came to grips with its shocking new political topography—no dividing wall between east and west but a country divided nevertheless between the prosperous and the desperate.

In fact, on 4 July 1991, the government summarily announced that planning for the Jewish Museum was being suspended, only to have it reinstated in September by the Berlin Senate. Despite continuing calls for the museum's suspension, the Senate voted unanimously in October to build the museum, however altered it may be by the new realities on the ground—both economic and topographical. It is significant perhaps that in the minds of civic leaders, Berlin's reunification could not proceed until the city had begun to be reunited with its missing Jewish past.

To trim the museum's costs, city planners ordered the angles of its walls to be straightened, among dozens of other changes, which helped keep it within its newly allotted budget of 117 million marks. In addition, a hall intended for outside the main building was absorbed into the ground floor, several of the outer "voids" were themselves voided, and the complex plan for the lower floor was vastly simplified so that it would come into line with the main building. At first, the architect resisted those changes that seemed to neutralize the difficulty of his design, especially those that removed the museum's estranging properties. Later, however, Libeskind offered a different, more philosophical explanation for what would be necessary changes. What was designed while the Berlin wall was standing would now be built in a newly reunified city. "As soon as Berlin was unified, I straightened all the walls," Libeskind has written. "My enemies told me I was no longer a deconstructivist, that I had chickened out, because I had straightened the walls. But I did it because I felt the project was no longer protected by the kind of schizophrenia developed out of the bilateral nature of the city."[39] . . . "The museum has to stand and open itself in a different way in a united and wall-less city."[40]

In fact, as Bernhard Schneider forcefully reminds us, no one who enters the building will experience it as a zigzag or as a jagged bolt of lightning. These are only its drawn resemblances as seen from above and will have virtually nothing to do with

Interior view of exhibition space at The Jewish Museum Extension to the Berlin Museum during construction, 1997.

the volumes of space located inside.[41] The building's radical design is barely apparent as one approaches it from the street. Though its untempered zinc plating is startlingly bright in its metallic sheen, when viewed from the entrance of the Berlin Museum on Lindenstrasse, the new building, opened to the public in 1999, also strikes one as a proportionately modest neighbor to the older baroque facade next door. Indeed, over time, the untempered zinc will weather into the same sky-blue shade as the untempered zinc window frames on the Berlin Museum next door. The echo of materials and hue between these buildings is thus subtle but distinct, the only apparent link between them at first sight.[42]

Libeskind's museum is also lower and narrower than the Berlin Museum, and its zinc-plated facade seems relatively self-effacing next to the ochre hues of its baroque neighbor. Though outwardly untouched, the stolid facade of the Berlin Museum itself is now recontextualized in its new setting adjacent the Jewish Museum. For as designed by Libeskind, the connection between the Berlin Museum and Jewish Museum Extension remains subterranean, a remembered nexus that is also no longer visible in the landscape, but buried in memory. The Berlin Museum and Jewish Museum are thus "bound together in depth," as Libeskind says. "The existing building is tied to the extension underground, preserving the contradictory autonomy of both on the surface, while binding the two together in depth. Under-Over-Ground Museum. Like Berlin and its Jews, the common burden—this insupportable, immeasurable, unshareable burden—is outlined in the exchanges between two architectures and forms which are not reciprocal: cannot be exchanged for each other."[43]

"The entrance to the new building is very deep, more than ten meters under the foundations of the Baroque building," Libeskind tells us. "From the entrance, one is faced with three roads: the road leading to the Holocaust tower which . . . has no entrance except from the underground level; the road leading to the garden; and the road leading to the main circulation stair and the void. The entire plane of the museum is tilted toward the void of the superstructure. The building is as complex as the history of Berlin."[44] As we enter the museum, in fact, the very plane of the ground on which we stand seems to slope slightly. It is an illusion created in part by the diagonal slant of narrow, turretlike windows, cut at thirty-five-degree angles across the ground-line itself. For on the "ground floor" we are actually standing just below ground level, which is literally visible through the window at about eye level. Only the earth line in the half-buried window establishes a stable horizon, a plumb line of dirt. Because the upper-floor windows are similarly angled, our view of Berlin is skewed, its skyline broken into disorienting slices of sky and buildings.

The exhibition halls themselves are spacious but so irregular in their shapes, cut through by enclosed voids and concrete trusses, that one never gains a sense of continuous passage. "I have introduced the idea of the void as a physical interference with chronology," Libeskind has said. "It is the one element of continuity throughout the complex form of the building. It is 27 meters high and runs the entire length of the building over 150 meters. It is a straight line whose impenetrability forms the central axis. The void is traversed by bridges which connect the various parts of the museum to each other."[45] In fact, a total of six voids cut through the museum on both horizontal and vertical planes. Of these six voids, the first two are accessible to visitors entering from the sacred and religious exhibition spaces. According to the architect's specifications, nothing is to be mounted on the walls of these first two voids, which may contain only free-standing vitrines or pedestals.

The third and fourth voids cut through the building at angles that traverse several floors, but these are otherwise inaccessible. Occasionally, a window opens into these voids, and they may be viewed from some thirty bridges cutting through them at different angles; but otherwise, they are to remain sealed off and so completely "unusable space" jutting throughout the structure and outside it. The fifth and sixth voids run vertically the height of the building. Of these, the fifth void mirrors the geometry of the sixth void, an external space enclosed by a tower: this is the Holocaust void, a negative space created by the Holocaust, an architectural model for absence. This concrete structure itself has no name, Libeskind says, because its subject is not its walls but the space enveloped by them, what is "between the lines." Though connected to the museum by an underground passageway, it appears to rise autonomously outside the museum walls and has no doors leading into it from outside. It is lighted only indirectly by natural light that comes through an acutely slanted window up high in the structure, barely visible from inside.

The spaces inside the museum are to be construed as "open narratives," Libeskind says, "which in their architecture seek to provide the museum-goer with new insights into the collection, and in particular, the relation and significance of the Jewish Department to the Museum as a whole."[46] Instead of merely housing the collection, in other words, this building seeks to estrange it from viewers' preconceptions. Such walls and oblique angles, he hopes, will defamiliarize the all-too-familiar ritual objects and historical chronologies, and cause museumgoers to see into these relations between the Jewish and German departments as if for the first time.

The interior of the building is thus interrupted by smaller, individual structures, shells housing the voids running throughout the structure, each painted

Interior view of the Holocaust void at The Jewish Museum Extension to the Berlin Museum, 1997.

Facing page: Interior view of bridges and voids at The Jewish Museum Extension to the Berlin Museum, 1997.

graphite black. They completely alter any sense of continuity or narrative flow and suggest instead architectural, spatial, and thematic gaps in the presentation of Jewish history in Berlin. The absence of Berlin's Jews, as embodied by these voids, is meant to haunt any retrospective presentation of their past here. Moreover, curators of both permanent and temporary exhibitions will be reminded not to use these voids as "natural" boundaries or walls in their exhibition, or as markers within their exhibition narratives. Instead, they are to design exhibitions that integrate these voids into any story being told, so that when mounted, the exhibition narrative is interrupted wherever a void happens to intersect it. The walls of the voids facing the exhibition walls will thus remain untouched, unusable, outside healing and suturing narrative.

Indeed, the void is a direct result of this battle between form and function. Useless space is the guiding criterion here, according to the architect. "The void is there because you cross it and yet cannot get to it; but had the void been there without one's awareness of it then it would cease to be a void—it would simply not be there. . . . You're crossing a space which, unlike a normal galleria, does not lead you to a collection; a passage which doesn't lead you to show you the goods of the museum. There is a passage but it doesn't get you anywhere; it doesn't show the museum as an attractive entity in that sense. It appears, however, as you walk through it, that you understand more about what is not being shown by what you have seen as not being able to be shown."[47]

Nor has this void passed unchallenged as a philosophical construct. In an essay on Libeskind's design, Jacques Derrida poses an "anxious question [that has] to do with the relation between this determined void, totally invested with history, meaningfulness, and experience, and place itself, place as a nonanthropological, nontheological possibility for this void to take place."[48] That is, Derrida wonders whether the void itself, once in place, doesn't lose its capacity as a kind of black hole or vacuum into which all stable meaning is sucked. In fact, as Derrida quite correctly observes, there are two kinds of void here: "One is the general spacing of the structure in discontinuity. The other is this very determinedly sealed space with nobody can experience or enter into."[49] One refers literally to the absence left behind by a murdered people, an absence that must be marked and that shapes (however negatively) the culture and society that brought it about. The other kind of void is that sealed-off place, which nobody can know. It is present but unknowable; it is like deep memory that gives shape and meaning to the surrounding present but remains hidden in and of itself.

Libeskind hopes, moreover, to create spaces wherein the apparent meaning in objects is always doubled, to include countermeanings, as well. "The function of the bridges in terms of exhibits is to double everything in the museum. Everything in Berlin has double meaning."[50] On one side would be Max Liebermann's paintings, Libeskind says, and on the other Liebermann's wife's desperate letters to the chief of the Gestapo pleading for her life in Auschwitz. On one side are Walter Benjamin's wonderful guidebooks to Berlin; on the other side is the suicide note he wrote in Spain while trying to escape the Nazis. All meanings, however contradictory and paradoxical, will be made palpable here in Libeskind's architecture; like uncanniness itself, such artifacts and works when thus contextualized will always contain their opposites.

Implied in any museum's collection is that what you see is all there is to see, all that there ever was. By placing architectural "voids" throughout the museum, Libeskind has tried to puncture this museological illusion. What you see here, he seems to say, is actually only a mask for all that is missing, for the great absence of life that now makes a presentation of these artifacts a necessity. The voids make palpable a sense that much more is missing here than can ever be shown. As Vera Bendt has aptly noted, the destruction itself caused the collection here shown to come into being. Otherwise, these objects would all be part of living, breathing homes— unavailable as museum objects. This is then an aggressively antiredemptory design, built literally around an absence of meaning in history, an absence of the people who would have given meaning to their history.

The only way out of the new building is through the Garden of Exile. "This road of exile and emigration leads to a very special garden which I call the E.T.A. Hoffmann Garden," Libeskind has said. "Hoffmann was the romantic writer of incredible tales, and I dedicated this garden to him because he was a lawyer working in a building adjacent to the site."[51] The Garden of Exile consists of forty-nine concrete columns filled with earth, each twenty-three feet high, four by five feet square, spaced three feet apart. Forty-eight of these columns are filled with earth from Berlin, their number referring to the year of Israel's independence, 1948; the forty-ninth column stands for Berlin and is filled with earth from Jerusalem. They are planted with willow oaks that will spread over the garden of columns into a great, green canopy. Although the columns stand at ninety-degree angles to the ground plate, the ground plate is tilted in two angles, so that one stumbles about as if in the dark, at sea without sea legs. We are sheltered in exile yet still somehow thrown off balance by it and disoriented at the same time.

At one point, before eventually rejecting it, Freud cites Jentsch's contention that "the central factor in the production of the feeling of uncanniness [is] intellectual uncertainty; so that the uncanny would always, as it were, be something one does not know one's way about in. The better oriented in his environment a person is, the less readily will he get the impression of something uncanny in regard to the objects and events in it."[52] If we allow our sense of uncanniness to include this sense of uncertainty after all, we might then ask how a building accomplishes this disorientation. In Libeskind's case, he has simply built into it any number of voided spaces, so that visitors are never where they think they are. Neither are these voids wholly didactic. They are not meant to instruct, per se but to throw previously received instruction into question. Their aim is not to reassure or console but to haunt visitors with the unpleasant—uncanny—sensation of calling into consciousness that which has been previously—even happily—repressed. The voids are reminders of the abyss into which this culture once sank and from which it never really emerges.

If modern architecture has embodied the attempt to erase the traces of history from its forms, postmodern architecture like Libeskind's would make the traces of history its infrastructure, the voids of lost civilizations literally part of the building's foundation, now haunted by history, even emblematic of it. The architecture of

Exterior view of the Holocaust void, left, and the E. T. A. Hoffmann Garden, right, at The Jewish Museum Extension to the Berlin Museum, 1997.

Exterior view of The Jewish Museum Extension to the Berlin Museum during construction, 1997.

what Libeskind calls "decomposition" derives its power not from a sense of unity but from what Anthony Vidler has called the "intimation of the fragmentary, the morselated, the broken."[53] Rather than suggesting wholeness and mending, salvation or redemption, such forms represent the breach itself, the ongoing need for *tikkun ha'olam* (mending the world) and its impossibility.

As historian Reinhart Koselleck has brilliantly intimated, even the notion of history as a "singular collective"—that is, an overarching and singularly meaningful History—is a relatively modern concept.[54] Alois M. Müller has elaborated, "Until the 18th century the word had been a plural form in German, comprising the various histories which accounted for all that had happened in the world. History as a singular noun had a loftier intent. In future, not only individual minor historical episodes were to be told. History suddenly acquired the duty to comprehend reality as a continuous whole and to portray the entire history of humankind as a path to freedom and independence. History was no longer to be 'just' the embodiment of many histories. History as a unity sought to make them comprehensible."[55] And as Müller also makes quite clear, this project of historical unification had distinctly redemptive, even salvational aims, the kind of history that its tellers hoped would lead to a "better world."

Libeskind's project, by contrast, promises no such relief. His is not, as Müller reminds us, a "revelatory monument to the 'good' in history, but to a historical crime perpetrated in the name of history."[56] By resisting continuous, homogeneous history-housing, Libeskind never allows memory of this time to congeal into singular, salvational meaning. His is partly integrationist, and partly disintegrationist, architecture. His is a project that allows for the attempt at integration as an ongoing, if impossible project, even as it formalizes disintegration as its architectural motif. Libeskind would deunify such history, atomize it, allow its seams to show, plant doubt in any single version, even his own. All toward suggesting an antiredemptory housing of history, one that expresses what Müller has called a systematic doubt, a lack of certainty in any attempt that makes it all process, never result.

Kurt W. Forster suggests that Libeskind's design literally bears the "double burden of representing both actual buildings and mental structures, and which therefore [has] to submit to being measured by both standards."[57] As a mental structure, it literally organizes the past it would house and support. Here we begin to answer the questions we opened with: we see that architecture cannot remain entirely distinct from, even oblivious to, the history it shelters; its spatial configuration is never really independent of its contents. Neither can we evaluate such architecture outside of the ways it makes (and unmakes) meaning in the present moment. "Beautiful architecture without Beauty" is how Daniel Libeskind ends an essay called "Countersigns," his coda to a collection of drawings, essays, and models.[58] Beautiful architecture without Beauty: the point is that beauty, like meaning and form, may have outlasted itself as a useful category when discussing architecture like this.

From the beginning, this project seemed to be defined as that which would be nearly impossible to complete. Planners initiated a nearly impossible project, selected a nearly unbuildable design, and have now succeeded in building a public edifice that embodies the paralyzing questions of contemporary German culture. The result leaves all questions intact, all doubts and difficulties in place. This museum extension is an architectural interrogation of the culture and civilization that built it, an almost unheard-of achievement.

But with its thirty connecting bridges, 75,000 square feet of permanent exhibition space, 4,800 square feet of temporary exhibition space, and 43,000 square feet of storage, office, and auditorium spaces, the Jewish Museum will have roughly three times the space of the Berlin Museum next door. Some have suggested that the Berlin Museum be allowed to spill into most of the newly available space, leaving the Jewish Museum department on the bottom floor only; others have suggested that the building in itself be designated the national "memorial to Europe's murdered Jews."[59] In any case, all the attention this design has received, both laudatory and skeptical, will generate a final historical irony. Where the city planners had hoped to return Jewish memory to the house of Berlin history, it now seems certain that Berlin history will have to find its place in the larger haunted house of Jewish memory. The Jewish wing of the Berlin Museum will now be the prism through which the rest of the world will come to know Berlin's past.

If "estrangement from the world is a moment of art," as Adorno would have it, after Freud, then we might say that the uncanniness of a museum like Libeskind's crystallizes this moment of art.[60] But if the "uncanny is uncanny only because it is secretly all too familiar, which is why it is repressed," as Freud himself would have it, then perhaps no better term describes the condition of a contemporary German culture coming to terms with the self-inflicted void at its center—a terrible void that is at once all too secretly familiar and unrecognizable, a void that at once defines a national identity, even as it threatens to cause such identity to implode.

CHAPTER SEVEN

Germany's Holocaust Memorial Problem—and Mine

"It is not up to you to complete the work, yet you are not free to abstain from it."

—*Rabbi Tarfon*, Pirkei Avot

ONCE, NOT SO LONG AGO, GERMANY had what it called a "Jewish Problem." Then it had a paralyzing Holocaust memorial problem, a double-edged conundrum: How would a nation of former perpetrators mourn its victims? How would a divided nation reunite itself on the bedrock memory of its crimes? In June 1999, after ten years of tortured debate, the German Bundestag voted to build a national "Memorial for the Murdered Jews of Europe" on a prime, five-acre piece of real estate between the Brandenburger Tor and Potsdamer Platz, a stone's throw from Hitler's bunker. In their vote, the Bundestag also accepted the design—a waving field of pillars—by American architect Peter Eisenman, which had been recommended by a five-member Findungskommission, for which I served as spokesman.

Proposed originally by a citizens' group headed by television talk-show personality and journalist Lea Rosh and World War II historian Eberhard Jäckel, the memorial soon took on a fraught and highly politicized life of its own. Although I had initially opposed a single, central Holocaust memorial in Germany for the ways it might be used to compensate such irredeemable loss, or even put the past behind a newly reunified Germany, over time I began to grow skeptical of my own skepticism. Eventually, I was invited to serve on the commission charged with choosing an appropriate design for Germany's national memorial to Europe's murdered Jews, the only foreigner and Jew on the panel. In this final chapter, I would like to tell the story of Germany's national Holocaust memorial and my own role in it, my evolution from a highly skeptical critic on the outside of the process to one of the arbiters on the inside. I find that as the line between my role as critic and arbiter began to collapse, the

issues at the heart of the Germany's memorial conundrum came into ever sharper, more painful relief.

The seeds of Germany's national Holocaust memorial were probably sown during President Ronald Reagan's disastrous wreath-laying visit, at Chancellor Helmut Kohl's invitation, to the military cemetery in Bitburg, where the tombstones of Waffen S.S. soldiers lay side by side those of Wehrmacht conscripts. Like other nations, Kohl believed, Germany should also have ready-made memorial sites where foreign dignitaries could pay their respects to their hosts' war dead and fallen heroes. This was a time-honored tradition and, Kohl seemed to feel, a crucial step toward Germany's normalization, its return to a respected place among nations. The problem, of course, was that unlike other nations, a memorial honoring both Germany's war dead and its heroes would in essence be a self-contradicting memorial. Those now considered its "heroes" had been regarded as treacherous enemies of the state during the war, whereas its fallen soldiers had been killed in Hitler's campaign to conquer Europe and murder its Jews. As the Green Party had put it, "State guests from abroad who want to honor the dead by laying a wreath . . . will understand that in the Federal Republic of Germany the erection of a national monument will run aground because of the danger of equating the deaths of perpetrators and victims of National Socialist crimes against humanity."[1]

Stung by the near-universal opprobrium generated by his ill-fated attempt to follow the protocol of other states, Kohl decided to take matters into his own hands. With the fall of the Berlin wall in 1989, he found what he believed was an ideal site for this protocol. The Neue Wache, or the "new guard," was a templelike, domed neoclassical building on Unter den Linden, designed by Karl Friedrich Schinkel in 1818 as the Prussian Royal Guardhouse. Located just beyond the wall in the eastern sector of the city, it had served both the Nazis and the communists as a "national memorial" and wreath-laying site during their respective regimes in Berlin. With the reunification of Berlin, Kohl believed it could be a central monument to all the victims of war and tyranny and thus provide a common site for the unification of a people, as well, a reconciliation of victims and perpetrators, east and west, all united now in their hatred of tyranny and war. Reportedly, a miniature of Käthe Kollwitz's modern pietà of a mother holding a dead son had always been a favorite object on his desk, so he proposed it as the central figure to be placed in the sanctuary of the Neue Wache. When critics protested the impropriety of remembering Jewish victims alongside their perpetrators—both in the quintessentially Christian image of sacrifice—Kohl responded simply that Kollwitz's was a universal figure of mourning appropriate to all who would mourn their war losses at the Neue Wache. Nevertheless, he allowed for bronze tablets specifically commemorating the Jewish, homosexual, and Gypsy victims of the Nazis to be installed underneath the Doric portico just before dedicating this, Germany's national Memorial to the Victims of Tyranny and War. Since its dedication in 1993, the Neue Wache has remained more a curiosity for tourists than a shrine for Germans, whose ambivalence to such mixed memory is reflected in their muted indifference to it.[2]

All of which only exacerbated and energized the ongoing debate surrounding a separate "Memorial for the Murdered Jews of Europe," which Lea Rosh and Eberhard Jäckel had proposed jointly in 1988. Along with a private citizens' initiative they had organized, Rosh and Jäckel at first hoped to place their memorial on the Gestapo-Gelände, a scarred wasteland and former site of the Gestapo headquarters in a no-man's-land near the wall in the center of Berlin. But the "Gestapo-terrain" had long been enmeshed in a complicated debate over its own future and how to commemorate all the victims of the Gestapo in a single place.[3] With the fall of the wall in 1989, however, the project gained the backing of both the federal government and the Berlin Senate, which recognized that such a memorial might serve as a strategic counterweight to the Neue Wache. Shortly after, the government designated an alternative site for the memorial, also at the heart of the Nazi regime's former seat of power. Bordered on one side by the "Todesstreifen," or "death-strip," at the foot of the Berlin wall, and on the other by the Tiergarten, the former site of the "Ministerial Gardens" was still a no-man's-land in its own right, slightly profaned by its proximity to Hitler's bunker and the Reichs Chancellery. But as almost five acres at the heart of a reunified capital, it would also become one of Berlin's most sought-after pieces of real estate—and was thus regarded as a magnanimous, if monumental, gesture to the memory of Europe's murdered Jews.

In 1994, about a year after the dedication of the Neue Wache, a prestigious international competition was called for designs for Germany's national "Memorial for the Murdered Jews of Europe," and some 528 designs were submitted from around the world. The designs ran the gamut of taste and aesthetic sensibilities, from the beautiful to the grotesque, from high modern to low kitsch, from the architectural to the conceptual. There was, for example, Horst Hoheisel's aforementioned proposal to blow up the Brandenburger Tor, as well as Dani Karavan's proposed field of yellow flowers in the shape of a Star of David. As described earlier, Renata Stih and Frieder

Käthe Kollwitz, Pietà — Mother with Dead Son, *1937–1938, installed in the Neue Wache, 1993.*

Schnock proposed a series of bus stops whence coaches would take visitors to the sites of actual destruction throughout Berlin, Germany, and Europe. Other designs included numerous variations on gardens of stone, broken hearts, and rent Stars of David. Round, square, and triangular obelisks were proposed, as well as a gigantic vat (130 feet tall), an empty vessel for the blood of the murdered. One artist proposed a Ferris wheel composed of cattle cars instead of carriages, rotating between "the carnivalesque and the genocidal."[4]

The jury was composed of some fifteen members, experts and laypeople, appointed by the three sponsoring agencies now involved—the Bundestag, the Berlin Senate, and the original citizens' group. Though the deliberations had been shielded from public view, many of the jurors subsequently told of rancorous, biting debate, with little meeting of the minds. The citizens' group resented the intellectuals and experts on the jury, with what they regarded as their elitist taste for conceptual and minimalist design. "This is not a playground for artists and their self-absorbed fantasies," Lea Rosh is reported to have reminded her colleagues on the jury. Meanwhile, the intellectuals sniffed at the lay jurors' middlebrow eye for kitsch and monumental figuration, their philistine emotionalism; and the Bundestag's appointees glanced anxiously at their watches as the right political moment seemed to be ticking away.

In March 1995, organizers announced the jury's decision: first prize would be shared by two teams who had submitted similarly inspired designs—one led by Berlin architect Christine Jackob-Marks and the other by a New York artist living in Cologne, Simon Ungers. Of these two, only that proposed by Jackob-Marks would be built, however, possibly with elements incorporated from the other, and an additional eight projects would be recognized as finalists in the competition. Jackob-Marks's winning design consisted of a gargantuan, twenty-three-foot thick concrete gravestone, in the shape of a three-hundred-foot square, tilted at an angle running from six feet high at one end to twenty-five feet high at the other. It was to be engraved with the recoverable names of 4.5 million murdered Jews, and in the Jewish tradition of leaving small stones at a gravesite to mark the mourner's visit, it was to have some eighteen boulders from Masada in Israel scattered over its surface.

Its literal-minded and misguided symbolism seemed to have paralyzed a jury as unable to resist it as to love it. Eighteen is the Hebrew number representing *chai*, or life, so the number of stones seemed right. But according to the early Jewish historian Josephus, Masada was the last stronghold against the Romans at the end of the Jewish revolt of 66–73 C.E. and also the site of a collective suicide of Jews that prevented the Romans from taking them as slaves. A German national Holocaust me-

Christine Jackob-Marks, Memorial for the Murdered Jews of Europe. *Winner of the voided 1995 competition for a Berlin Holocaust memorial.*

morial with Jewish self-sacrifice as part of its theme? Within hours of the winner's announcement, the monument's mixed memorial message of Jewish naming tradition and self-sacrifice generated an avalanche of artistic, intellectual, and editorial criticism decrying this "tilted gravestone" as too big, too heavy-handed, too divisive, and finally just too German. Even the leader of Germany's Jewish community, Ignatz Bubis, hated it and told Chancellor Kohl that the winning design was simply unacceptable. Kohl threw up his hands in exasperation, pronounced the design as "too big and undignified," and obligingly rescinded the government's support for the winner of the Holocaust memorial competition. Germany's "Memorial for the Murdered Jews of Europe" seemed to have been sunk by its own monumental weight—and once again, Germany was left pondering its memorial options.

Between the announcement of the winner and its subsequent rejection, the organizers showed all 528 designs in a grand memorial exhibition at Berlin's Stadtratshaus. Good, I wrote at the time. Better a thousand years of Holocaust memorial competitions and exhibitions in Germany than any single "final solution" to Germany's memorial problem. This way, I reasoned, instead of a fixed icon for Holocaust memory in Germany, the debate itself—perpetually unresolved amid ever-changing conditions—might now be enshrined. Of course, this was also a position that only an academic bystander could afford to take, someone whose primary interest lay in perpetuating the process.

At the same time, dozens of articles and op-ed pieces appeared in the daily press, most castigating the winning design, and many others lamenting the whole sorry spectacle of Germany's memorial self-flagellation. *Der Spiegel* columnist Henryk Broder, as acerbic as ever, suggested that the exhibition of 528 designs best be regarded as a "quarry [where] anthropologists, psychologists, and behaviorists could examine the condition of a confused nation wanting to create a monument to its victims in order to purify itself."[5] An entire volume was produced in a matter of weeks comprising the objections of some three dozen critics, artists, and intellectuals, with my own words emblazoned epigrammatically on the back cover: "If the aim is to remember for perpetuity that this great nation once murdered nearly six million human beings solely for having been Jews, then this monument must remain uncompleted and unbuilt, an unfinishable memorial process."[6]

My Holocaust Memorial Problem

After yet another year of stormy debate over whether a new competition should be called, whether a new site should be found, or whether the winners should be invited to refine their proposals further still, the memorial's organizers again took the high road. They called for a series of public colloquia on the memorial to be held in January, March, and April 1997, which they hoped would break the memorial deadlock and ensure that the memorial be built before the Holocaust receded further into the history of a former century. Toward this end, they invited a number of distinguished artists, historians, critics, and curators to address the most difficult issues and to suggest how the present designs might best be modified. I was among those invited to speak at the last colloquium, in April 1997, and was asked to explore the memorial iconography of other nations' Holocaust memorials in order to put the Germans' process into international perspective.

The first two colloquia, in January and March 1997, roused considerable public interest, but as the exchanges between organizers of the memorial and invited speakers grew more acrimonious, a gloomy sense of despair settled over the proceedings. The organizers, led by Lea Rosh, insisted that the "five aims" of the project remain inviolable: (1) this would be a memorial only to Europe's murdered Jews; (2) ground would be broken for it on 27 January 1999, Germany's newly designated "Holocaust Remembrance Day" marked to coincide with the liberation of Auschwitz in 1945; (3) its location would be the five-acre site of the Ministerial Gardens, between the Brandenburg Gate and Potsdamer Platz; (4) the nine finalists' teams from the 1995 competition would be invited to revise their designs and concepts after incorporating suggestions and criticism from the present colloquia; and (5) the winning design would be chosen from the revised designs of the original nine finalists.[7]

Not only did the designs continue to come under withering attack by the invited experts but the aims of the project itself were now called strongly into question. Among other speakers at the first colloquium, historian Jürgen Kocka suggested that although there was an obvious need for a memorial to Europe's murdered Jews, the need for a memorial to encompass the memory of the Nazis' other victims was just as clear. Other speakers, such as Michael Stürmer, then questioned the site itself, whether its gargantuan dimensions somehow invited precisely the kind of monumentality that had already been rejected. Other critics focused more narrowly on the first colloquium's theme: "Why There Should Be a Holocaust Memorial in Berlin," concluding that with the authentic sites of destruction and memory scattered throughout Berlin, there shouldn't be a central memorial at all.

These vociferous challenges to the memorial were met by a seemingly stony indifference by the speaker of the Berlin Senate, Peter Radunski, who had been appointed to convene the proceedings. Because these criticisms had no place on the agenda, he said, they need not be addressed here. Lea Rosh's response was less measured. She opened the third colloquium with a bitter attack on what she called the "leftist intellectual establishment" responsible for undermining both the process and by extension memory of Europe's murdered Jews. The aim here was how to go forward, she said, not to debate the memorial's raison d'être, which was already established. Her angry words, in turn, simply antagonized the critics and hardened the positions of the memorial's opponents, who included many of Germany's elite historians, writers, and cultural critics, including Reinhart Koselleck, Julius Schoeps, Solomon Korn, Stefanie Endlich, Christian Meier, and eventually Günter Grass and Peter Schneider.

By the time I spoke at the third colloquium in mid-April, both the organizers and a large public audience at the Stadtratshaus in Berlin had grown visibly and audibly agitated by the spectacle of their tortured memorial deliberations. Over and over again, the other speakers—senators, art historians, and artists—bemoaned the abject failure of their competition. All of which was compounded by their acute embarrassment over the incivility of it all, the petty bickering, the name-calling, the quagmire of politics into which the process seemed to be sinking. Bad enough we murdered the Jews of Europe, one senator whispered to me, worse that we can't agree on how to commemorate them.

When my turn to speak came, I discarded my carefully prepared lecture, which had already been translated and printed in the morning papers that day anyway. I began instead by trying to reassure the audience: decorum is never a part of the memorial-building process, not even for a Holocaust memorial. "You may have failed to produce a monument," I said, "but if you count the sheer number of design-hours that 528 teams of artists and architects have already devoted to the memorial, it's clear that your process has already generated more individual memory-work than a finished monument will inspire in its first ten years." I proceeded to tell the stories of other, equally fraught memorial processes in Israel and the United States, the furious debate in Israel's Knesset surrounding the day of remembrance there, the memorial paralysis in New York, Los Angeles, and Washington, D.C., that had eventually resulted in several competing memorials, all of them contested. I could almost hear the collective sigh of relief.

In fact, here I admitted that until that moment, I had been one of the skeptics. Rather than looking for a centralized monument, I was perfectly satisfied with the national memorial debate itself. Better, I had thought, to take all these millions of Deutsch marks and use them to preserve the great variety of Holocaust memorials already dotting the German landscape. Because no single site can speak for all the victims, much less for both victims and perpetrators, the state should be reminding its citizens to visit the many and diverse memorial and pedagogical sites that already exist: from the excellent learning center at the Wannsee Conference House to the enlightened exhibitions at the Topography of Terror at the former Gestapo headquarters, both in Berlin; from the brooding and ever-evolving memorial landscape at Buchenwald to the meticulously groomed grounds and fine museum at Dachau; from the hundreds of memorial tablets throughout Germany marking the sites of deportation to the dozens of now-empty sites of former synagogues—and all the spaces for contemplation in between.

Here I also admitted that with this position, I had made many friends in Germany and was making a fine career out of skepticism. Most colleagues shared my fear that Chancellor Kohl's government wanted a "Memorial for the Murdered Jews of Europe" as a great burial slab for the twentieth century, a hermetically sealed vault for the ghosts of Germany's past. Instead of inciting memory of murdered Jews, we suspected, it would be a place where Germans would come dutifully to *unshoulder* their memorial burden, so that they could move freely and unencumbered into the twenty-first century. A finished monument would, in effect, finish memory itself.

On one hand, I said, we must acknowledge the public need and political necessity for a German national Holocaust memorial; at the same time, we must recognize the difficulty of answering this need in a single space. If the aim of a national Holocaust memorial in Berlin is to draw a bottom line under this era so that a re-unified Germany can move unencumbered into the future, then let us make this clear. But if the aim is to remember for perpetuity that this great nation once murdered nearly six million human beings solely for having been Jews, then this monument must also embody the intractable questions at the heart of German Holocaust memory rather than claiming to answer them. Otherwise, I feared that whatever form the monument takes near the Potsdamer Platz would not mark the memory of Europe's murdered Jews so much as bury it altogether.[8]

These were persuasive arguments against the monument, and I am still ambivalent about the role a central Holocaust monument will play in Berlin. But at the same time, I said, I have also had to recognize that this was a position of luxury that perhaps only an academic bystander could afford, someone whose primary interest was in perpetuating the process. As instructive as the memorial debate had been, however, it had neither warned nor chastened a new generation of xenophobic neo-Nazis—part of whose identity depends on forgetting the crimes of their forebears. And although the memorial debate has generated plenty of shame in Germans, it is largely the shame they feel for an unseemly argument—not for the mass murder once committed in their name. In good academic fashion, we had become preoccupied with the fascinating issues at the heart of the memorial process and increasingly indifferent to what was supposed to be remembered: the mass murder of Jews and the void it left behind.

The self-righteous and self-congratulatory tenor of our position had also begun to make me uneasy. Our unimpeachably skeptical approach to the certainty of monuments was now beginning to sound just a little too certain of itself. My German comrades in skepticism called themselves "the secessionists," a slightly self-flattering gesture to the turn-of-the-century movement of artists, many of whom would be Jewish victims of the Nazis. What had begun as an intellectually rigorous and ethically pure interrogation of the Berlin memorial was taking on the shape of a circular, centripetally driven, self-enclosed argument. It began to look like so much hand-wringing and fence-sitting, even an entertaining kind of spectator sport. "But can such an imperfect process possibly result in a good memorial?" parliamentarian Peter Conradi asked me at one point. I replied with an American aphorism that was altogether unfamiliar to his German ears: "Yes," I said, "for perfect is always the enemy of good." To this day, I'm not sure he understood my point.

And here, I realized, my personal stake in the memorial had begun to change. The day after I returned from that third colloquium in April, Speaker of the Berlin Senate Peter Radunski, called to ask if I would join a Findungskommission of five members appointed to find a suitable memorial design. Who were the other four, I asked. He replied with the names of the directors of the German Historical Museum in Berlin (Christoph Stölzl) and the Museum of Contemporary Art in Bonn (Dieter Ronte), as well as one of Germany's preeminent twentieth-century art historians (Werner Hoffmann) and one of Berlin's most widely respected and experienced arbiters of postwar architecture (Josef Paul Kleihues)—all authorities he believed to be above reproach. We would be given free rein to extend the process as we saw fit, to invite further artists, and to make an authoritative recommendation to the chancellor and the memorial's organizers. I was to be the only true expert on Holocaust memorials, he said. And, as I then realized, I would be the only foreigner and Jew.

Before answering, I had to ask myself a series of simple but cutting questions: Did I want Germany to return its capital to Berlin *without* publicly and visibly acknowledging what had happened the last time Germany was governed from Berlin? With its gargantuan, even megalomaniacal restoration plans and the flood of big-industry money pouring into the new capital in quantities beyond Albert Speer's wildest dreams, could there really be no space left for public memory of the victims of Berlin's last regime? How, indeed, could I set foot in a new German capital built on the presumption of inadvertent historical amnesia that new buildings always breed? As Adorno had corrected his well-intentioned but facile (and now hackneyed) "Nach Auschwitz . . ." dictum, maybe it was also time for me to come down from my perch of holy dialectics and take a position.

But as one of the newly appointed arbiters of German Holocaust memory, I would also find myself in a strange and uncomfortable predicament. The skeptics' whispered asides echoed my own apprehensions: a mere decoration, this American Jew, a sop to authority and so-called expertise. I asked myself: Was I invited as an academic authority on memorials or as a token American and foreigner? Is it my expertise they want, or are they looking for a Jewish blessing on whatever design is finally chosen? If I can be credited for helping arbitrate official German memory, can I also be held liable for another bad design? In fact, just where is the line between my role as arbiter of German memory and my part in a fraught political process far beyond my own grasp?

And yet, I wondered, how is Germany to make momentous decisions like this *without* the Jewish sensibility so mercilessly expunged from its national consciousness? When Germany murdered half of its Jewish population and sent the rest into exile, and then set about exterminating another 5.5 million European Jews, it deliberately—and I'm afraid permanently—cut the Jewish lobe of its culture from its brain, so to speak. As a result, Germany suffers from a self-inflicted Jewish aphasia. Good, sensible Jewish leaders like Ignatz Bubis counsel wisdom and discretion. But even that is not a cure for this aphasia. A well-meaning German like Lea Rosh takes a Jewish name and initiates a monument. Neither is this a cure. No, the missing Jewish part of German culture remained a palpable and gaping wound in the German psyche—and it must appear as such in Berlin's otherwise reunified cityscape.

The problem was that in voiding itself of Jews, Germany had forever voided itself of the capacity for a normal, healthy response to Jews and their ideas. Instead, it was all a tortured bending over backwards, biting one's tongue, wondering what "they" really thought of Germans. It is a terrible, yet unavoidable consequence of the Holocaust itself, this Jewish aphasia, a legacy of mass murder. Thus, I began to grasp just this need for a foreigner and a Jew on the Findungskommission. Without a Jewish eye to save it from egregiously misguided judgments (like the winner of the first competition), anything was possible. This might be as practical a matter as it was political.

So when asked to serve on this Findungskommission for Berlin's "Memorial for the Murdered Jews of Europe," I agreed, but only on the condition that we write a precise conceptual plan for the memorial. Perhaps the greatest weakness in the first competition had been its hopelessly vague conceptual description of the memorial, leaving artists to founder in an impossible sea of formal, conceptual, and political ambiguities. In contrast, we would be clear, for example, that this memorial will not displace the nation's other memorial sites, and that a memorial to Europe's murdered Jews would not speak for the Nazis' other victims but may, in fact, necessitate further memorials to them. Nor should this memorial hide the impossible questions driving Germany's memorial debate. It should instead reflect the terms of the debate, the insufficiency of memorials, the contemporary generation's skeptical view of official memory and its self-aggrandizing ways. After all, I had been arguing for years that a new generation of artists and architects in Germany—including Christian Boltanski, Norbert Radermacher, Horst Hoheisel, Micha Ulmann, Stih and Schnock, Jochen Gerz, and Daniel Libeskind—had turned their skepticism of the monumental into a radical countermonumentality. In challenging and flouting every one of the monument's conventions, their memorials have reflected an essentially German ambivalence toward self-indictment, where the void was made palpable yet remained unredeemed. If the government insisted on a memorial in Berlin for "Europe's murdered Jews," then couldn't it, too, embody this same countermonumental critique?

Rather than prescribing a form, therefore, we described a concept of memorialization that took into account: a clear definition of the Holocaust and its significance; Nazi Germany's role as perpetrator; current reunified Germany's role as rememberer; the contemporary generation's relationship to Holocaust memory; and the aesthetic debate swirling around the memorial itself. Instead of providing answers, we asked questions: What are the national reasons for remembrance? Are they redemptory, part of a mourning process, pedagogical, self-aggrandizing, or inspiration against contemporary xenophobia? To what national and social ends will this memorial be built? Just how compensatory a gesture will it be? How antiredemptory can it be? Will it be a place for Jews to mourn lost Jews, a place for Germans to mourn lost Jews, or a place for Jews to remember what Germans once did to them? These questions must be made part of the memorial process, I suggested, so let them be asked by the artists *in* their designs, even if they cannot finally be answered.

Here I also reminded organizers that this would not be an aesthetic debate over how to depict horror. The Holocaust, after all, was not merely the annihilation of nearly 6 million Jews, among them 1.5 million children, but also the extirpation of a thousand-year old civilization from the heart of Europe. Any conception of the Holocaust that reduces it to the horror of destruction alone ignores the stupendous loss and void left behind. The tragedy of the Holocaust is not merely that people died so terribly but that so much was irreplaceably lost. An appropriate memorial design will acknowledge the void left behind and not concentrate on the memory of terror and destruction alone. What was lost needs to be remembered here as much as how it was lost.

In addition, I suggested that organizers must be prepared to accept the fact that this memorial was being designed in 1997, more than fifty years after the end of World War II. It will necessarily reflect the contemporary sensibility of artists, which includes much skepticism over the very appropriateness of memorials, their traditional function as redemptory sites of mourning, national instruction, and self-aggrandizement. To this end, I asked organizers to encourage a certain humility among designers, a respect for the difficulty of such a memorial. It is not surprising that a memorial such as Jackob-Marks's was initially chosen: it represented very well a generation that felt oppressed by Holocaust memory, which would in turn oppress succeeding generations with such memory. But something subtler, more modest, and succinct might suggest a balance between being oppressed by memory and being inspired by it, a tension between being permanently marked by memory and being disabled by it. As other nations have remembered the Holocaust according to their founding myths and ideals, their experiences as liberators, victims, or fighters, Germany will also remember according to its own complex and self-abnegating motives, whether we like them or not. Let Germany's official memorial reflect its suitably tortured relationship to the genocide of Europe's Jews, I said.

Before proceeding, we had to address two further concerns shared both by us, as members of the Findungskommission, and the memorial's opponents: Should it be a contemplative site only, or pedagogically inclined as well? By extension, would this memorial serve as a center of gravity for the dozens of memorials and pedagogical centers located at the actual sites of destruction, or would it somehow displace them and even usurp their memorial authority? Because we did not see Holocaust memory in Germany as a zero-sum project, we concluded that there was indeed room in Berlin's new landscape for *both* commemorative spaces and pedagogically oriented memorial institutions. In fact, Berlin and its environs were already rich with excellent museums and permanent exhibitions on the Holocaust—from the Wannsee Villa to the Topography of Terror, from the new Jewish Museum on Lindenstrasse and the proposed Institute for the Study of Anti-Semitism to the critical and insightful exhibitions at Buchenwald and Sachsenhausen.

The question was never whether there would be only a memorial or a museum. But rather: In addition to these existing pedagogical houses of memory, was there room for a commemorative space meant for memorial contemplation and national ceremonies? Again, we concluded that in Berlin's constellation of memorial sites, there was indeed room for a central memorial node in this landscape, one that would inspire public contemplation of the past even as it encouraged the public to visit and learn the specifics of this past in the many other museums nearby and throughout the country.

In fact, though still suspicious of the monument as a form, I began to see how important it would be to add a space to Germany's restored capital deliberately designed to remember the mass murder of Europe's Jews. This would not be a space for memory designed by the killers themselves, as the concentration camp sites inevitably are, but one designed specifically as a memorial site, one denoting the current generation's deliberate attempt to remember. Of course, the government must continue to support the dozens of other memorial and pedagogical sites around the country. But these are, after all, already there. To build a memorial apart from these sites of destruction, however, is not merely the passive recognition and preservation of the past. It is a deliberate act of remembrance, a strong statement that *memory must be created* for the next generation, not simply preserved.

Eventually, this question was also addressed at some length by Jürgen Habermas in an article appearing in *Die Zeit.* Here he wrote that it is precisely because historical institutions change and "can tacitly be turned into something else, once the climate shifts," that Germany has a crucial need for a permanent monument in addition to the many fine interpretive centers already in place. In Habermas's words, "The monument should be a sign that the memory of the Holocaust remains a constitutive feature of the ethico-political self-understanding of the citizens of the Federal Republic."[9]

Finally, I would have to reserve the right to dissent publicly over any final design that I could not stand by. I would agree to serve on such a Findungskommission even as I still held strong doubts that a resolution was possible. I would suspend judgment on whether such a resolution was desirable until the end. If in the end we arrived at nothing we could justify to the organizers, then my early skepticism would have been justified. But if we did find something in a collaborative effort with artists and architects, it would be our responsibility to explain our choice to the public. For if we could not justify it formally, conceptually, and ethically, then how could we expect the public to accept it?[10]

Berlin's "Memorial for the Murdered Jews of Europe"

How to proceed? In what we would call an extension of the original process and not its replacement, we agreed to invite the nine finalists of the 1995 competition in addition to a dozen or so other world-class artists and architects to submit new designs. Over the next few weeks—via trans-Atlantic phone, telefax, and e-mail—we hammered out a list of twenty-five artists and architects who would be invited to submit a sketch and conceptual abstract. Each of us had been asked to name five or six possible invitees, after which we agreed on those names who had overlapped on all our lists. Among those who had initially accepted our invitations were Peter Eisenman, Jochen Gerz, Rebecca Horn, Dani Karavan, Daniel Libeskind, James Turrell, and Rachel Whiteread. Christian Boltanski replied that he already had his memorial in *Missing House*. After initially accepting our invitation, Rachel Whiteread withdrew, explaining that with her Vienna monument still in flux, she just didn't have the stomach for a similarly fraught contest in Berlin. We never heard again from James Turrell. In June, we submitted both our plan and list to organizers in a closed-door session chaired by the speaker of the Berlin Senate and attended by a deputy from Chancellor Kohl's office. They accepted it, congratulated us, and then publicly announced that the members of our Findungskommission would be choosing a new design from this list of artists by November 1997 and that ground would be broken in January 1999—to coincide with both the official return of Germany's capital to Berlin and Germany's Holocaust remembrance days.

None of which quelled the raging controversy. The German newspapers were still rife with dissent: Who elected this search committee, anyway? Why these artists? Why this site? Why not another open competition? I also wondered whether such a précis would justify going forward with the search. In the end, our précis was vindicated by the great strength of the submissions we received in October 1997. Of the artists we invited, including some of the most radically skeptical, nearly all agreed to participate. Their designs ranged across the spectrum of contemporary aesthetic sensibilities—from the conceptual to the figurative, from minimalist to landscape art, from constructivist to deconstructivist architecture. Over the course of three days in October, the five of us held private, two-hour seminars in front of each design board, reading aloud the designers' rationale, weighing concept against execution, the liabilities and promise in each proposal.

In the first of the nineteen submitted designs we studied, Reinhard Matz and Rudolf Herz proposed taking a about a half-mile stretch of autobahn just south of

Kassel and paving it over in cobblestones, slowing traffic down to a traitorously slow twenty-five miles an hour, and marking this stretch as a "memorial for Europe's murdered Jews." Too bad, we concluded, that it wasn't in Berlin; maybe the state of Hesse would approve it for the autobahn below Kassel. Then we turned to the sharp-edged and gigantic geometric forms submitted by Simon Ungers, Arno Dietch and Anna Simon-Dietch, and Gerhard Merz. To our eyes, each suggested a self-certainty of form we had deemed incompatible with the project; if this were to be a self-interrogating memorial, altogether uncertain of its form, the monumental cubes, regular angles, and formal stability in these designs would not suffice. Still others, like Christine Jackob-Marks's new design, an abstracted map of Europe marked with a stele for every Jewish community wiped out during the Holocaust, struck us as entirely inoffensive—altogether inanimate and therefore benign.

In the end, we compiled a list of what we regarded as the eight strongest designs and invited the artists to present their work to us and the organizers in November 1997. For half an hour each, the artists reflected on their designs and we asked questions. Occasionally, the questions, however tactfully posed, proved devastating. In the case of Markus Lüpertz's conciliatory figure of the biblical matriarch Rachel, it was clear that he wanted to bridge Jewish and Christian sensibilities, to illustrate the common source of both traditions. But, we asked, had he considered the possibility that in her disfigured nakedness, this twenty-foot-tall statue of *Rachel-imeinu* (Rachel, our mother) perched atop a grassy hillock would have been forbidden viewing to the huge number of Hasidic Jews murdered? There could, of course, be no answer. The artist's intentions were wholly honorable, but born in a land without Jews, he could not know what would be offensive to Jewish sensitivities. We were also anxious to hear Rebecca Horn's description of her design, an extremely subtle and gently kinetic work in keeping with her overall oeuvre. But because it included ash (intended here only to represent inanimacy) encased behind a glass cylindrical wall descending into the ground, the possible confusion over its source and meaning made this particular work untenable in our eyes.

Dani Karavan had resubmitted his yellow flower garden in the shape of a Jewish star, and it held much appeal for the ways it would change seasonally, demand tending, and even fade into a haunting palimpsest of the star during the winter. At the same time, we wondered whether Europe's murdered Jews would want to be remembered by "the badge of shame" assigned them by their tormentors—even as we liked the notion that the German landscape itself would now have to wear this star as its own national badge of shame. Zvi Hecker's "pages of the book" appealed to all in

Rolf Storz and Hans Jörg Wörhle, Empty Memorial Plaza. *Proposal for Berlin's "Memorial for the Murdered Jews of Europe," 1997.*

its underdetermined reference to a murdered "people of the book," but in its mix of pages, gates, benches, trees, and Hebrew lettering, its formal parts seemed to complicate the succinctness of its concept.

Finally, even though the designs by Daniel Libeskind and Jochen Gerz had been on all of our final lists of four, the strength of their designs did not seem equal to their brilliant conceptions. Libeskind's great broken wall—what he called *Stone-Breath*—certainly evoked a spectacular vision of irreparability, irredeemable voids, and a scarred landscape; but insofar as this seemed to be an extension of the void he had built into his Jewish Museum design, it also appeared to be an extension of the Jewish Museum itself, which already had a Holocaust void built into it. And for all the brilliant interactive potential in Jochen Gerz's *Warum?* plaza of stainless-steel pillars, we resisted the possible mystification of the Holocaust in such a question, even as we couldn't help but see echoes of a trade fair and flagpoles in its layout.

In thus weighing the power of concept against formal execution in this final group of designs, the members of the Findungskommission unanimously agreed that the two proposals by Gesine Weinmiller and Peter Eisenman–Richard Serra far transcended the others in their balance of brilliant concept and powerful execution. Though equally works of terrible beauty, complexity, and deep intelligence, the designs by Weinmiller and Eisenman–Serra derived their power from very different sources. The choice here was not between measures of brilliance in these two works but between two very different orders of memorial sensibilities: Weinmiller's was the genius of quietude, understatement, and almost magical allusiveness; the collaboration of Eisenman and Serra resulted in an audacious, surprising, and dangerously imagined form. One was by a young German woman of the generation now obligated to shoulder the memory and shame of events for which she was not to blame; the other was by two well-known Americans, architect and artist, one of whose Jewish family left Germany two generations ago. Together, we felt, these two designs would offer the public, government, and organizers of the memorial an actual and

Rudolf Herz and Reinhard Matz, Cobblestone Autobahn Kilometer. *Proposal for Berlin's "Memorial for the Murdered Jews of Europe," 1997.*

stark choice. Their cases were equally strong, but in the end one would have to gather the force of consensus over the other.

In Gesine Weinmiller's three-sided plaza, visitors would descend into memory and wend their way through eighteen wall-segments composed of giant sandstone blocks scattered in a seemingly random pattern in the square. The walls surrounding the area on three sides created a rising horizon as one came further into their compass, slowly blocking out the surrounding buildings and traffic noise. This space would be both part of the city and removed from it. And only gradually would the significance of these forms and spaces begin to dawn on visitors: the eighteen sections of stone wall recall *life* in Hebrew gematria (*chai*); the descent into memory space countered the possible exaltation of such memory and suggested a void carved out of the earth, a wound; the stacking of large stone blocks recalled the first monument in Genesis, a *Sa'adutha*, or witness-pile of stones, a memorial cairn; the rough texture and cut of the stones visually echoed the stones of the Western Wall in Jerusalem, the ruin of the Temple's destruction; their rough fit would show the seams of their construction; the pebbles on which visitors tread would slow their

Gerhard Merz, Open-topped Mausoleum, Hole in Ground. *Proposal for Berlin's "Memorial for the Murdered Jews of Europe,"1997.*

Dani Karavan, Jewish Star Garden of Yellow Flowers. *Proposal for Berlin's "Memorial for the Murdered Jews of Europe," 1997.*

pace and mark their visit in sound as well as in the visible traces their steps would leave behind.

Then there was a striking, yet altogether subtle perspectival illusion created from the vantage point in one corner above the plaza: the seemingly random arrangement of scattered wall segments would suddenly compose themselves into a Star of David and then fall apart as one moved beyond this point. The memory of Jews murdered would be constituted momentarily in the mind's eye before decomposing again, the lost Jews of Europe reconstituted only in the memorial activity of visitors here. Built into this design was also space for historical text on the great wall at the bottom of the decline into memory. Such a text would not presume to name all the victims of the crime but would name the crime itself. Built into this space was the capacity for a record of Holocaust history and for the changing face of its memory.

In its original conception, the proposal by Peter Eisenman and Richard Serra also suggested a startling alternative to the very idea of the Holocaust memorial. Like Weinmiller's, theirs was a pointedly antiredemptory design: it found no compensa-

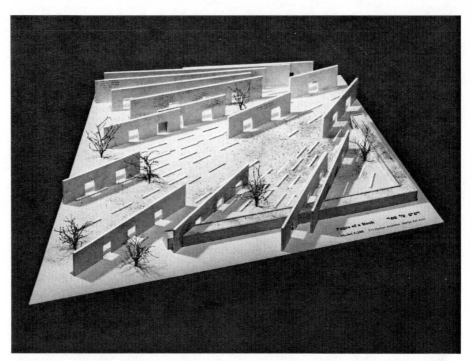

Zvi Hecker, Pages of the Book. *Proposal for Berlin's "Memorial for the Murdered Jews of Europe,"*
1997.

tion for the Holocaust in art or architecture. In its waving field of four thousand pillars, it at once echoed a cemetery, even as it implied that such emblems of individual mourning were inadequate to the task of remembering mass murder. Toward this
end, it took the vertical forms of its pillars—sized from ground level to 16 feet high,
spaced three feet apart—and turned their collected mass into a horizontal plane.
Rather than pretending to answer Germany's memorial problem in a single, reassuring form, this design proposed multiple, collected forms arranged so that visitors
have to find their own path to the memory of Europe's murdered Jews. As such, this
memorial provided not an answer to memory but an ongoing process, a continuing
question without a certain solution.

Part of what Eisenman called its *Unheimlichkeit,* or uncanniness, derived precisely from the sense of danger generated in such a field, the demand that we now
find our own way into and out of such memory. And because the scale of this installation would be almost irreproducible on film shot from the ground, it demanded
that visitors enter the memorial space and not try to know it vicariously through

their snapshots. What would be remembered here are not photographic images but the visitors' experiences and what they remembered in situ. As might have been expected in a piece partly designed by Richard Serra, this design also implied a certain physical danger in such memory, a danger meant to remain implicit but so close to being actualized in its scale and forms as to suggest something more than a mere figure of threatening memory.

To the designs by Weinmiller and Eisenman–Serra recommended by the Findungskommission, the memorial's organizers added the proposals by Jochen Gerz (discussed at length in Chapter 5) and Daniel Libeskind. At the time, we strongly recommended that these names not be added to the final list, since it might create the appearance of competing lists of finalists. But for reasons that were never clear to the Findungskommission, Lea Rosh insisted that Gerz's *Warum?* proposal be added, and Speaker Peter Radunski insisted that Libeskind's broken wall be added as well. The appearance of an "A" list and a "B" list was indeed created, but not much was made of it,

Daniel Libeskind, Stone-Breath. *Proposal for Berlin's "Memorial for the Murdered Jews of Europe," 1997.*

as large audiences turned out to hear the public presentations of proposals by each of these final four teams of artists and architects. Before long, consensus (though far from unanimous) gathered around the design by Peter Eisenman and Richard Serra. It was reported that Chancellor Kohl also strongly favored the design by Eisenman and Serra and even invited the team to Bonn to hear them explain their proposal to him.

At this point, I wondered whether Weinmiller's design had been eliminated from consideration on the basis of its subtlety or for what the press had called its kitschy "Aha-effect." Or maybe Eisenman and Serra had been chosen for the same reason I had been asked to serve as the Findungskommission's spokesman: so mistrustful were the Germans of their own judgment that they could not assign such responsibility—at either the artistic or evaluative level—to themselves alone. In any case, during their visit with the chancellor in January 1998, Eisenman and Serra were asked to consider a handful of design changes that would make the memorial acceptable to organizers. As an architect who saw accommodation to his clients' wishes as part of his job, Eisenman agreed to adapt the design to the needs of the project. As an artist, however, Richard Serra steadfastly refused to contemplate any changes

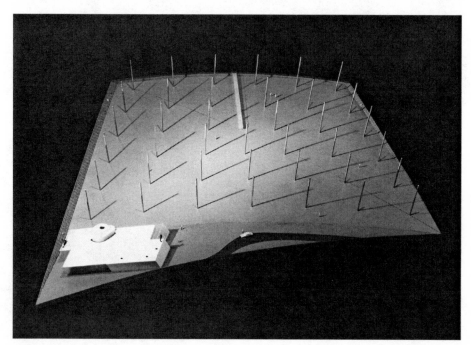

Jochen Gerz, Warum? *Proposal for Berlin's "Memorial for the Murdered Jews of Europe," 1997.*

Gesine Weinmiller, Eighteen Scattered Sandstone Wall Segments. *Proposal for Berlin's "Memorial for the Murdered Jews of Europe," 1997.*

in the design whatsoever. As a result, he withdrew from the project, suggesting that once changed, the project would in effect no longer be his.

Although we were sorry to see Richard Serra withdraw from the project, we understood the artist's prerogative to resist recommended changes in what he regarded as a finished work. Here, in fact, the artist's and the architect's modes of operation may always diverge: where the architect generally sees an accommodation to the clients' requests as part of the job, the artist is more apt to see suggested changes, however slight, as a threat to the work's internal logic and integrity. This conflict, too, is normal in the course of collaborations between artists and architects.

In spite of our enthusiastic recommendation of Eisenman and Serra's proposal, in the sheer number of its pillars and its overall scale in proportion to the allotted space, the original design left less room for visitors and commemorative activities than we had wanted. Some of us also found a potential for more than figurative danger in the memorial site: at sixteen feet high, the tallest pillars might have hidden some visitors from view, thereby creating the sense of a labyrinthine maze, an effect desired by neither designers nor commissioners. The potential for a purely visceral experience that might occlude a more contemplative memorial visit was greater than some of us would have preferred.

Among the modifications we therefore requested of Peter Eisenman, now acting on his own, was a slight downscaling of both the size of individual pillars and their number. In June 1998, I spent a day in Peter Eisenman's New York City studio to hear his rationale and to see the changes he had made, a day before he sent his newly designed model off to Berlin for safe-keeping. Shortly after, I could report to the other commissioners not only that Eisenman had expertly incorporated our suggestions into the design but that they worked, in unexpected ways, to strengthen the entire formalization of the concept. Here I also found that I had, in effect, collapsed my roles as arbiter, critic, and advocate—all toward finding the language that the chancellor himself might use in justifying his decision to a still-skeptical public.

Eisenman's revised design reduced both the number of pillars (from forty-two hundred to about three thousand) and their height, so that they would now range from one and a half feet tall to about ten feet tall or so in one section of the field. Where the "monumental" has traditionally used its size to humiliate or cow viewers into submission, this memorial in its humanly proportioned forms would put people on an even footing with memory. Visitors and the role they play as they wade knee-, or chest-, or shoulder-deep into this waving field of stones will not be diminished by the monumental but will be made integral parts of the memorial, now invited into a memorial dialogue of equals. Visitors will not be defeated by their memorial obligation here nor dwarfed by the memory-forms themselves, but rather enjoined by them to come face to face with memory.

Able to see over and around these pillars, visitors will still have to find their way through this field of stones even as they are never actually lost in or overcome by the memorial act. In effect, they will make and choose individual spaces for memory, even as they do so collectively. The implied sense of motion in the gently undulating field also formalizes a kind of memory that is neither frozen in time nor static in space. The sense of such instability will help visitors resist an impulse toward closure in the memorial act and heighten their own role in anchoring memory in themselves.

In their multiple and variegated sizes, the pillars are both individuated and collected: the very idea of "collective memory" is broken down and replaced with the collected memories of individuals murdered, the terrible meanings of their deaths now multiplied and not merely unified. The land sways and moves beneath

Peter Eisenman and Richard Serra, Waving Field of Pillars. *Proposal for Berlin's "Memorial for the Murdered Jews of Europe," 1997.*

these pillars so that each one is some three degrees off vertical: we are not reassured by such memory, not reconciled to the mass murder of millions but now disoriented by it.

In practical terms, the removal of some twelve hundred pillars has dramatically opened up the plaza for public commemorative activities. It has also made room for tourist buses to discharge visitors without threatening the sanctity of the pillars on the edges of the field. By raising the height of the lowest pillar tops from nearly flush with the ground to approximately a one and a half feet tall, the new design also ensures that visitors will not step on or walk out over the tops of pillars. Because the pillars will tilt at the same degree and angle as the roll of the ground-level topography into which the pillars are set, this, too, will discourage climbing or clambering-over. In fact, because these pillars are neither intended nor consecrated as tomb-stones, there would be no desecration were someone to step or sit on one of them. But in Jewish tradition, it is also important to avoid the appearance of a desecration, so the minor change in the smallest pillars was still welcome.

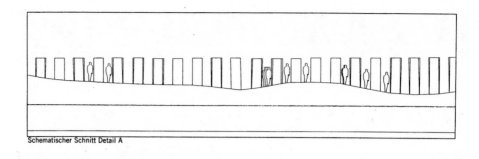

Schematischer Schnitt Detail A

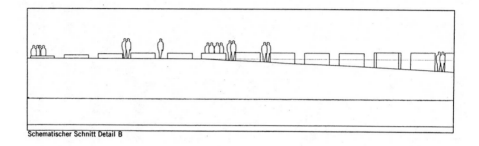

Schematischer Schnitt Detail B

DENKMAL FÜR DIE ERMORDETEN JUDEN EUROPAS
EISENMAN ARCHITECTS AND RICHARD SERRA

Schematischer Schnitt Details A und B
Maßstab 1:250

Peter Eisenman and Richard Serra, architects' sketch of original design, Memorial for the Murdered Jews of Europe, *1997.*

In their warm, sandy tone, the concrete-form pillars will reflect the colors of the sun and sky on one hand and remain suggestive of stone, even sandstone, on the other. The concrete will not have the rough lines of their pour forms but will be smooth, close to the texture of sidewalk. They can also be impregnated with an anti-graffiti solution to make them easy to clean. Over time, it will be important to remove graffiti as it appears, in order not to allow it to accumulate. The crushed-stone ground surface is also an excellent idea, in that it inhibits running, frolicking, or lying on the ground even as it marks the visitors' footsteps in both sound and space.

The architect prefers that the pillars, though stonelike, remain underdetermined and open to many readings: they are alternately stones, pillars, blank tablets, walls, and segments. This said, in their abstract forms, they will nevertheless accommodate the references projected onto them by visitors, the most likely being the tombstone. This is not a bad thing and suggests the need to keep these pillars blank-faced. With written text, they would look very much like tombstones, in fact, and might begin to generate a dynamic demanding some sort of formal treatment as tombstones, even symbolic ones.

For this reason, I suggested that a permanent, written historical text be inscribed on a large tablet or tablets set into the ground and tilted at a readable angle. This position will bring visitors into respectful, even prayerful repose as they read the text, with heads slightly bowed in memory. These could be placed at the entrance or on the sides, under the trees lining the perimeter of the field, leaving the integrity of

Peter Eisenman, revised design, Memorial for the Murdered Jews of Europe, *1998.*

the field itself formally intact while still denoting what is to be remembered here. Thus placed, the memorial texts will not create a sense of beginning or end of the memorial field, leaving the site open to the multiple paths visitors take in their memorial quest. This, too, will respect the architect's attempt to foster a sense of incompleteness; it will not be a memorial with a narrative beginning, middle, and end built into it.

The introduction of rows of evergreen trees and linden trees was also welcome, insofar as they simultaneously demarcate this space, even buffering it from the city, while integrating the site into the cityscape by connecting it visually to the trees of the Tiergarten on the west side of the street. Because the lower branches of the

Peter Eisenman, revised design, Memorial for the Murdered Jews of Europe, *detail with trees, 1998.*

Peter Eisenman, revised design, Memorial for the Murdered Jews of Europe, *overview with bus-loading area, 1998.*

trees will be trimmed upward to a height of ten feet or so, the memorial site itself will be fully visible from the street, sidewalk, and adjacent buildings. When visitors enter the area, their line of sight will take in the surrounding skyline, but as they come further into the center of the field of pillars, the horizon of treetops will gradually rise to screen out all but the tops of surrounding buildings, thereby removing visitors from the urban landscape and immersing them gently into the memorial space.

It was for these reasons that the Findungskommission approved Eisenman's revised design and unanimously recommended it to the chancellor and memorial commissioners. We had hoped for a memorial that would evolve over time to reflect every generation's preoccupations, the kinds of significance every generation will find in the memory of Europe's murdered Jews. In this memorial, which insists on its incompleteness, its working through of an intractable problem over any solution, we found a memorial that was as suggestive in its complex conception as it was eloquent in its formal design. As such, it came as close to being adequate to Germany's impossible task as is humanly possible. This is finally all we could ask of Germany's national attempt to commemorate the Nazis' murder of European Jewry.

Memory Meets Politics

By this time, the summer of 1998, national elections were looming, and Helmut Kohl's Christian Democratic Union had suffered several losses in preliminary regional elections earlier in the spring. All watched and waited as deadlines for the chancellor's announced decision passed without comment. Into this void other politicians occasionally leaped. Berlin's CDU mayor, Eberhard Diepgen, declared that he did not want Berlin turned into a "capital of remorse" and that it would be best to suspend the process indefinitely.[11] And then, with national elections only weeks away, Social Democratic Party leader Gerhard Schroeder's culture minister-designate, Michael Naumann, was asked whether or not an SPD government led by Schroeder would support the building of Eisenman's Holocaust memorial. No, he answered, for two reasons: first, he was skeptical of any monument's adequacy to remember the Holocaust, believing that any such monument would serve merely as a "suspension of guilt in art"; second, though he had not yet seen a model of Eisenman's design, photographs of it suggested a certain "Speer-like monumentality," which he found inappropriate in such a memorial.[12] Naumann's response to this question on his first day as culture-minister designate was as refreshingly honest as it may have been impolitic. For whether or not he had intended it, the memorial had now become an electoral issue dividing the two candidates and their party agendas. Among many in the Social Democratic Party, there seemed to be an underlying belief that this memorial and its design had become so closely associated with Chancellor Kohl that it would have to be defeated with him. In German interviews, Schroeder publicly backed his minister-designate on this issue; but in the United States, he diplomatically sidestepped the question. By the time of the elections, in September 1998, the fate of the memorial seemed to be hanging on the result of the elections alone.

Indeed, even though every memorial has built into it a political calculus, by inadvertently turning the national question of Holocaust memory in Germany into a partisan electoral issue, the Social Democrats also raised a number of questions as to their motives. Would a Schroeder era include a moratorium on new memorials everywhere in Germany for their intrinsic incapacity to memorialize history? Or would there be a moratorium only on new Holocaust memorials? Had German Social Democrats actually moved away from their traditional, reconciliative position promoting memory of the Holocaust, as embodied in Willy Brandt's kneeling at the foot of the Warsaw Ghetto Monument in 1970, or their embrace of Richard von Weiszäcker's speech of May 1985, as Jeffrey Herf pointedly asked?[13]

Or if there was simple political gain in such a position, where was its source? A shadow constituency in Germany that secretly but fervently wanted no sign of Germany's past crimes marring their capital's magnificent new landscape? Or worse, those who were secretly happy that at least the war against the Jews was won, even if the larger war was lost? Could this constituency actually comprise a swing vote in Germany in 1998? At the time, I wondered whether the party's position on the memorial was based in principled, if theoretical doubts as to the efficacy of any Holocaust memorial or whether, more cynically, it stemmed from a cold electoral calculation, a seemingly elevated gesture actually aimed at Germany's sullen minority.

As it turned out, once it became clear that as an electoral issue, the memorial would only burn any politician who came too close to it, a truce of sorts was called. On the eve of a vote in the Berlin Senate on 26 August to determine whether the city of Berlin would continue to support a central "Memorial for the Murdered Jews of Europe," Mayor Diepgen announced that he had enough votes to block the memorial. In response, the memorial's organizers asked me to publish my assessment of Eisenman's revised design. It would be the first public presentation of the new design, and the organizers hoped it would sway the vote toward the memorial.[14] Whether it was as a result of my article or not, two days after the assessment appeared, Chancellor Kohl and Mayor Diepgen agreed to defer further discussion on the memorial until after the elections on 27 September.

After handily defeating Helmut Kohl and his Christian Democratic Union, Gerhard Schroeder and his Social Democratic Party entered into a so-called red-green governing coalition with Joshka Fischer's Green Party. Because the Greens supported the memorial for Europe's murdered Jews, the coalition agreement stipulated that the memorial be put to a vote in the Bundestag sometime in the new year. With the memorial itself now seemingly ratified by the coalition agreement, the new minister of culture, Michael Naumann, began to float a series of alternatives to Eisenman's field of pillars, which was, procedurally at least, still the project's winning design.

Naumann, a former journalist and recent president of the German-owned Henry Holt Publishing Company in New York, made it clear that if Germany was going to build a Holocaust memorial, he preferred that it be as pedagogically inclined as possible, a center for learning and research, not just contemplation. Toward this end, the he proposed, among other possibilities, a permanent installation for screening Holocaust survivors' video testimony from Steven Spielberg's Shoah Oral History Project. When asked about this project, Spielberg demurred and suggested that this was a German question to be decided by Germans only. Besides, the new Jewish Museum in Berlin had already agreed to house an archive of these testimonies and to show them, as well. A few weeks later, Naumann proposed building a complex of three institutions in the memorial's place: a Leo Baeck Institute, a Holocaust Museum, and an Institute for the Comparative Study of Genocides. In a heated response, the directors of all of Berlin's existing Holocaust research archives and institutes objected that not only had they not been consulted, but how would such centers be coordinated with their own, without making them redundant? At about the same time, editorial writers began to ask whether the memorial procedure already in place had been abandoned, or whether the previous memorial procedure itself had been secretly abrogated.[15] Government lawyers initiated an inquiry to determine just what the legal status of the memorial procedure actually was.

They found that in spite of the Findungskommission's explicit recommendation of Peter Eisenman's revised design for the memorial (now called Eisenman-II), and the support of two out of the three groups of organizers (the Citizens' Committee headed by Lea Rosh and the federal government), the coalition agreement's stipulated vote in the Bundestag on whether to accept the winning design had yet to be taken. But even here, the issue as to what constituted the "winning design" had become almost hopelessly muddled. For as it became clear to all that the original procedure was still in place, and that there were enough votes on both sides of the aisle in the Bundestag to approve Eisenman's design, the culture minister hoped to reach a compromise whereby both Eisenman's memorial *and* Naumann's plan for an interpretive center might be adopted together in the same space.

With this in mind, and with the tacit approval of members of parliament, the Findungskommission, and the memorial commissioners, Peter Eisenman and Naumann began unofficial discussions on how a synthesis might be achieved between

Eisenman-II (now supported by Naumann) and the minister of culture's own desire for an added "interpretive center, library, and research center." These discussions were moderated by Michael Blumenthal, director of Berlin's Jewish Museum, amid consultations with members of the Findungskommission and the commissioners. In appearing to reach a synthesis in which both the memorial and an added interpretive center would be acceptable to the minister of culture and the architect, all parties hoped that the process could go forward. Michael Naumann would now support Eisenman-II, and the architect would agree to consider possible additions to the memorial.

But here a public relations fiasco erupted. Asked by the minister of culture what such an addition might look like, Eisenman presented a beautifully constructed model and computer-generated images of a possible archive and library complex built into his field of pillars. In his proposal for a Holocaust memorial archive, Eisenman seemed to lift one corner of his field of pillars so that they would rise into a series of color-blended buildings, which would in turn be connected by pedestrian ramps to a gigantic, freestanding glass wall of one million books, visible from the memorial area. Exhibition space would be built underground to house a permanent installation on the Holocaust, as well as a lecture hall, research facilities, and offices.

When this project was unveiled, however, it assumed the mantle of an accomplished fact. For almost all in the press and public sphere, this seemed to be a new proposal altogether, a departure from the process. Even among the project's most vocal supporters, many viewed this as an opportunistic betrayal of the process by the architect, by which the architect himself had replaced Eisenman-II with something now called Eisenman-III. In fact, this provisional design was never intended by Eisenman to replace Eisenman-II but had been presented, somewhat ingenuously, as an act of good faith on Eisenman's part to repay Naumann's own act of good faith on agreeing to support the memorial. At this point, nobody seemed to know where the memorial stood, which design was even being debated, or what the procedure itself allowed.

In what seemed to be a last-ditch effort to save the memorial from itself, SPD member of Parliament and chair of the Bundestag Committee on Cultural and Media Affairs Elke Leonhard convened a public hearing in the Bundeshaus on 3 March 1999 intended to address the "state of deliberations" surrounding Berlin's "Memorial for the Murdered Jews of Europe." If the Bundestag was going to vote on the memorial, as mandated by the coalition agreement, it now needed to know exactly what it would

Peter Eisenman, proposed archive addition (not to be realized), Memorial for the Murdered Jews of Europe, *1999.*

be voting for or against. As the so-called speaker for the Findungskommission, I was invited to open the hearing with a short history of the project and answers to four pointed questions: What is the state of deliberations on the question of (1) *why* a monument should be erected; (2) *where* a monument should be erected; (3) *how* a monument to the murdered Jews of Europe should be designed; and (4) what conclusions can be drawn from the current state of deliberations for the further discussions and decision-making process of the German Bundestag? In the next six hours, my presentation was followed with statements by two other members of the Findungskommission (Josef Paul Kleihues and Dieter Ronte), as well as by representatives of the memorial's organizers, including Lea Rosh for the Citizens' Committee, Peter Radunski for the Berlin Senate, and Michael Naumann for the federal government. In addition, two of the memorial's leading opponents—György Konrad, president of Berlin's Academy of Art, and cultural critic Solomon Korn—were invited to make presentations against the memorial. After each presentation, members of the parliamentary committee asked questions of the speakers. In my presentation, I described both my initial opposition to the memorial and my eventual role in trying to accomplish it—basically an extemporaneous version of this chapter. Michael Naumann eloquently detailed his own initial opposition to the memorial and his qualified support for it now. György Konrad and Solomon Korn both questioned the premises of such a memorial and suggested that by definition it would have to result in bad and bombastic art and that, in fact, Eisenman's design only proved their point. And in a somewhat startling formulation, Speaker of the Berlin Senate Peter Radunski confounded all by suggesting that the Berlin Senate could not vote on whether to support the memorial until the Bundestag itself had voted on it—even though the procedure seemed to demand just the opposite sequence.

At the end of the six-hour session, which had proceeded without a break, I was asked by Elke Leonhard for a concluding statement. Here I suggested that now it was time for the Bundestag to vote on Eisenman-II only, to approve it or reject it on the basis of the arguments we had made that day. Once the memorial had been voted into existence, then the question of whether a library and research center should be added and what that might consist of could be considered by the organizers. I cautioned that attaching an addition to the memorial before a vote could introduce a number of complicating dimensions, some of them possibly fatal—especially questions of institutional redundancy and sources of archival material already housed elsewhere. Such an addition would demand its own debate and process, I said, separate from and subsequent to the Bundestag's approval of Eisenman-II. Proponents of such an addition may well make a persuasive case for it, but without consulting and collaborating closely with the directors of other well-established pedagogical centers (such as those at the Wannsee Villa, Topographie des Terrors, Sachsenhausen, and Buchenwald, among others), such a project will never find the support it needs among existing memorial and research centers.

Should the memorial go forward? I asked. Past decisions to proceed with it, even if made for wrong-headed reasons, have also created their own set of political realities, no less consequential for all their political logic. At this point, I concluded, the only thing worse than making the monument now would be to reverse course and deliberately choose not to make it. The unwelcome guest of Holocaust memory has already been invited to Germany's millennial party. To disinvite this guest now, as unpopular as he may be, would seem to give grave offense to the memory of all whom this guest represents.

So, yes, I said. Gerhard Schroeder's government should build the memorial and give the German public a choice, even an imperfect choice: let them choose to remember what Germany once did to the Jews of Europe by coming to the memorial, by staying at home, by remembering alone or in the company of others. Let the people decide whether to animate such a site with their visits, with their shame, their sorrow, or their contempt. Or let the people abandon this memorial altogether, if that is what they choose, and let the memorial itself now become the locus for further debate. Then let the public decide just how hollow or how substantial a gesture this memorial is, whether any memorial can ever be more than a ritual gesture to an unredeemable past. With these words, I sat down.

The Bundestag committee chair, Elke Leonhard, thanked me and adjourned the hearing. Having beaten us all into exhaustion on that day in March, the question of Germany's national "Memorial for the Murdered Jews of Europe" was returned to parliamentary committee, where it was drafted for a vote in the Bundestag on 25 June 1999. There it became enmeshed yet again in parliamentary politics, but it was also back in German hands, where it belonged. Michael Naumann continued to lobby for as large an interpretive center as possible, something approaching a national museum to share Eisenman's field of waving pillars. Other proposals included theologian Richard Schroeder's suggestion that a single tablet be installed, inscribed in both the Hebrew original and several other languages, "Thou shalt not kill."

Beginning that morning at nine and running until after two in the afternoon, a full session of the German Bundestag met in public view to debate and finally vote on Berlin's "Memorial for the Murdered Jews of Europe." Both opponents and proponents were given time to make their cases, each presentation followed by noisy but civil debate. By this time, in fact, the positions of all the members of parliament were well known and counted in advance. A number of alternative measures to the memorial were duly proposed and defeated, including a memorial for all of the Nazis' victims and the above-mentioned tablet with "Thou shalt not kill." Finally, by a vote of 314 to 209, with 14 abstentions, the Bundestag approved the memorial in three separate parts:

> (1) The Federal Republic of Germany will erect in Berlin a memorial for the murdered Jews of Europe on the site of the former Ministerial Gardens in the middle of Berlin;
> (2) The design of Peter Eisenman's field of pillars will be realized, as well as a small place of information that will detail the fate of the victims and the authentic sites of destruction; and

(3) A public foundation will be established by the Bundestag to oversee the completion of the memorial. It will be composed of representatives from the Bundestag, the city of Berlin, and the citizens' initiative for the establishment of the memorial, as well as the directors of other memorial museums, members of the Central Committee for the Jews of Germany, and other victim groups. The foundation will begin its work with the memorial's groundbreaking in the year 2000.[16]

When asked by reporters if I was sorry the debate was finally over, whether this might actually mean the end of Germany's Holocaust memory-work, as I had initially feared, I could answer honestly that only half the debate was over. Now that the parliament had decided to give Holocaust memory a central place in Berlin, an even more difficult job awaits the organizers: defining exactly what it is to be remembered here in this waving field of pillars. What will Germany's national Holocaust narrative be? How will the memorial's text actually read? Who will write it and to whom will it be written? The question of historical content begins at precisely the moment the question of memorial design ends. Memory, which has followed history, will now be followed by still further historical debate.

In the end, by choosing to create a commemorative space in the center of Berlin—a place empty of housing, commerce, or recreation—the Bundestag reminds Germany and the world at large of the self-inflicted void at the heart of German culture and consciousness. It is a courageous and difficult act of contrition on the part of the government and reflects Germany's newfound willingness *to act* on such memory, as it did the summer of 1999 in Kosovo, and not be merely paralyzed by it. But because the murdered Jews can respond to this gesture only with a massive silence, the burden of response now falls on living Germans—who in their memorial visits will be asked to recall the mass murder of a people once perpetrated in their name, the absolute void this destruction has left behind, and their own responsibility for memory itself.

Notes

INTRODUCTION

1. Kaplan, "Theweleit and Spiegelman," 160.
2. See Hirsch, "Family Pictures," 8–9. Also see Hirsch's excellent elaboration of this notion in her *Family Frames*.
3. In responding to my call for interweaving a history of events with a reflection on how Holocaust history comes to be told, for example, a well-respected historian, Peter Hayes, suggested that such a study, "as well as Saul Friedlander's recent work, lavishes talents on a project not quite worthy of [Young and Friedlander]. Their preoccupations reflect a sort of scholasticism now quite rampant in the academy in which commonplace problems of technique are mistaken for profound matters of substance, in which how we learn and relate what we know becomes as intellectually significant and preoccupying as the knowledge itself, and in which—in self-flattering fashion—the scholars who interpret and the students who learn become the subject of inquiry, inevitably displacing the participants themselves."

   Here I am grateful to Peter Hayes for sending me his "Comment in Response" to an early version of "Toward a Received History of the Holocaust," both delivered as parts of a panel on "Contemporary Interpretations of the Holocaust," at the annual Social Science History Association Conference, New Orleans, 12 October 1996.
4. Bartov, *Murder in Our Midst*, 116.
5. Friedlander, *Reflections of Nazism*, 19.
6. For a brilliant illustration of history that includes the art and literature of the era under discussion, see Friedlander, *Nazi Germany and the Jews*, vol. 1.
7. Adorno, "Engagement," 125–127.
8. Friedlander, *Memory, History, and Extermination*, 61.
9. Ibid., 55.
10. Adorno, *Prisms*, 27, 19.
11. For an insightful elaboration on the "ever-dying" of the avant-garde, see Mann, *Theory-Death of the Avant-Garde*.
12. See Friedlander, *Nazi Germany and the Jews*, 1:3.
13. For a detailed discussion of the Harburg counter-monument, see Young, *Texture of Memory*, 27–48. Also see Könneke, ed., *Das Harburger Mahnmal gegen Faschismus*.
14. Here I refer to my earlier book, *The Texture of Memory*, as well as to the catalogue of essays I introduced and edited for an exhibition at the Jewish Museum in New York, *The Art of Memory*.
15. Here I must acknowledge some of the important discussions of this "cutting-edge" art

already under way. For example, see van Alphen's fine study, *Caught by History*; Liss, *Trespassing through Shadows*; and Sicher, ed., *Breaking Crystal*.

For exhibition catalogues to shows on contemporary Holocaust art, see Feinstein, ed., *Witness and Legacy*; and Snyder, ed., *Impossible Evidence*.

16. Here I am indebted to Bernstein's *Foregone Conclusions*.

CHAPTER ONE Art Spiegelman's *Maus* and the After-Images of History

1. See Friedlander, *Nazi Germany and the Jews*, vol. 1.
2. Friedlander, "Trauma, Transference," 55. In his earlier *Reflections of Nazism*, Friedlander was more skeptical of what he would later call postmodern responses to the Holocaust and more deeply ambivalent toward the very motives for such art (see citation in Introduction).
3. Friedlander, "Trauma, Transference," 41.
4. Ibid.
5. Spiegelman, *Maus*, 2:135.
6. Friedlander, "Trauma, Transference," 41.
7. Friedlander, *Memory, History, and Extermination*, 132.
8. Ibid., 53.
9. Broszat and Friedlander, "Controversy About Historicization," 129.
10. See Hirsch, "Family Pictures," 8. For more on my own notion of "received history," see Young, "Toward a Received History," 21–43.
11. Hirsch, "Family Pictures," 8–9.
12. From author's interview with Spiegelman, as well as from Spiegelman, "Commix," 61.
13. Spiegelman, "Artist's Statement," 44.
14. Spiegelman, "Commix," 61.
15. From Kalir, "Road to *Maus*," 2.
16. Spiegelman, "Commix," 61.
17. Ibid.
18. Kalir, "Road to *Maus*," 1.
19. Spiegelman, *Breakdowns*.
20. Ibid., unpaginated.
21. Spiegelman, "Commix," 71.
22. Varnedoe and Gopnik, *High and Low*, 154. For an overview of the comics' place in modern art, see 153–229.
23. Laub, "Bearing Witness," 57.
24. For a full elaboration of this kind of "side-shadowed" history telling, see Bernstein, *Foregone Conclusions*.
25. Though Spiegelman wrote and conceived of *Maus* as a single work from the beginning, he agreed to allow Pantheon Books to divide it into two volumes, the first published in 1986. This was partly to preempt possible copy-cat "comics" and animated cartoons by those familiar with the sections of *Maus* already published in *Raw Comics*, the journal Spiegelman and his wife, Françoise Mouly, co-edit.

26. Kaplan, "Theweleit and Spiegelman," 162.
27. See Miller's deeply insightful essay, "Cartoons of the Self," 49.
28. From author's interview with Spiegelman, November 1993.
29. Gopnik, "Comics and Catastrophe," 33.
30. Storrs, "Making Maus," 1.
31. Author interview with Spiegelman, November 1993.
32. Rosen, "Trivialization of Tragedy," 85.
33. "Letter to the Editor."
34. Miller, "Cartoons of the Self," 46.
35. Hutton, *History as an Art of Memory*, 72.
36. Amichai, "Tourists," as quoted in Bernstein, *Foregone Conclusions*, 127.

CHAPTER TWO   David Levinthal's *Mein Kampf*

1. Levinthal quoted in *Wild West*, 5.
2. In an eye-opening essay on the work of Hans Bellmer, Herbert Lust wrote that "any artist interested in the female body's endless possibilities or 'forbidden' mental states must reckon with [Hans] Bellmer" ("For Women Are Endless Forms," 47).
   Although this is undoubtedly so, it may be equally true that neither can viewers today see any of these contemporary artists' work without recalling Bellmer's early conceptual photographs of his violently reconstituted doll. Moreover, when we recall that Bellmer made and photographed this doll in 1934 Germany as an explicit protest, dissent, and challenge to the unyielding absolutism of the Nazis, Levinthal's images of erotic dolls as Holocaust victims begin to resonate as a kind of protest art and further breaking of cultural taboos.
3. For a fuller elaboration of both Levinthal's place among the "photo-conceptual vanguard" and the place of his *Mein Kampf* series in his larger corpus of work, see Stainback and Woodward, *David Levinthal*.
4. This chapter is adapted from my catalogue essay, "David Levinthal's *Mein Kampf*," in Levinthal, *Mein Kampf*, 67–83.
5. Chandler and Ride, "Foreword," unpaginated.
6. Levinthal and Trudeau, *Hitler Moves East*, 7.
7. "Toying with History," 29.
8. From *Wild West*, 7.
9. From interview with Woodward in *David Levinthal*, 153.
10. From Von Dräteln, "Jochen Gerz's Visual Poetry," 47.
11. See Kuspit, "Sings in Suspense," as cited by Mellors, "David Levinthal," in *Dark Light*.
12. Reviews of Levinthal's *Mein Kampf* were generally, if warily, positive. In almost every case, reviewers were moved by the power of the images, even as they were made intensely uncomfortable by their subject—and its relentlessly cool treatment. "Lovely to look at, horrific to behold" was how Robin Cembalist put it in her review of *Mein Kampf* in *Forward* ("Levinthal's Disturbing Photos," 9). Others, like Sarah Boxer, wonder whether Levinthal

can't help but become part of the pornographic culture he proposes to be exploring ("Hardly Child's Play").

13. For an elaboration of the ways women's corpses, in particular, have have been represented as emblematic in our culture, see Bronfen, *Over Her Dead Body*.

14. Sontag, *On Photography*, 11–12.

15. These images are available for viewing in the U.S. Holocaust Memorial Museum Photo Archives, WIS nos. 136–138.

16. *Hitler Moves East*, 8.

17. From interview with Woodward in *David Levinthal*, 153.

18. Friedlander, *Reflections of Nazism*, 19.

CHAPTER THREE   Sites Unseen

1. Nora, "Between Memory and History," 19.

2. Attie, "Writing on the Wall Project," 9.

3. Ibid.

4. Attie quoted in Axelrod, "Time Exposures," 40.

5. Attie quoted in Chazan, "Ghosts of the Ghettos."

6. As related by the artist to the author in an interview. The exchange is also described by Attie in *Writing on the Wall*, 12.

7. Michael André Bernstein, "Shimon Attie," 6.

8. As quoted from a handbill supplied to the author, courtesy of the artist (my translation).

9. See, for example, Ido de Haan's work in Holland, a preview of which I received in a copy of "Invention of a National Trauma," a paper delivered at "Memory and the Second World War," the Netherlands State Institute for War Documentation, Amsterdam, 27 April 1995.

10. For more in this vein, see Young, "Anne Frank House," 131–137.

11. As described by Attie in an unpublished project description for "Walk of Fame," provided to the author.

12. Ibid.

13. Ibid.

14. As described in Palowski, "Retracing Schindler's List," a travel booklet published by Kraków's Ministry of Tourism.

15. Protzman, "Artist Projects a Ghostly Past," 10.

16. Attie, project description for "Walk of Fame."

CHAPTER FOUR   Memory, Countermemory, and the End of the Monument

1. Here I elaborate and expand on themes I first explored in "Counter-Monument," 267–296. Also see Young, *Texture of Memory*, 27–48.

2. For a record of this competition, see *Denkmal für die ermordeten Juden Europas*. For a col-

lection of essays arguing against building this monument, see *Der Wettbewerb für das "Denkmal für die ermordeten Juden Europas."*

On his proposal to blow up the *Brandenburger Tor*, see Hoheisel, "Aschrottbrunnen—Denk-Stein-Sammlung—Brandenburger Tor," 253–266.

3. Nietzsche, *Use and Abuse of History*, 14–17.
4. Mumford, *Culture of Cities*, 438.
5. Ibid., 434.
6. Broszat, "Plea for Historicization," 129.
7. Krauss, *Originality of the Avant-Garde*, 280.
8. Nora, "Between Memory and History," 13.
9. Huyssen, "Monument in a Post-Modern Age," 11. Also see Huyssen's elaboration of this essay in his *Twilight Memories*, 249–260.
10. Elsen, *Modern European Sculpture*, 122–125.
11. For elaboration of this theme, see Winzen, "Need for Public Representation," 309–314.
12. From Hoheisel, "Rathaus-Platz-Wunde." Subsequent quotations from Hoheisel on this memorial are drawn from this booklet.
13. See Fischer and Glameier, eds., *Missing House*.
14. See Bradley, ed., *Rachel Whiteread*, 8. Other essays in this exhibition catalogue for the retrospective of Rachel Whiteread's work at the Tate-Liverpool Gallery by Stuart Morgan, Bartomeu Mari, Rosalind Krauss, and Michael Tarantino also explore various aspects of the sculptor's gift for making absence present.
15. *Judenplatz Wien 1996*, 94.
16. Ibid., 109.
17. See Stih and Schnock, *Arbeitsbuch für ein Denkmal in Berlin*.
18. Stih and Schnock, *Bus Stop Fahrplan*, 6.
19. Ibid., 9.
20. Nicolai, "Bus Stop—The Non-Monument," unpaginated brochure on the project published by Stih and Schnock.

CHAPTER FIVE   Memory Against Itself in Germany Today

1. As quoted in Lichtenstein and Wajeman's interview, "Jochen Gerz," E-3.
2. In Gerz's difficult-to-translate words,

"Ihr Vorhandensein ist der Beweis ihrer Unverfanglichkeit. Die im Museum Dachau reproduzierten—hier nicht aufgenommenen—Beschriftungen aus dem KZ Dachau zeigen, dass die gleiche Funktion den Schriftzeichen eigen ist, im Museum und im KZ. Sie sind das Medium, das beide möglich macht.

"Latent beinhaltet die Beschriftung im KZ Dachau das Museum Dachau und die im Museum das KZ. Sie selbst ist das Dachau-Projekt." From text panel for "EXIT / Materialien zum Dachau-Projekt," Neuer Berliner Kunstverein e.V. Zusammenarbeit mit dem Berliner Kunslterprogramm des DAAD und den Berliner Festspielen, 1975.
3. This project was reinstalled as part of the mammoth exhibition at the Martin Gropius Bau

in Berlin, "Deutschlandbilder," 7 September 1997–11 January 1998, where I saw it.

For further details on the installation and its reception, see Gerz and Levy, *EXIT*.

4. Nasgaard, "Book of Gestures," 39.
5. "Between the real and its reproduction, there is a *no man's land*," Gerz has said. "My work is situated in this zone." Quoted in Stephen Snoddy, "25 May 1991 . . . ," 67.
6. From author's interview with the artists, June 1989.
7. From Gintz, "'L'Anti-Monument,'" 87.
8. Parts of this section on the Gerzes' Harburg monument appeared in Young, "Counter-monument," 267–296, and then in Young, *Texture of Memory*, 28–37.
9. For further insights into the Harburg monument's commissioning, building, and reception, see essays by Achim Könneke, Karl Weber, Marcia Tucker, Jean-Pierre Salgas, Thomas Wagner, and myself in Könneke, ed., *Das Harburger Mahnmal gegen Faschismus*.
10. See North, "Public as Sculpture," 861. As North shows, such an impulse has a long history in its own right.

For further discussion of these dimensions to contemporary sculpture, see Sayre, *Object of Performance*; Lippard, *Changing*, 261–264; and Crimp, "Serra's Public Sculpture."
11. Gerz quoted in Von Dräteln, "Jochen Gerz's Visual Poetry," 47.
12. Ibid.
13. From Gintz, "'L'Anti-Monument,'" 80.
14. From a public presentation by the Gerzes on the "Gegen-Denkmal," at a conference on "Kunst und Holocaust," at Evangälischen Akademie Loccum, West Germany, 20 May 1989. Speaking in German to a German audience, Jochen Gerz was making an obvious, if ironic, allusion to the Nazis' own, notoriously literal-minded reference to being "stabbed in the back" by enemies internal, external and imagined. Appropriating the Nazis' language in this way was clearly intended both as a provocation and as an ironic self-identification by the Gerzes as "enemies of the Reich." See *Kunst und Holocaust*.
15. Quoted in Gibson, "Hamburg," 106–107.
16. Ibid., 106.
17. Ibid., 107.
18. From "Forwort," in *Sefer Yizkor*, 130, as quoted in Kugelmass and Boyarin, eds., *From a Ruined Garden*, 11.
19. On the "missing gravestone syndrome," see Merloo, "Delayed Mourning in Victims," in Krystal, ed., *Massive Psychic Trauma*, 74.
20. For the details of this project, I am indebted to personal correspondence and conversations with Jochen Gerz, as well as these articles, among others: Jhering, "Duell mit der Verdrängung"; Haase, "Mahnmale gegen Faschismus und Rassismus," 12–14; and Lichtenstein and Wajeman, "Jochen Gerz," E1–E6.
21. See essays by Rogoff, "Dieses Obskure Objekt der Begierde," and Kugler, "Menschen Verstummen, Steine Reden Immer . . . ."
22. Rogoff, "Aesthetics of Post-History," 138.
23. Gerz quoted in Friese, ed., *Die Bremer Befragung*, 8 (emphasis added).
24. Ibid., 103.

25. Ibid., 104.

26. For answers to this implied question, see Gerz, *Monument Vivant*.

27. From interview with Snoddy, "25 May 1991 . . . ," 67.

28. Gerz, "Why Did It Happen?" 1.

29. Ibid., 2.

30. Ibid., 6.

CHAPTER SIX   Daniel Libeskind's Jewish Museum in Berlin

1. Freud, "Uncanny," 17:241.

2. Vidler, *Architectural Uncanny*, 7.

3. Ibid., x.

4. See Lydenberg, "Freud's Uncanny Narratives," 1076. Here she also shows how the *unheimlich* (alien and threatening) contains within it its own lexical opposite (*heimlich*, familiar and agreeable). That is, part of uncanny's power to affect us is just its familiarity, which is all the more disturbing when estranged.

5. Simon, *Berlin Jüdische Museum*, 9, quoted in Weinland and Winkler, *Jüdische Museum*, 10.

6. Ibid.

7. See Bendt, "Jüdische Museum," in 200–209.

8. Simon, *Berlin Jüdische Museum*, 34, quoted in Weinland and Winkler, *Jüdische Museum im Stadtmuseum Berlin*, 10.

9. The issue of what constitutes Jewish art remains as fraught as ever in contemporary discussions of national and ethnic art. Among others, see Gutmann, "Is There a Jewish Art?" 1–20.

10. Weinland and Winkler, *Jüdische Museum im Stadtmuseum Berlin*, 10.

11. From an interview Robin Ostow had with Reiner Gunzer, the Museumsreferant who negotiated with Galinski at this time. I am grateful to Robin Ostow for sharing with me her essay "(Is It) a Jewish Museum," in Jeffrey Peck and Claus Leggewie, eds., *Jewish Communities* (forthcoming), where these details are cited.

12. From *Berlinische Notizen* 1–2 (1975): 11, cited in Weinland and Winkler, *Jüdische Museum*, 17.

13. "Palais auf dem Prufstein," *Die Welt*, 19 October 1985, quoted in Weinland and Winkler, *Jüdische Museum*, 28.

14. Ibid.

15. Weinland and Winkler, *Jüdische Museum*, 30.

16. *Berlinische Notizen* 4 (1987): 120ff., as cited in Weinland and Winkler, *Jüdische Museum*, 32.

17. Ibid.

18. See Bothe and Bendt, "Ein eigenstandiges Jüdisches Museum," 12.

19. "Nichts in Berlins Geschichte hat die Stadt jemals mehr verandert als die Verfolgung, Verteibung und Ermordung ihrer jüdischen Burger—dies war eine Veranderung nach Innen, die ins Herz der Stadt traf." Ibid., 12.

20. Ibid., 159.

21. Though this was Libeskind's first full commission, it was not his first building. Other projects subsequently commissioned have been built in Wiesbaden and Osnabrück, among other places.

22. As cited by Vidler, *Architectural Uncanny,* 135.
23. *Realisierungs Wettbewerb,* 169.
24. Ibid., 166.
25. Libeskind, *Between the Lines,* 3.
26. Libeskind, "Between the Lines," 63.
27. As noted by Bendt, "Model of Integration," 29.
28. For further insightful reflection on the role these voids play in Berlin generally and in Libeskind's design in particular, see Huyssen, "Voids of Berlin," 57–81.
29. Eisenman, "Representation of the Limit," 120.
30. Ibid.
31. Forster, "Monstrum Mirabile et Audax," 19.
32. *Realisierungs Wettbewerb,* 169.
33. Libeskind, *Between the Lines,* 8.
34. *Realisierungs Wettbewerb,* 166.
35. Ibid., 58.
36. Ibid., 168.
37. Ibid.
38. Ibid.
39. Libeskind, *Radix-Matrix,* 113.
40. Libeskind, "Between the Lines," 65.
41. Schneider, "Libeskind's Architecture," 120.
42. "I got the idea of using Zinc from Schinkel," Libeskind has said. "Before his very early death, he recommended that any young architect in Berlin should use as much zinc as possible.... In Berlin, untreated zinc turns to a beautiful blue-gray. Many of Schinkel's Berlin buildings, particularly at the Kleinglienicke Park, are built of zinc which has been painted white. When you knock them, you can tell that they are just covers. That is very Berlin-like." Libeskind, "1995 Raoul Wallenberg Lecture," 40.
43. *Realisierungs Wettbewerb,* 169.
44. Libeskind, "1995 Raoul Wallenberg Lecture," 34.
45. Ibid., 35.
46. *Realisierungs Wettbewerb,* 169.
47. *Between the Lines,* 12.
48. Derrida, "Response to Libeskind," 111.
49. Ibid., 115.
50. Libeskind, "1995 Raoul Wallenberg Lecture," 37.
51. Ibid., 33.
52. Freud, "Uncanny," 17:221.
53. Vidler, *Architectural Uncanny,* 70.
54. See Koselleck, *Futures Past,* 92–93.
55. Müller, "Daniel Libeskind's Muses," 117.
56. Ibid.
57. Forster, "Mildew Green Is the House of Forgetting," 7.
58. Libeskind, "Countersign," 135.

59. In the next and final chapter, I explore briefly Libeskind's separate design proposal for Germany's national "memorial for the murdered Jews of Europe," to be located in Berlin. In submitting a design for this memorial, the architect made clear that he did not want his museum design for a Jewish Museum to be turned into a Holocaust memorial.

60. Adorno, *Aesthetic Theory*, 262.

CHAPTER SEVEN   Germany's Holocaust Memorial Problem—and Mine

1. As quoted in Reichel, *Politik mit der Erinnerung*, 242. The Greens' statement is also cited by Michael Wise in his excellent study of Berlin's architectural problems during reunification, *Capital Dilemma*, 146.

2. For an excellent account of the entire *Neue Wache* debate, see *Streit um die Neue Wache*.

3. For more on the debate surrounding the discovery of ruins on the Gestapo-Gelände and subsequent architectural competitions to memorialize this site, see Young, *Texture of Memory*, 81–90.

4. See *Denkmal für die ermordeten Juden Europas*.

5. Broder, "Deutschmeister des Trauens," 222.

6. From Young, "Gegen das Denkmal, für Erinnerung," 178.

7. From Radunski's "Opening Remarks" to the First Colloquium on Berlin's Memorial to the Murdered Jews of Europe, 11 January 1997.

8. For articulate arguments against the memorial, see Koselleck, "Wer das vergessen werden?"; and Konrad, "Abschied von der Chimäre," 41.

9. Habermas, quoted from a letter he wrote to Peter Eisenman, 16 December 1998. The article from which he was drawing appeared as "Der Zeigefinger," *Die Zeit*, 31 March 1999.

10. I raised many of these same issues, in slightly different form, in Young, "Gegen Sprach-losigkeit," 28.

11. For further details and an insightful summary of the entire process up to September 1998, see Wise, "Totem and Taboo," 38–46.

12. As recalled by Michael Naumann in a conversation with the author in April 1999; also cited in Cowell, "Opponent of Kohl."

13. On the implications of this issue for traditional stances in the CDU and SPD, see Herf's insightful essay, "Naumann und Schroeder's 'Nein' zur Denkmal." Also see Herf's excellent book, *Divided Memory*.

14. I published this as "Die menschenmögliche Losung des Unlosbaren," 25.

15. On the eve of a planned visit between Peter Eisenman and Michael Naumann, I was invited to write a op-ed piece for the *Berliner Zeitung*, in which I asked just these questions, among others. See James E. Young, "Was keine andere Nation je versucht hat," 13–14.

16. For sending me the actual wording of the measure, I thank Dagmar Schwermer of Bay-erischer Rundfunk (Bavarian Radio).

Bibliography

Adorno, Theodore W. *Aesthetic Theory*. Translated by C. Lenhardt. New York: Routledge and
　　Kegan Paul, 1984.
——— . "Engagement." In *Noten zur Literatur,* vol. 3, 125–127. Frankfurt: Suhrkamp
　　Verlag, 1965.
——— . *Prisms*. Translated by Samuel and Shierry Weber. Cambridge: MIT Press, 1981.
Amichai, Yehuda. "Tourists." In *Selected Poetry of Yehuda Amichai,* edited and translated by
　　Chana Bloch and Stephen Mitchell, 137–138. New York: Harper and Row, 1986.
Amishai-Maisels, Ziva. *Depiction and Interpretation: The Influence of the Holocaust on the
　　Visual Arts*. Oxford: Pergamon, 1993.
Attie, Shimon. *Sites Unseen: European Projects: Installations and Photographs*. Burlington,
　　Vt.: Verve Editions, 1998.
——— . "The Writing on the Wall Project." In Attie, *The Writing on the Wall: Projections in
　　Berlin's Jewish Quarter,* 9–12. Heidelberg: Edition Braus, 1994.
Axelrod, Toby. "Time Exposures: Resurrecting Berlin's Jews, in Photographs." *Jewish Week,*
　　3 February 1995, 40.
Baigell, Matthew. *Jewish-American Artists and the Holocaust*. New Brunswick, N.J.: Rutgers
　　University Press, 1997.
Bal, Mieke, Jonathan Crewe, and Leo Spitzer. *Acts of Memory: Cultural Recall in the Present*.
　　Hanover, N.H.: University Press of New England, 1998.
Bartov, Omer. *Murder in Our Midst: The Holocaust, Industrial Killing, and Representation*.
　　Oxford: Oxford University Press, 1996.
Bendt, Vera. "Das Jüdische Museum." In *Wegweiser durch das jüdische Berlin: Geschichte und
　　Gegenwart,* 200–209. Berlin: Nicolai Verlag, 1987.
Benjamin, Walter. *Illuminations*. Edited by Hannah Arendt and translated by Harry Zohn.
　　New York: Schocken, 1973.
Bernstein, Michael André. *Foregone Conclusions: Against Apocalyptic History*. Berkeley:
　　University of California Press, 1994.
——— . "Shimon Attie: Images as Memory—Memory of Images." In Shimon Attie,
　　Writing on the Wall: Projections in Berlin's Jewish Quarter, 6–8. Heidelberg: Edition
　　Braus, 1994.
Bersani, Leo. *The Culture of Redemption*. Cambridge: Harvard University Press, 1990.
Böhm-Duchen, Monica, ed. *After Auschwitz: Responses to the Holocaust in Contemporary
　　Art*. London: Lund Humphries, 1995.
Boltanksi, Christian. *Lessons of Darkness*. Chicago: Museum of Contemporary Art, 1988.
Boorstin, Daniel. *The Image: A Guide to Pseudo-Events in America*. New York: Macmillan,
　　1987.

Bothe, Rolf, and Vera Bendt. "Ein eigenstandiges Jüdisches Museum als Abteilung des Berlin Museums." In *Realisierungs Wettbewerb: Erweiterung Berlin Museum mit Abteilung Jüdisches Museum,* 12–13. Berlin: Senatsverwaltung für Bau- und Wohnungswesen, 1990.

Boxer, Sarah. "Hardly Child's Play: Shoving Toys into Darkest Corners." *New York Times,* 24 January 1997.

Boyarin, Jonathan. *Storm from Paradise: The Politics of Jewish Memory.* Minneapolis: University of Minnesota Press, 1992.

Boyarin, Jonathan, and Daniel Boyarin. *Jews and Other Differences: The New Jewish Cultural Studies.* Minneapolis: University of Minneapolis Press, 1997.

Bradley, Fiona, ed. *Rachel Whiteread: Shedding Life.* London: Tate Gallery, 1996.

Broder, Henryk. "Deutschmeister des Trauens." *Der Spiegel,* 17 April 1995, 222.

Bronfen, Elisabeth. *Over Her Dead Body: Configurations of Feminity, Death and the Aesthetic.* New York: Routledge, 1992.

Broszat, Martin. "Plea for a Historicization of National Socialism." In *Reworking the Past: Hitler, the Holocaust, and the Historians' Controversy,* edited by Peter Baldwin, 77–87. Boston: Beacon Press, 1990.

Broszat, Martin, and Saul Friedlander. "A Controversy about the Historicization of National Socialism." In *Reworking the Past: Hitler, and Holocaust, and the Historians' Controversy,* edited by Peter Baldwin, 102–134. Boston: Beacon Press, 1990.

Caruth, Cathy. *Unclaimed Experience: Trauma, Narrative, and History.* Baltimore: Johns Hopkins University Press, 1996.

Cembalist, Robin. "Levinthal's Disturbing Photos of Nazis in Toyland." *Forward,* 11 November 1994, 9.

Champagne, Lenora, ed. *Out from Under: Texts by Women Performance Artists.* New York: Theatre Communications Group, 1990.

Chandler, David, and Peter Ride. "Foreword." In *Dark Light: David Levinthal Photographs, 1984–1994,* edited by David Chandler. London: Photographers' Gallery, 1994.

Chazan, Guy. "Ghosts of the Ghettos." *The Times* (London), 25 January 1995.

Christenberry, William, and Merry Foresta. "Toying with History: A Conversation with David Levinthal." *See: A Journal of Visual Culture* 1, no. 2 (1995): 29–31.

Cowell, Alan. "An Opponent of Kohl Puts Taboo Topic into Election." *New York Times,* 26 July 1998.

Crane, Susan. "(Not) Writing History: Rethinking the Intersections of Personal History and Collective Memory with Hans von Aufsess." *History and Memory* 8, no. 1 (Spring–Summer 1996): 5–29.

Crimp, Douglas. "Serra's Public Sculpture: Redefining Site Specificity." In *Richard Serra/Sculpture,* edited by Rosalind Krauss. New York: Museum of Modern Art. 1986.

Czaplicka, John. "History, Aesthetics and Contemporary Commemorative Practice in Berlin." *New German Critique* 65 (Spring–Summer 1995): 155–187.

Danto, Arthur. *After the End of Art: Contemporary Art and the Pale of History.* Princeton, N.J.: Princeton University Press, 1997.

de Haan, Ido. "The Invention of a National Trauma: The Memory of the Persecution of the

Jews in the Netherlands." Paper presented at "Memory and the Second World War in International Comparative Perspective," the Netherlands State Institute for War Documentation, Amsterdam, 27 April 1995.

Denkmal für die ermordeten Juden Europas: Kunstlierischer Wettbewerb — Kurzdokumentation. Berlin: Senatsverwaltung für Bau und Wohnungswesen, 1995.

Derrida, Jacques. "Response to Daniel Libeskind." In Daniel Libeskind, *Radix-Matrix: Architecture and Writings,* translated by Peter Green, 110–112. Munich: Prestel Verlag, 1997.

Douglas, Lawrence. "The Memory of Judgment: The Law, the Holocaust, and Denial." *History and Memory* 7, no. 2 (1996): 100–120.

Dufour, Gary, ed. *Jochen Gerz: People Speak.* Vancouver, B.C.: Vancouver Art Gallery, 1994.

Eisenman, Peter. "Representation of the Limit: Writing a 'Not-Architecture." In *Daniel Libeskind: Countersign,* 120–121. London: Academy Editions, 1991.

Elsen, Albert. *Modern European Sculpture, 1918–1945: Unknown Beings and Other Realities.* New York: G. Braziller, 1979.

Ezrahi, Sidra Dekoven. "The Holocaust and the Shifting Boundaries of Art and History." *History and Memory* 1, no. 2 (1989): 77–98.

Feinstein, Stephen C. "Mediums of Memory: Artistic Responses of the Second Generation." In *Breaking Crystal: Writing and Memory After Auschwitz,* edited by Ephraim Sicher, 201–275. Urbana: University of Illinois Press, 1998.

Feinstein, Stephen C., ed. *Witness and Legacy: Contemporary Art About the Holocaust.* Minneapolis, Minn.: Lerner, 1995.

Feireiss, Kristin, ed. *Daniel Libeskind: Erweiterung des Berlin Museums mit Abteilung Jüdisches Museum.* Berlin: Ernst & Sohn, 1992.

Felman, Shoshana, and Dori Laub. *Testimony: Crisis of Witnessing in Literature, Psychoanalysis, and History.* New York: Routledge, 1992.

Fischer, Andreas, and Michael Glameier, eds. "The Missing House." Berlin: Berliner Kunstlerprogram des DAAD für das Heimatmuseum Berlin-Mitte, 1990.

Forster, Kurt. "Mildew Green Is the House of Forgetting." In Daniel Libeskind, *Radix-Matrix: Architecture and Writings,* 7. Munich: Prestel Verlag, 1997.

——— . "Monstrum Mirabile et Audax." In *Erweiterung des Berlin Museums mit Abteilung Jüdisches Museum,* edited by Kristin Feireiss, 17–23. Berlin: Ernst & Sohn, 1992.

Foster, Hal. *The Anti-Aesthetic: Essays on Postmodern Culture.* Port Townsend, Wash.: Bay Press, 1983.

Freud, Sigmund. "The Uncanny." In *The Standard Edition of the Complete Psychological Works of Sigmund Freud,* translated by James Strachey. Vol. 17, 219–252. London: Hogarth Press, 1955.

Friedlander, Saul. *Memory, History, and the Extermination of the Jews of Europe.* Bloomington: Indiana University Press, 1993.

——— . *Nazi Germany and the Jews.* Vol. 1. New York: HarperCollins, 1997.

——— . *Reflections of Nazism: An Essay on Kitsch and Death.* New York: Harper and Row, 1984.

——— . "Trauma, Transference, and 'Working Through' in Writing the History of the

Shoah." *History and Memory* 4 (Spring–Summer 1992): 39–59.

———. *When Memory Comes.* New York: Farrar, Straus and Giroux, 1979.

Friedlander, Saul, ed. *Probing the Limits of Representation: Nazism and the "Final Solution."* Cambridge: Harvard University Press, 1993.

Friese, Peter, ed. *Die Bremer Befragung/The Bremen Questionnaire: Sine Somno Nihil, 1990–1995.* Bremen: Cantz Verlag, 1995.

Geis, Deborah. "'And This Strength Is in Me Still': Embodying Memory in Works by Jewish Women Performance Artists." *Yearbook of English Studies* 24 (1994): 172–179.

Gerz, Jochen. *Jochen Gerz: Life After Humanism — Photo/Text, 1988–1992.* Bremen: Edition Cantz, 1992.

———. *Le Monument vivant de Biron: la question secrète.* Arles: Actes Sud, 1996.

———. *2146 Steine: Mahnmal gegen Rassismus—Saarbrücken.* Stuttgart: Verlag Gerd Hätje, 1993.

———. "Why Did It Happen?" Proposal for Berlin's "Memorial to the Murdered Jews of Europe." Unpublished submission to the *Senatsverwaltung für Wissenschaft, Forschung und Kultur,* Berlin, 1997.

Gerz, Jochen, and Francis Levy. *EXIT: Das Dachau Projekt.* Frankfurt: Verlag Roter Stern, 1978.

Gibson, Michael. "Hamburg: Sinking Feelings." *Art News* (Summer 1987): 105–106.

Giedeon, Siegfried, Fernand Léger, and José Luis Sert. "Nine Points on Monumentality." In *Architecture, You and Me: The Diary of a Development,* edited by Siegfried Giedion, 48–51. Cambridge: Harvard University Press, 1958.

Gillis, John, ed. *Commemorations: The Politics of National Identity.* Princeton, N.J.: Princeton University Press, 1994.

Gilman, Sander. *Jewish Self-Hatred: Anti-Semitism and the Hidden Language of the Jews.* Baltimore: Johns Hopkins University Press, 1986.

———. *The Jew's Body.* New York: Routledge, 1991.

Gintz, Claude. "'L'Anti-Monument' de Jochen & Esther Gerz." *Galeries Magazine* 19 (June–July 1987): 80–82, 130.

Gopnik, Adam. "Comics and Catastrophe." *New Republic,* 22 June 1987.

Gutmann, Joseph. "Is There a Jewish Art?" In *The Visual Dimension: Aspects of Jewish Art,* edited by Claire Moore, 1–20. Boulder, Colo.: Westview Press, 1993.

Haase, Amine. "Mahnmal gegen Faschismus und Rassismus." *Kunst und Antiquitäten* 1/2 (1992): 12–14.

Habermas, Jürgen. "Concerning the Public Use of History." *New German Critique* 44 (Spring–Summer 1988): 40–50.

———. "Der Zeigefinger: Die Deutschen und ihr Denkmal." *Die Zeit,* 31 March 1999.

Hartman, Geoffrey. *The Longest Shadow: In the Aftermath of the Holocaust.* Bloomington: Indiana University Press, 1996.

———. "Public Memory and Its Discontents." *Raritan* 13, no. 4 (1993): 24–40.

Hass, Aaron. *The Aftermath: Living with the Holocaust.* New York: Cambridge University Press, 1995.

———. *In the Shadow of the Holocaust: The Second Generation.* New York: Cambridge University Press, 1990.

Hayes, Peter. "Comment in Response to Contemporary Interpretations of the Holocaust." Remarks delivered at the annual Social Science History Association Conference, New Orleans, 12 October 1996.

Herf, Jeffrey. *Divided Memory: The Nazi Past in the Two Germanys.* Cambridge: Harvard University Press, 1997.

——— . "Naumann und Schroeders 'Nein' zur Denkmal: Eine Neue Vergesslichkeit aus einer unerwartete Ecke?" *Die Zeit,* 12 August 1998.

Himmelblau, Coop. *Die Faszination der Stadt: The Power of the City.* Darmstadt: n.p., 1988.

Hirsch, Marianne. *Family Frames: Photography, Narrative, and Postmemory.* Cambridge: Harvard University Press, 1997.

——— . "Family Pictures: *Maus,* Mourning, and Post-Memory." *Discourse* 15, no. 2 (1992–1993): 3–29.

Hoffmann, Detlef, and Karl Ermert. *Kunst und Holocaust: Bildiche Zeugen von Ende der Westlichen Kultur.* Rehburg-Loccum, Germany: n.p., 1990.

Hoheisel, Horst. "Aschrottbrunnen—Denk-Stein-Sammlung—Brandenburger Tor— Buchenwald: Vier Erinnerungsversuche." In *Shoah—Formen der Erinnerung: Geschichte, Philosophie, Literatur, Kunst,* edited by Nicolas Berg, Jess Jochimsen, and Bernd Stiegler, 253–266. Munich: Wilhelm Fink Verlag, 1996.

——— . "Rathaus-Platz-Wunde." In *Aschrott-Brunnen: Offene Wunde der Stadtgeschichte.* Kassel, Germany: City of Kassel, 1989.

Holtzman, Karen, ed. *Burnt Whole: Contemporary Artists Reflect on the Holocaust.* Washington, D.C.: Washington Project for the Arts, 1994.

Horowitz, Sara R. *Voicing the Void: Memory and Muteness in Holocaust Fiction.* Albany: State University of New York Press, 1997.

Hutton, Patrick H. *History as an Art of Memory.* Hanover, N.H.: University Press of New England, 1993.

Huyssen, Andreas. "Anselm Kiefer: The Terror of History, the Temptation of Myth." *October* 48 (Spring 1989): 25–45.

——— . "The Monument in a Post-Modern Age." In *The Art of Memory: Holocaust Memorials in History,* edited by James E. Young, 9–17. Munich: Prestel Verlag, 1994.

——— . "Monumental Seduction." In *Acts of Memory: Cultural Recall in the Present,* edited by Mieke Bal, Jonathan Crewe, and Leo Spitzer, 191–207. Hanover, N.H.: University Press of New England, 1998.

——— . *Twilight Memories: Marking Time in a Culture of Amnesia.* New York: Routledge, 1995.

——— . "The Voids of Berlin." *Critical Inquiry* 24, no. 1 (1997): 57–81.

Johnson, Ken. "Art and Memory." *Art in America,* November 1993, 90–99.

Judenplatz Wien 1996: Wettbewerb Mahnmal und Gedenkstätte für die jüdischen Opfer des Naziregimes in Österreich, 1938–1945. Vienna: Stadt Wien/Kunsthalle Wien, 1996.

Kalir, Jane. "The Road to *Maus.*" Exhibit at Galerie St. Etienne, New York City, 17 November 1992–9 January 1993.

Kaplan, Alice Yeager. "Theweleit and Spiegelman: Of Mice and Men." In *Remaking History: DIA Art Foundation Discussions in Contemporary Culture, Number 4,* edited by Barbara Kruger and Phil Marian, 151–172. Seattle, Wash.: Bay Press, 1989.

Kirschenblatt-Gimblett, Barbara. *Destination Culture: Tourism, Museums, and Heritage.* Berkeley: University of California Press, 1998.

Könneke, Achim, ed. *Das Harburger Mahnmal gegen Faschismus / The Harburg Monument Against Fascism.* Hamburg: Hätje, 1994.

Konrad, György. "Abschied von der Chimäre: Zum Streit um das Holocaust-Denkmal." *Frankfurter Allgemeine Zeitung,* 26 November 1997, 41.

Koselleck, Reinhard. *Futures Past: On the Semantics of Historical Time.* Translated by Keith Tribe. Cambridge: MIT Press, 1985.

——— . "Wer das vergessen werden? Das Holocaust-Mahnmal heirarchisiert die Opfer." *Die Zeit,* 19 March 1998.

Krauss, Rosalind. *The Originality of the Avant-Garde and Other Modernist Myths.* Cambridge: MIT Press, 1988.

Kugelmass, Jack, and Jonathan Boyarin, eds. *From a Ruined Garden: The Memorial Books of Polish Jewry.* New York: Schocken Books, 1983.

Kugler, Lieselotte. "Menschen Verstummen, Steine Reden Immer . . . ." In Jochen Gerz, *2146 Steine: Mahnmal gegen Rassismus: Saarbrücken,* 168–179. Stuttgart: Verlag Gerd Hätje, 1993.

Kushner, Tony. *The Holocaust and the Liberal Imagination: A Social and Cultural History.* Cambridge, Mass.: Blackwell, 1994.

Kuspit, Donald. "Sings in Suspense." *Arts Magazine,* April 1991.

LaCapra, Dominick. *Representing the Holocaust: History, Theory, Trauma.* Ithaca, N.Y.: Cornell University Press, 1996.

Lang, Berel. *Act and Idea in the Nazi Genocide.* Chicago: University of Chicago Press, 1990.

Langer, Lawrence L. *Holocaust Testimonies: The Ruins of Testimony.* New Haven and London: Yale University Press, 1991.

——— . *Preempting the Holocaust.* New Haven and London: Yale University Press, 1998.

Laub, Dori. "Bearing Witness or the Vicissitudes of Listening." In Shoshana Felman and Dori Laub, *Testimony: Crises of Witnessing in Literature, Psychoanalysis, and History,* 57–74. New York: Routledge, 1992.

Levinthal, David. *The Wild West: Photographs by David Levinthal.* Washington, D.C.: Smithsonian Institution Press, 1993.

Levinthal, David, and Garry Trudeau. *Hitler Moves East: A Graphic Chronicle, 1941–43.* New York: Laurence Miller Gallery, 1977.

Libeskind, Daniel. *Between the Lines: Extension to the Berlin Museum with the Jewish Museum.* Amsterdam: Joods Historisch Museum, 1991.

——— . *Daniel Libeskind: Countersign.* London: Academy Editions, 1991.

——— . "1995 Raoul Wallenberg Lecture." Ann Arbor, Mich.: College of Architecture and Urban Planning, 1995.

——— . *Radix-Matrix: Architecture and Writings.* Translated by Peter Green. Munich: Prestel Verlag, 1997.

Lichtenstein, Jacqueline, and Gerard Wajeman. "Jochen Gerz: Invisible Monument." *Art Press,* April 1993.

Lippard, Lucy R. *Changing: Essays in Art Criticism.* New York, 1971.

Liss, Andrea. "(Im)possible Evidence." In *Contemporary Artists View the Holocaust,* edited by Jill Snyder. Reading, Pa.: Freedman Gallery, 1994.

———. *Trespassing Through Shadows: Memory, Photography, and the Holocaust.* Minneapolis: University of Minnesota Press, 1998.

Lust, Herbert. "For Women Are Endless Forms: Hans Bellmer's Dark Art." *Sulfur,* Spring 1990, 34–53.

Lydenberg, Robin. "Freud's Uncanny Narratives," *PMLA* 112 (October 1997): 1072–1086.

Lyotard, Jean-François. *The Postmodern Condition: A Report on Knowledge.* Minneapolis: University of Minnesota Press, 1984.

Maier, Charles S. "A Surfeit of Memory? Reflections on History, Melancholy and Denial." *History and Memory* 5, no. 2 (Fall–Winter 1993): 136–152.

———. *The Unmasterable Past: History, Holocaust, and German National Identity.* Cambridge: Harvard University Press, 1988.

Mann, Paul. *The Theory-Death of the Avant-Garde.* Indianapolis: Indiana University Press, 1991.

Merloo, Joost. "Delayed Mourning in Victims of Extermination Camps." In *Massive Psychic Trauma,* edited by Henry Krystal. New York: International Universities Press, 1968.

Miller, Nancy. "Cartoons of the Self: Portrait of the Artist as a Young Murderer: Art Spiegelman's *Maus.*" *M/e/a/n/i/n/g,* Fall 1992, 43–54.

Mitchell, W. J. T. *Iconology: Image, Text, Ideology.* Chicago: University of Chicago Press, 1986.

Mitscherlich, Alexander and Margarete. *The Inability to Mourn: Principles of Collective Behavior.* Translated by Beverley R. Placzek. New York: Grove Press, 1975.

Müller, Alois M. "Daniel Libeskind's Muses." In Daniel Libeskind, *Radix-Matrix: Architecture and Writings,* 116–119. Munich: Prestel Verlag, 1997.

Mumford, Lewis. *The Culture of Cities.* New York: Harcourt, Brace, Jovanovich, 1938.

Nasgaard, Roald. "The Book of Gestures: Some Thoughts on the Early Work." In *Jochen Gerz: People Speak,* edited by Gary Dufour, 33–48. Vancouver, B.C.: Vancouver Art Gallery, 1994.

Nicolai, Bernd. "Bus Stop—The Non-Monument: On the Impossibility of a Final Memorial to the Murdered Jews of Europe." Unpaginated brochure on the project published by Renata Stih and Frieder Schnock, 1996.

Nietzsche, Friedrich. *The Use and Abuse of History.* Translated by Adrian Collins. New York: Macmillan, 1985.

Nora, Pierre. "Between Memory and History: *Les Lieux de Mémoire.*" *Representations* 26 (Spring 1989): 13–25.

———. *Realms of Memory: Rethinking the French Past.* Vol. 1. New York: Columbia University Press, 1996.

North, Michael. "The Public as Sculpture: From Heavenly City to Mass Ornament." *Critical Inquiry* 16 (Summer 1990): 860–879.

Palowski, Franciszek. "Retracing Schindler's List." Travel booklet published by the Ministry of Tourism, Kraków.

Protzman, Ferdinand. "An Artist Projects a Ghostly Past." *Forward,* 21 April 1995, 10.

Rabinbach, Anson. "The Jewish Question in the German Question." *New German Critique* 44 (Spring–Summer 1988): 159–192.

Reichel, Peter. *Politik mit der Erinnerung: Gedächtnisorte im Streit um die Nationalsozialistische Vergangenheit.* Munich: Carl Hanser Verlag, 1995.

Rogoff, Irit. "The Aesthetics of Post-History: A German Perspective." In *Vision and Textuality,* edited by Stephen Melville and Bill Readings, 115–146. Durham, N.C.: Duke University Press, 1995.

———. "Dieses Obskure Objekt der Begierde." In Jochen Gerz, *2146 Steine: Mahnmal gegen Rassismus: Saarbrücken,* 156–165. Stuttgart: Verlag Gerd Hätje, 1993.

Rosen, Jonathan. "The Trivialization of Tragedy." *Culturefront,* Winter 1997, 80–85.

Rosenthal, Rachel. "My Brazil." In *Out from Under: Texts by Women Performance Artists,* edited by Lenora Champagne, 71–87. New York: Theatre Communications Group, 1990.

Roth, Beatrice. "The Father." *Out from Under: Texts by Women Performance Artists,* edited by Lenora Champagne, 33–44. New York: Theatre Communications Group, 1990.

Roth, Michael. *The Ironist's Cage: Memory, Trauma, and the Construction of Identity.* New York: Columbia University Press, 1995.

Sack, Leeny. "The Survivor and the Translator." In *Out from Under: Texts by Women Performance Artists,* edited by Lenora Champagne, 119–151. New York: Theatre Communications Group, 1990.

Saltzman, Lisa. *Anselm Kiefer and Art After Auschwitz.* New York: Cambridge University Press, 1999.

Santner, Eric L. *Stranded Objects: Mourning, Memory, and Film in Postwar Germany.* Ithaca, N.Y.: Cornell University Press, 1990.

Sayre, Henry M. *The Object of Performance: The American Avant-Garde Since 1970.* Chicago: University of Chicago Press, 1989.

Schama, Simon. *Landscape and Memory.* New York: HarperCollins, 1995.

Schneider, Bernhard. "Daniel Libeskind's Architecture in the Context of Urban Space." In Daniel Libeskind, *Radix-Matrix: Architecture and Writings.* Munich: Prestel Verlag, 1997.

Sicher, Ephraim, ed. *Breaking Crystal: Writing and Memory After Auschwitz.* Urbana: University of Illinois Press, 1998.

Simon, Hermann. *Das Berlin Jüdische Museum in der Oranienburger Strasse.* Berlin: n.p., 1988.

Snoddy, Stephen. "25 May 1991 . . . ." In *Jochen Gerz: Life After Humanism—Photo/Text, 1988–1992,* 67–68. Bremen: Edition Cantz, 1992.

Snyder, Jill, ed. *Impossible Evidence: Contemporary Artists View the Holocaust.* Reading, Pa.: Freedman Gallery/Albright College, 1994.

Sontag, Susan. "Fascinating Fascism." *New York Review of Books,* 6 February 1975, 26.

———. *On Photography.* New York: Farrar, Straus and Giroux, 1973.

Spiegelman, Art. "Artist's Statement." In *Jewish Themes/Contemporary American Artists*, edited by Susan Tumarkin Goodman, vol. 2, 44. New York: Jewish Museum, 1986.

———. *Breakdowns: From Maus to Now—An Anthology of Strips by Art Spiegelman*. New York: Nostalgia Press, 1977.

———. "Commix: An Idiosyncratic Historical and Aesthetic Overview." *Print*, November–December 1988, 61–73, 195–196.

———. "Letter to the Editor." *New York Times Book Review*, 29 December 1991, 4.

———. *Maus: A Survivor's Tale*. Vols. 1 and 2. New York: Pantheon, 1986, 1991.

Stainback, Charles, and Richard B. Woodward. *David Levinthal: Work from 1975–1996*. New York: International Center of Photography, 1997.

Stih, Renata, and Frieder Schnock. *Arbeitsbuch für ein Denkmal in Berlin: Orte des Erinnerns im Bayerischen Viertel—Ausgrenzung und Entrechtung, Vertreibung, Deportation und Ermordung von Berlin Juden in den Jahren 1933 bis 1945*. Berlin: Gatza Verlag, 1993.

———. *Bus Stop Fahrplan*. Berlin: Neue Gesellschaft für bildende Kunst, 1995.

Storrs, Robert. "Making Maus." Pamphlet for Projects Room Exhibition, Museum of Modern Art, New York.

Streit um die Neue Wache: Zur Gestaltung einer zentralen Gedenkstätte. Berlin: Akademie der Künste, 1993.

Theweleit, Klaus. *Male Fantasies*. Translated by Stephen Conway. Minneapolis: University of Minnesota Press, 1987.

Tucker, Marcia, ed. *The Art of Memory: The Loss of History*. New York: New Museum of Contemporary Art, 1987.

van Alphen, Ernst. *Caught by History: Holocaust Effects in Contemporary Art, Literature, and Theory*. Stanford, Calif.: Stanford University Press, 1997.

Varnedoe, Kirk, and Adam Gopnik. *High and Low: Modern Art and Popular Culture*. New York: Museum of Modern Art, 1991.

Vidler, Anthony. *The Architectural Uncanny: Essays in the Modern Unhomely*. Cambridge: MIT Press, 1996.

von Ankum, Katharina. "German Memorial Culture: The Berlin Holocaust Monument Debate." *Response* 68 (Fall 1997–Winter 1998): 41–48.

von Dräteln, Doris. "Jochen Gerz's Visual Poetry." *Contemporanea*, September 1989, 42–47.

von Jhering, Barbara. "Duell mit der Verdrängung." *Die Zeit*, 14 February 1992.

Weinland, Martina, and Kurt Winkler. *Das Jüdische Museum im Stadtmuseum Berlin: Eine Dokumentation*. Berlin: Nicolai, 1997.

Weinstein, Andrew. "Art After Auschwitz." *Boulevard* 9 (1994): 187–196.

Der Wettbewerb für das "Denkmal für die ermordeten Juden Europas": Eine Streitschrift. Berlin: Verlag der Kunst/Neue Gesellschaft für Bildende Kunst, 1995.

Winzen, Matthias. "The Need for Public Representation and the Burden of the German Past." *Art Journal* 48 (Winter 1989): 309–314.

Wise, Michael. *Capital Dilemma: Germany's Search for a New Architecture of Democracy*. New York: Princeton Architectural Press, 1998.

———. "Totem and Taboo: The New Berlin Struggles to Build a Holocaust Memorial." *Lingua Franca*, December–January 1999, 38–46.

Young, James E. "The Anne Frank House: Holland's Memorial 'Shrine of the Book.'" In *The Art of Memory: Holocaust Memorials in History*, edited by James E. Young, 131–137. Munich: Prestel Verlag, 1994.

———. "The Counter-Monument: Memory Against Itself in Germany Today." *Critical Inquiry* 18 (Winter 1992): 267–296.

———. "David Levinthal's *Mein Kampf*: Memory, Toys, and the Play of History." In David Levinthal, *Mein Kampf*, 67–83. Santa Fe, N.Mex.: Twin Palms, 1996.

———. "Gegen das Denkmal, für Erinnerung." In *Der Wettbewerb für "Das Denkmal für die ermordeten Juden Europas: Eine Streitschrift*, 174–178. Berlin: Verlag der Kunst/Neue Gesellschaft für Bildende Kunst, 1995.

———. "Gegen Sprachlösigkeit hilft kein Kreischen und Lachen: Berlins Problem mit dem Holocaust-Denkmal—und meines." *Frankfurter Allgemeine Zeitung*, 2 January 1998, 28.

———. "Germany's Memorial Question: Memory, Counter-Memory, and the End of the Monument." *South Atlantic Quarterly* 96, no. 4 (Fall 1997): 853–880.

———. "The Holocaust as Vicarious Past: Art Spiegelman's *Maus* and the Afterimages of History." *Critical Inquiry* 24 (Spring 1998): 666–699.

———. "Die menschenmögliche Losung des Unlosbaren." *Der Tages Spiegel*, 22 August 1998, 25.

———. "Sites Unseen: Shimon Attie's Acts of Remembrance, 1991–1996." In Shimon Attie, *Sites Unseen: European Projects: Installations and Photographs*, 10–17. Burlington, Vt.: Verve Editions, 1998.

———. *The Texture of Memory: Holocaust Memorials and Meaning*. New Haven and London: Yale University Press, 1993.

———. "Toward a Received History of the Holocaust." *History and Theory* 36, no. 4 (December 1997): 21–43.

———. *Writing and Rewriting the Holocaust: Narrative and the Consequences of Interpretation*. Bloomington: Indiana University Press, 1988.

Young, James E., ed. *The Art of Memory: Holocaust Memorials in History*. Munich: Prestel Verlag, 1994.

Zizek, Slavoj. *For They Know Not What They Do: Enjoyment as a Political Factor*. London: Verso, 1991.

———. *The Sublime Object of Ideology*. London: Verso, 1989.

Illustration Credits

Chapter 1

Pages 13, 16, 23, 25, 27, 28, 29, 30, 31, 33, 37, 38, 40: Reprinted by permission of Pantheon Books, a division of Random House, Inc.; *17, 20, 21, 22:* Reprinted by permission of Art Spiegelman.

Chapter 2

Pages 48, 52, 53, 56, 57, 60: David Levinthal; *58:* Etablissement Cinématographie et Photographie des Armées, Paris.

Chapter 3

Pages 64, 65, 68, 69, 73, 76, 77, 81, 84, 88, 89: Shimon Attie.

Chapter 4

Pages 92, 93, 98, 99, 100, 101, 102, 103, 104, 105: Horst Hoheisel; *106:* Henning Langenheim; *108, 112:* Photos by author; *109*: Micha Ullman; *110, 111:* Rachel Whiteread and the Anthony d'Offay Gallery, Ltd., London; *113, 114, 115, 116, 117:* Renata Stih and Frieder Schnock.

Chapter 5

Pages 122, 125, 141, 142, 143, 148: Jochen Gerz; *128, 129, 136, 137:* Jochen Gerz and Esther Shalev-Gerz; *131, 132, 133:* Photos by author.

Chapter 6

Pages 162, 164, 167, 168: Daniel Libeskind; *169, 172, 173, 176, 177, 180, 181:* Fotografie Bitter-Bredt.

Chapter 7

Page 188: Photo by author; *190, 202, 203, 204, 205, 206, 207, 208, 209, 211:* Senatswervaltung für Bauen und Wohnen, Berlin; *212, 213, 214, 215, 220:* Peter Eisenman Architects.

Index